Richard Wagner, Edward L. Burlingame, William Foster Apthorp

Art Life and Theories of Richard Wagner

selected from his writings and translated by Edward L. Burlingame - with a preface,

a catalogue of Wagner's published works and drawings of the Bayreuth opera

house

Richard Wagner, Edward L. Burlingame, William Foster Apthorp

Art Life and Theories of Richard Wagner

selected from his writings and translated by Edward L. Burlingame - with a preface, a catalogue of Wagner's published works and drawings of the Bayreuth opera house

ISBN/EAN: 9783337394943

Printed in Europe, USA, Canada, Australia, Japan

Cover: Foto ©Thomas Meinert / pixelio.de

More available books at **www.hansebooks.com**

ART LIFE AND THEORIES

OF

RICHARD WAGNER

Selected from his Writings and Translated

BY

EDWARD L. BURLINGAME

WITH A PREFACE, A CATALOGUE OF WAGNER'S
PUBLISHED WORKS AND DRAWINGS OF
THE BAYREUTH OPERA HOUSE.

NEW YORK
HENRY HOLT AND COMPANY
1875

TABLE OF CONTENTS.

DRAWINGS OF· THE

BAYREUTH OPERA HOUSE.

INTRODUCTION.

O UTSIDE of Germany, only the most devoted students of Wagner's theories have any true knowledge of him as a writer—or at all events, as a writer of anything beyond the texts of his operas. And even among those most interested, either as upholders or opponents of his beliefs, such knowledge has been confined to readers who have a much better understanding of German than is sufficient to follow the general course of an ordinary treatise. Thus, although many have an excellent acquaintance with his ideas as interpreted by others, very few know them as interpreted by himself; and it is safe to say that only a small minority of those who take a keen interest in the new school, know of even the existence of the nine stout octavo volumes of " collected works," which entitle Wagner to the name of its first literary and philosophical expositor, as he is otherwise entitled to that of its first composer.

Only a few of his pamphlets, essays, and letters, have been translated into English. The essay on Beethoven (not included in this volume) has been translated in America, and I believe in England also ; but it does not form a very appropriate or, indeed, a very inviting, introduction to Wagner's works. The letter on "The Music of the Future" was translated in England by Mr. Dannreuther, but the version is practically unknown to American readers, and attracted little attention at a time when Wagner had fewer English-speaking followers than now. The nine volumes present a great but rather formidable field of choice ; the difficulty in selecting from them matter that will form a just exposition of the composer's theories, without alarming the reader by essays of unfit length and technicality, is very great ; and these facts are perhaps the reasons why the present is, so far as I know, the first venture made in this direction ;—they are certainly the reasons why my volume claims no higher title than that of " Miscellanies," and does not pretend to include more than enough to furnish a synopsis of Wagner's creed.

Without asking any undue indulgence for the translations here given, justice to Herr Wagner himself makes it necessary to say something of the very unusual difficulties in the way of rendering his style satisfactorily into English—or, into satisfactory English—the reader may interpret the phrase in whichever way he will. No explanation of these difficulties will be needed by anyone who has ever read any of the original German ; but to anyone who has not, I can perhaps best explain the hardness of the labor, by asking him to imagine such .an undertaking as the endeavor to render Carlyle's English into French ;—a task which does not seem to me, as I look back over my work, to present a greatly exaggerated comparison. Indeed, as far as the mere use of language is concerned, Wagner's style has not a few characteristics of Carlyle's. The absolute independence with which he (coins words) is one of these ; and he indulges to the full in that inexhaustible resource of the German metaphysician,— that immense length of sentence which does not hinder the intelligibility of his own language, but works much ruin if we endeavor to transfer it into our own. The very nature of his subject compels the coining of words and even phrases ; the purely metaphysical character of much of it often renders almost necessary the length and intricacy of his clauses ; but behind this, the chief difficulty in rendering his writings is a certain diffuseness of style, the result of his being essentially a poet and an artist, rather than one accustomed to express himself in exact and careful prose. He constantly acknowledges this in his essays, expressing his dislike for critical and speculative writing ; but his translator is forced to refer to it also ; and while I have no wish to escape from any judgment of my work, I feel justified in believing that some passages which may appear too diffuse and vague are only unchanged representatives of similar parts in the original,—passages where Wagner forgets the expositor, in a moment's dreaming over ideals that need no explanation for himself.

The short, dry, and somewhat stiff sentences in the little autobiographical sketch preceding the Miscellanies, presented difficulties of another kind. They were so much of the nature of disconnected notes, that it was hard to give them enough of the character of a continuous record.

I have not tried to translate any one of Wagner's poems—even of those shorter ones in his collected works which it might have been possible to include in such a volume as this. Apart from my belief in the German proverb which declares that it needs a poet to translate a poet, I had not leisure to make even the audacious attempt. But I earnestly hope we may some time have an English version of the best of those noble dramatic works, which sufficiently prove to every reader of German that we should have known Wagner as a true poet, if we had not first seen his rare genius in another aspect. The great drama of the Nibelungen would be a worthy study for any translator ambitious enough and confident enough to begin the labor; and English readers would gain from a really noble rendering of it, a new idea of the capacity and power of the man whom they now know only from a single side.

I have spoken of the difficulty of selecting from the

voluminous collected works, "matter that will form a just exposition of the composer's theories without alarming the reader by essays of great length and technicality;" a brief explanation of the reasons for the choice I have made for this volume will show that at least an earnest effort has been made to solve the problem.

The account of the production of the "Liebesverbot" (the title of which is a piece of word-coinage that compelled me to the imitative "Love-Veto") was selected because it is the only thing besides the Autobiography which gives us a glimpse of Wagner's earlier youth, and shows him in a stage altogether prior to the development of his later views. The "Pilgrimage to Beethoven," the "End in Paris" (*Ein Ende in Paris*), and the two papers on the Parisian performance of "Der Freischütz," are what seemed to me to be the best of a series of sketches written in Paris itself, during the period of great want and distress referred to in the Autobiography; and in their original arrangement, as well as in the collected works, they were presented in the character of papers found in the portfolios of the author's fictitious friend "N.," whose death is described in "An End in Paris," and who might have been drawn from Wagner himself at this time of his greatest misery. They present Wagner in a different light from that given by any others of his writings; the "Pilgrimage" and the "End in Paris" are, I think, the only bits of prose fiction we have from him.

The choice of the essay on "The Music of the Future" needs, of course, no explanation. With the exception of the extended treatise on "The Opera and the Drama" (*Oper und Drama*), by itself occupying an entire volume, and therefore inadmissible here, it is the most complete general explanation of his most important art-theory that Wagner has written. It must be said here, that in the original edition of the Collected Works, the title of the essay (*Zukunftsmusik*) was placed between ironical quotation marks,—the writer's method of showing that he had himself adopted a phrase at first applied derisively by his enemies. I did not repeat the inverted commas in my translation, partly because I was in doubt whether their meaning would be appreciated there, and partly because I feared they would be generally taken for additions of my own, made on the supposition that the term was only half-seriously used by us. In spite of its origin as a mere chaffing phrase, it has really become the only designation under which all the theories of Wagner's school are at once understood.

The account of the production of Tannhäuser in Paris seemed to me one of the most important of those letters in which we get a little autobiography, and to be valuable for other reasons also, as the author's own version of a well-remembered musical event, and as containing some candid confessions about the Parisians, which partly offset the bitterness of the paper ironically entitled "*Le Freischutz.*"

The "Purpose of the Opera" (I think this the only translation of the title that makes it cover the whole ground in English) needs as little explanation as "The Music of the Future," though as an essay it is much less clear and satisfactory. The extracts from the letter on "Musical Criticism" are valuable as suggestions; and the "Legend of the Nibelungen" is the original scheme made out by Wagner to indicate the arrangement he intended to give to the myth in his great trilogy. It is inserted chiefly on this account; for the extreme conciseness which has been given to it here, takes away all its beauty as a version of the Nibelungen story.

Finally, the account of the inception and progress of the Bayreuth Opera-house undertaking, seemed so timely as to come within the limits of the collection, although it is wanting in the clearness and definiteness needed for a good description, and is largely occupied with an explanation of the theories governing the construction of the building, rather than with such an account of the result as would at this time gratify many readers. The two plates which have been selected from a considerable number affixed to the German edition of the two papers, will, however, aid in giving a clear idea of the interior arrangements of the building, and the way in which Wagner's desires have been carried out in them.

I have avoided including in this collection any of those polemic writings to which Wagner has frequently been aroused by the intense hostility formerly displayed against him. Strong and biting as they are, and well as they show still another side of his power and intense individuality, I regard them as of too temporary and merely national interest to find place among these selections. The insertion of any one of them, it is true, might give English and American readers a clearer understanding of the intensity of the musical war that raged in Germany during the growth of Wagner's theories; but even the briefest of his defensive essays would occupy space more useful for other matters.

I desire to express my hearty thanks to my friend, Mr. William F. Apthorp, of Boston, for the great service he has done the readers of these translations, by preparing the list of Wagner's published works which closes the volume. It is of the greatest value in following the growth of the composer's theories and production—what may be called his art-biography; and I do not know of so complete a catalogue elsewhere, though scattered materials for an even fuller one no doubt exist in Germany, in a style inaccessible to the ordinary reader. I have also to thank Mr. Apthorp for frequent aid and suggestions, of a kind which his thorough musical knowledge and experience as a critic made particularly serviceable. Had I been able to avail myself of his criticism in any other way than by occasional correspondence, I might have avoided any errors in the use of technical terms—errors into which I may have had the misfortune to fall, but which I have earnestly endeavored to avoid, in spite of the many cases where an English equivalent is difficult to find. In many such cases I profited by the kind aid of a very thorough musical student among my friends here.

I also wish to express my thanks to Mr. Fitzgerald, of the Popular Science Monthly, the able translator of Strauss' " Preface," etc., for taking part, when I was somewhat hurried, in the translation of the Bayreuth article, and in that of the extracts on " Musical Criticism."

E. L. B.

NEW YORK, *March*, 1875. .

AUTOBIOGRAPHY.

M Y name is WILHELM RICHARD WAGNER, and
I was born in Leipzig on the twenty-second
day of May, 1813. My father, who was a police actu-
ary, died six months after my birth.

My step-father, Ludwig Geyer, was an actor and a
painter, and had written several comedies,—one of
which, " The Slaughter of the Innocents," had considerable success. The family went to live with him
in Dresden. He wished to make a painter of me,
but I had decidedly no talent for drawing.

My step-father, too, died early—when I was only
seven years old. A little while before his death I had
learned to play on the piano " Ueb' immer Treu und
Redlichkeit " and the " Jungfernkranz," then quite a
novelty ; and on the day before he died he had me
play them both over to him in an adjoining room. I
heard him say in a faint voice to my mother, " What
if he should have a talent for music ? "

Early the next day, after he was dead, our mother
came into the nursery, and said something to each of
us children ; to me she said, " He hoped that something worth having might be made of you."

And I remember that I long imagined something
would be made of me.

With my ninth year I entered the Dresden Kreuz-schule. I wanted to study; I had no thought of music. Two of my sisters were learning to play the piano; but I listened to them without taking lessons myself.

Nothing pleased me so much as "Der Freischütz." I often saw Weber pass our house when he came out of the rehearsals. I always looked upon him with religious awe.

At last my private tutor, who taught me to construe Cornelius Nepos, had to give me piano lessons as well. I had hardly finished the first exercises in fingering when I began secretly to study the overture to the "Freischütz," at first without notes. My teacher once overheard me doing this, and pronounced that I would come to nothing. He was right; I have never in my life learned to play the piano. Still, I played then for myself alone,—nothing but overtures, and these with the most terrible fingering. It was impossible for me to play a passage clearly, and in this way I came to have a great horror of all "runs."

In Mozart's music I only liked the overture to the "Magic Flute;" "Don Juan" I disliked because it had the Italian text under it; this seemed to me supremely ridiculous.

This whole connection with music, however, was entirely a thing of secondary importance. Greek, Latin, Mythology, and Ancient History made up my chief employment. I made verses, too. On one occasion a school-fellow of ours had died, and the teachers set us the task of writing a poem on his death. The best poem was to be printed. Mine was printed, but only after I had cut out of it a good deal of bombast. I was then eleven years old.

I now longed to be a poet. I projected tragedies after the Greek model, incited thereto by reading Apel's tragedies, '' Polyidos,'' '' The Ætolians,'' and the rest. I was thought at school to be apt at literary studies ; even while I was in the third form I had translated the first twelve books of the Odyssey. At one time I began to learn English solely that I might know Shakespeare thoroughly. I even made a metrical translation of Romeo's monologue.

My English, however, I soon dropped ; but Shakespeare remained my model. I projected a great tragedy, more or less a compound of Hamlet and Lear. The plan was on the most stupendous scale. Forty-two persons perished in the course of the piece ; and in order to perform it I found myself compelled to reintroduce the majority of them as ghosts ; for otherwise I should have exhausted my *personnel.*

This piece occupied my attention for two years, during which time I left Dresden and the Kreuzschule and went to Leipzig. There, at the Nicholas seminary, I was put into the third form, after I had been in the second at the Dresden school ; and this circumstance so embittered me that from this time I let all my philological studies go by the board. I was idle and disorderly ; and only my great tragedy kept its place in my heart.

While I was finishing it, I made, at the Leipzig Gewandhaus concerts, my first acquaintance with Beethoven's music. The impression it made upon me was powerful to the last degree. I made friends with

Mozart, too, especially through his Requiem. Beethoven's music in Egmont so excited me, that I determined that my now completed tragedy should not proceed a step farther without being provided with just such accompaniment.

Without hesitation I put full confidence in my own ability to write this necessary music myself; at the same time I thought it best to get a few of the chief rules of thorough-bass clearly in my mind. In order to do this rapidly I borrowed Logier's " Thorough-bass Method " for a week, and studied it zealously ; but the study did not bear such quick fruit as I had imagined. The difficulties delighted and fascinated me. I decided to be a musician.

Meanwhile, however, my great tragedy had been discovered by the family. They were extremely annoyed at it ; for it was now revealed that I had utterly neglected my school studies for it ; and I was thenceforth kept rigidly to their diligent continuance. Under these circumstances I kept my secret profession of music to myself ; but I nevertheless composed, in the greatest secrecy, a sonata, a quartette, and an aria.

When I felt my musical studies sufficiently advanced, I at last came out with the disclosure. Naturally, I had to meet with much opposition ; for my relatives looked upon my inclination for music as also nothing but a passing fancy, since it was not justified by any preparatory studies, or especially by skill in any instrument.

I was then in my sixteenth year, and infected with the wildest mysticism by reading Hoffman ; during the day, while half dozing, I had visions in which fundamentals, thirds, and fifths appeared to me incarnate, and revealed to me their wonderful meaning ; what I wrote of them was the purest nonsense. At last I was put under the teaching of a capable music-master. The poor man had sad trouble with me ; he had to explain to me that what I looked upon as marvellous figures and powers were really intervals and chords. What could be more disappointing for my family than to find that I proved myself careless and unsystematic in this study also ?

My teacher shook his head ; and it certainly looked as though in this, too, I should come to nothing sensible. My zeal for study gradually died away, and I preferred to write overtures for a full orchestra, one of which was once produced in the Leipzig theatre.

These overtures formed the culminating-point of my absurdities. I chose, to aid the clearer comprehension of any one who should study the parts, to write them in three different inks,—the stringed instruments red, the reed instruments green, and the brass instruments black. Beethoven's ninth symphony was to be a mere Pleyel's sonata beside this wonderfully composed overture.

When it came to be performed I was especially injured by the regular repetition, every four bars throughout the piece, of a recurring *fortissimo* pound upon the drum : the audience soon passed from their original wonder at the obstinacy of the drummer, into unconcealed disgust ; and thence into a levity that wounded me deeply. This first performance of a piece of my composition left a deep impression upon me.

Now came the revolution of July (1830). With one bound I became a revolutionist, and adopted the opinion that every man with any aspiration should devote himself exclusively to politics. I enjoyed nothing but association with political literati; I even began an overture dealing with a political theme.

Thus I left school and entered the university; not, indeed, to pursue any one of the studies of the faculties, for I had really determined upon musical study; but to hear lectures on philosophy and æsthetics.

From this opportunity to educate myself, I derived practically no profit; I rather gave myself up to every kind of student's excesses, and with such recklessness and ardor that they soon disgusted me. At this period I gave my people great trouble, and my music was almost utterly neglected.

I soon came to my senses, however; I felt the necessity of beginning anew, and strictly disciplining myself in my musical studies; and Providence led me to the right man to inspire me with new love for the pursuit, and to rectify it by the most thorough teaching. This man was Theodor Weinlig, cantor at the St. Thomas seminary in Leipzig. Though I had already made some attempts at the study of fugue, I began with him for the first time the really thorough study of counterpoint, which he had the happy faculty of making the pupil learn as he played.

At this period I first learned to really know and love Mozart. I composed a sonata, in which I freed myself from all bombast, and committed myself to a natural and unforced style. This very simple and

modest work appeared in print, published by Breitkopf and Härtel.

My studies with Weinlig were over in less than half
a year; he himself let me leave his teaching after he
had carried me so far that I was able to solve easily
the most difficult problems of counterpoint.

"What you have gained through this dry study,"
he said to me, "is self-reliance."

During these same six months I also wrote an overture after the model of Beethoven, whom I now understood somewhat better; and it was played amid
encouraging applause at one of the Gewandhaus
concerts. After several other works, I also set to
work at a symphony; and to my chief model, Beethoven, I joined Mozart, especially his great symphony
in C major. Clearness and strength were what I
strove for in this, though amid many singular errors.

On the completion of the symphony, I made, in the
summer of 1832, a journey to Vienna, with the sole
object of making a hurried acquaintance with the
much-praised musical city. What I heard and saw
there improved me little; wherever I went I heard
"Zampa," and *pot-pourris* of Zampa by Strauss.
Both—especially at that time—were horrors for me.
On my return I stayed awhile in Prague, where I
made the acquaintance of Dionysius Weber, and
Tomaschek; the former had several of my compositions, among them my symphony, played in the Con-
servatory. There, too, I composed the text for a
tragic opera—"The Nuptials" (*Die Hochzeit*). I no
longer remember where I got the mediæval material
for it;—a mad lover climbs to the chamber-window of

his friend's bride, where she awaits her bridegroom. The bride struggles with the madman, and hurls him down into the court, where he, crushed by the fall, expires. At his burial, the bride, with a shriek, sinks dead beside the corpse. When I returned to Leipzig, I at once composed the first number of this opera, which contained a grand sextette which pleased Weinlig greatly ; but my sister disliked the libretto, and I destroyed it all.

In January, 1833, my symphony was performed in a Gewandhaus concert, and received much encouraging applause. About this time I became acquainted with Laube.

I made a journey to Wurzburg to visit my brother, and remained there during the whole year 1833 ; my brother was very useful to me, for he was an experienced singer. During the year, I wrote a romantic opera in three acts,—" The Fairies " (*Die Feen*),— for which I had composed the libretto after Gozzi's " Serpent Woman." Beethoven and Weber were my models. Many of the general effects were good ; the finale of the second act especially gave promise of considerable effect. Whatever I had played in concerts at Wurzburg was also successful ; and I went back to Leipzig with high hopes for the work I had finished, and offered it to the director of the theatre there for public production.

In spite of the willingness he expressed at first to carry out my wishes, I soon learned what every German composer has to learn in these days,*—that we

---

* It must be remembered that this was written in 1840.—TRANSLATOR.

have been crowded from our own stage by the success of Frenchmen and Italians, and that the production of our operas is a favor that we must beg for. My " Fairies'" was delayed indefinitely.

In the meantime I heard Devrient sing in Bellini's " Romeo and Juliet." I was amazed to hear such a remarkable performance of such utterly insignificant music. I was driven to despair at the means that could lead to so great a success. I was far from attributing any great merit to Bellini ; yet the material of which his music was made seemed to me nevertheless better calculated to diffuse life and warmth than the careful and anxious conscientiousness with which we Germans generally brought about only a tortured semblance of reality. The feeble tameness of the modern Italians, and the trifling frivolities of the French, seemed to challenge the earnest, conscientious Germans to make themselves masters of the better chosen and elaborated material of their rivals in order to vastly improve upon them by using it for real works of art.

I was one-and-twenty then, full of the enjoyment of life, and of a sanguine fashion of looking at the world ; " Ardinghello " * and " Young Europe " tingled through all my veins ; Germany seemed but a very small portion of the earth. I had emerged from my abstract mysticism, and was learning to love the material. Beauty of matter, wit, esprit, seemed to me excellent things; and as far as music was concerned, I found them all among the Italians and French. I abandoned my model, Beethoven. His last symphony seemed to me like the limit of a great

* " Ardinghello "—a romance by Heinse, defending the revival of the sensuous element in literature ; published about 1785.—TRANSLATOR.

1*

epoch in art, beyond which no one could pass, but within which no one could attain independence. Mendelssohn seemed to me to have felt this, when he came forward with his lesser orchestral compositions, leaving untouched the great exclusive form of the Beethoven symphony; it seemed to me as though, beginning with a minor but thoroughly independent form, he meant to *create* a greater one for himself.

Everything about me appeared to be in a state of fermentation—a "working"; to abandon myself to this seemed the most natural thing to do.

On a charming summer tour to the watering-places in Bohemia, I projected the scheme of a new opera, *Das Liebesverbot* (The Love-veto), for the libretto of which I made use of the material of Shakespeare's "Measure for Measure," with this difference—that I laid aside the serious element there prevailing, and modelled it entirely in the spirit of "Young Europe"; free and unconcealed sensuousness won the victory over puritanical hypocrisy.

In the summer of the same year, 1834, I accepted the position of musical director at the Magdeburg theatre. I very soon succeeded in the practical application of my musical knowledge to the duties of a leader, and the novel association with the singers and songstresses behind the scenes precisely suited my fancy for varying amusement.

I brought out the overture to my "Fairies" at a concert, and I had excellent success; but in spite of it I lost my liking for this opera, and as I could no longer personally attend to my affairs in Leipzig, I soon after decided not to trouble myself any further about it—which decision was practically the same as giving it up altogether.

For a New Year festival in 1835 I contributed some hastily composed music which met with general praise. Such easily won successes strongly confirmed me in the theory that to gain applause one must not be at all scrupulous in his choice of means; and I went on according to this idea in the composition of my *Liebesverbot*, giving myself no trouble whatever to avoid echoes of the French and Italian schools. After a trifling interruption I took up the work again in the winter of 1835-'36, and had it finished just before the breaking up of the opera troupe at the Magdeburg theatre. I had twelve days before the departure of the leading singers; and my opera must be studied in this interval if I wished to have it brought out by them.

With more recklessness than thought I let my opera, which included some decidedly difficult parts, go on the stage after only ten days' study—trusting to the prompter and my leader's baton. But in spite of these I could not banish the fact that the singers only half knew their rôles. The performance was like a dream to everybody; no one could get a reasonable conception of the thing, yet whatever went off even decently was fairly applauded. For a variety of reasons no second performance took place.

But in the meanwhile the serious side of life had made itself known to me. The outward independence I had been so quick to seize had led me into every kind of absurdity—pecuniary necessities and debts tortured me on every side. It was time for me to

make some extraordinary venture, that I might not actually fall into the common ruts of want.   With no prospects whatever of success, I went to Berlin, and offered
my " Liebesverbot " to the director of the royal
theatre for production.   Received at first with the
brightest promises, I was forced after long delay to
learn that no one of them was honestly meant.

I left Berlin in the most wretched state, to apply for
the situation of musical director at the theatre at
Königsberg in Prussia—a position that I afterward received.   In that town I was married in the fall of
1836, while I was in the most wretched outward circumstances.   The year that I spent in Königsberg
passed among the pettiest cares—utterly a loss for my
art.   I wrote nothing but one overture—" Rule Brit-
annia."

In the summer of 1837 I made a short visit to
Dresden, and there the reading of Bulwer's novel of
" Rienzi " brought me back to a favorite idea upon
which I had already dwelt—that of making the last of
the Roman tribunes the hero of a great tragic opera.
But kept from the execution of the plan by adverse
outward circumstances, I did not employ myself any
further with projects for it.   In the fall of the year I
went to Riga, to assume the position of first musical
director at the new theatre just opened there under Hol-
tei.   There I found excellent material collected for my
opera, and I set to work thoroughly *con amore* to make
use of it.   Several passages in my works were composed at that time for individual singers.   I also wrote
the libretto for a two-act comic opera, " Die glück-
liche Bärenfamilie," taking the material for it from a

story in the Arabian Nights. I had composed two
numbers of it, when I found to my annoyance that I
was again fairly on the way to the composition of
music à *la* Adam, and my spirits, my deeper feelings,
were inconsolably hurt by the discovery. I put aside
the work in disgust. The daily practice and conducting of Auber's, Adam's, and Bellini's music did their
part to thoroughly do away with the thoughtless pleasure I had taken in them.

The utter childishness of the theatrical public of our
provincial towns in the matter of what might by
chance be a first judgment of any new work of art
presented to them—since they are only accustomed
to seeing the performance of works that have already
been judged and accredited elsewhere—brought me to
the decision on no account to let an important work
have its first performance at the smaller theatres.
When I felt anew the earnest desire to undertake
some great work, I gave up all idea of a speedy performance of it to be brought about somewhere near
at hand. I thought of some leading theatre that
should some time produce it, and troubled myself very
little about where and when such a theatre might be
found.

So, then, I projected the scheme of a great tragic
opera in five acts ;—" Rienzi, the Last of the Tribunes " ; and I laid out the whole from the beginning on
so great a scale that it would have been impossible to
produce the piece—for the·first time, at least—at any
minor theatre. Indeed, the grandeur of the subject
permitted no other course, and I was governed in my
action less by choice than by necessity. In the sum-

mer of 1838 I worked at the subject-matter. At this period I was teaching our opera troupe, with real gratification and spirit, Mehül's " Jacob and his Sons."

When, in the fall, I began my " Rienzi," I bound myself to nothing but the single object of giving my subject fitting expression ; I set up no model for myself, but abandoned myself entirely to the feeling that preyed upon me—the feeling that I had now reached a point where I could demand of my artistic powers something really of importance, and expect from them something significant. The thought of being consciously shallow or trivial even in a single measure, was terrible to me. I continued the composition through the winter with full enthusiasm, so that in the spring of 1839 I had the first two acts completed. At the same time my contract with the director of the theatre came to an end, and various circumstances made it disagreeable for me to remain longer in Riga.

I had for two years cherished the plan of going to Paris ; even in Königsberg I had sent the scheme of a libretto to Scribe, with the proposition that if it pleased him he should work it out for his own benefit, and should in return get for me the engagement to compose this opera for Paris. Of course Scribe let this proposal pass almost unnoticed. Nevertheless I did not give up my plans, but took them up again in the summer of 1839 with new earnestness, and promptly persuaded my wife to set out with me in a sailing vessel which was to carry us to London.

I shall never forget this voyage ; it lasted three weeks and a half, and abounded in mishaps. We

were three times caught in violent storms, and once
the captain was compelled to put into a Norwegian
port. The passage through the Norwegian groups
made a singular impression on my fancy ; the legend
of the Flying Dutchman, as I heard it confirmed by
the lips of the sailors, took on for me a definite, peculiar coloring, such as only the adventures I had passed
through at sea could have given it.

We passed a week in London, resting from the terribly fatiguing voyage. Nothing interested me so ·
much as the city itself and the houses of Parliament.
I went to none of the theatres. I stayed a month at
Boulogne-sur-Mer. There I first made Meyerbeer's
acquaintance. I submitted the two completed acts of
my " Rienzi " to him, and he most kindly promised
me his assistance in Paris.

I entered Paris at last, with little money, but the
highest hopes. Entirely without introduction as I
was, I found myself altogether dependent upon Meyerbeer. He seemed to prepare for me with the most
thorough care everything that could further my wishes
in any way ; and it would certainly have seemed to
me that I was well on the way to the desired goal, if
it had not happened, unfortunately for me, that
during the whole time of my stay in Paris Meyerbeer
was for the most part—indeed, almost always—absent
from the city. Even at a distance he wished to be of
use to me ; but, as he warned me beforehand, any
pains taken by letter could be of no use where only
the most persistent personal effort could gain success.

At first I entered into relations with the Théâtre de
la Renaissance, which at that time produced both

dramas and operas. The arrangement of my "Liebesverbot" seemed to me best fitted for this theatre; and the somewhat trivial subject would have been good matter to work over for the French stage. I was so urgently recommended to the director of the theatre by Meyerbeer, that he could not but make me the best of promises. Shortly after, one of the most prolific of the Parisian dramatic poets, Dumersan, offered his services to me to undertake the re-arrangement of the subject. He translated with the greatest success three pieces which were selected for a trial hearing, so that my music fitted the new French text even better than the original German; it was just such music as the French most easily understand, and everything promised me the best results, when all at once the Théâtre de la Renaissance went into bankruptcy. All the trouble and hope had been in vain.

In the same winter, 1839-'40, I composed, besides an overture to the first part of Goethe's "Faust," several French songs; among others, a translation, made for me, of Heinrich Heine's "Two Grenadiers." I never thought of a possible production of my "Rienzi" in Paris, for I foresaw with certainty that I should have to wait at least five or six years before such a plan would be practicable, even under the most favorable circumstances; besides which, the translation of the libretto of the already half-finished opera would have put insurmountable obstacles in the way.

Thus I entered upon the summer of 1840 entirely without any prospects for the immediate future. My acquaintance with Habeneck, Halévy, Berlioz, and others, certainly led to no particular approach to any ; no artist has leisure in Paris to make friends with another ; each is in a rush and hurry on his own account. Halévy, like all Parisian composers nowadays, was only burning with enthusiasm for his art as long as it was necessary to win a great success ; as soon as this was attained, and he had entered the list of privileged lions among composers, he thought of nothing further but to make operas and get money for them. Celebrity is everything in Paris ; at once the good fortune and the ruin of the artist.

Berlioz, in spite of his repellent nature, attracted me far more ; he is separated by the whole breadth of the heavens from his Parisian colleagues, for he does not make his music for money. But he cannot write for pure art, either ; the whole sense of beauty escapes him. He stands, in his peculiar line, in an entirely isolated position ; on his side he has only a troop of idolators, who, themselves mediocre and without the slightest judgment, welcome in him the creator of a brand-new musical system, and entirely turn his head ; —and all others avoid him as a madman.

The Italians gave the last blow to my earlier trivial views regarding the material for music. These most-lauded heroes of song, Rubini at their head, thoroughly disgusted me with their performance. The public before which they sang did its part in producing this effect upon me. The Grand Opera of Paris left me utterly unsatisfied, by the want of all genius in what it accomplished. I found it all only ordinary and mediocre. The *mise en scène* and the decorations are, to speak frankly, what pleases me most in the whole *Academie Royale de Musique*. The *Opéra Comique* might have come much nearer to satisfying me ; it has the best talent, and its performances have a completeness, a character of their own, that we do not know in Germany. What is written for this theatre, however, belongs to the worst matter ever produced in a time of the decadence of art ; whither has the grace of Mehül, Isouard, and the younger Auber, fled before the unworthy quadrille-rhythms that alone nowadays clatter through the theatre ?

The only things that Paris contains that are worth the consideration of a musician, are the orchestral concerts in the salon of the conservatoire. The performance of German instrumental compositions at these concerts made a deep impression on me, and initiated me anew into the wondrous secrets of true art. Whoever desires to know the ninth symphony of Beethoven in its perfection, must hear it performed by the orchestra of the conservatoire in Paris. These concerts, however, stand absolutely alone ; nothing else is to be joined with them.

I hardly associated at all with musicians ; savants, painters, etc., made up my circle. I had many pleasant experiences of friendship in Paris.

As I was so utterly without prospects for the immediate future at Paris, I again took up the composition of my " Rienzi." I designed it now for Dresden, first, because I knew that there was the best material at that theatre—Devrient, Tichatschek, and others ; secondly, because I could hope, at my first introduction there, to depend upon the acquaintances of my early days. I now almost entirely gave up my

" Liebesverbot." I felt that as a composer I could no longer feel proud of it. I followed all the more independently my true artistic faith in continuing the composition of my " Rienzi."

Manifold difficulties and very bitter want encompassed my life at this period. Meyerbeer came suddenly to Paris for a short time ; he inquired with the most friendly sympathy about the position of my affairs, and wished to help me. He also put me into communication with Léon Pillet, the director of the grand opera. There was some idea of a two or three act opera, the composition of which should be entrusted to me for this theatre. I had already provided myself for the occasion with the scheme for a libretto. " The Flying Dutchman," whose intimate acquaintance I had made at sea, continually enchained my fancy. I had become acquainted, too, with Heinrich Heine's peculiar treatment of the legend in one portion of his " Salon." Especially the treatment of the delivery of this Ahasuerus of the ocean (taken by Heine from a Dutch drama of the same title) gave me everything ready to use the legend as the libretto of an opera. I came to an understanding about it with Heine himself, drew up the scheme, and gave it to M. Léon Pillet, with the proposition that he should have a French libretto made from it for me.

Everything was brought thus far when Meyerbeer again left Paris, and had to leave the fulfilment of my wishes to fate. Soon after I was astounded at being informed by Pillet that the scheme I had handed in pleased him so much that he would be glad to have me part with it altogether to him. He was, it ap-

peared, under the necessity, in fulfilment of an earlier
promise, of at once giving another composer a
libretto ; the scheme I had prepared was precisely
fitted for the purpose, and I should probably have little hesitation in consenting to the proposed surrender
of it, when I recollected that I could not possibly have
any hope of securing an immediate personal engagement
to compose an opera within the next four years, inasmuch as he must first fulfil his agreements with several candidates for the grand opera. Of course it
would be too long for me to carry the scheme of this
opera about with me all that while ; I should certainly
find some new one, and should soon console myself
for the sacrifice ! I obstinately opposed this presumption, but without being able to arrange anything more
than a postponement of the whole question for the
time being. I counted on the speedy return of Meyerbeer, and so kept silence.

During this time, I was commissioned by Schlesinger
to write for his *Gazette Musicale.* I contributed several articles of considerable length on German music,
etc. A little sketch called " A Pilgrimage to Beethoven " was especially praised. These performances
were of not a little help to me in making myself known
and esteemed in Paris. In November of this year I
entirely completed the score of my " Rienzi," and
sent it without delay to Dresden. This period was
the culminating-point of my want and misery ; it was
then that I wrote for the *Gazette Musicale* my little
story, " *Das ende eines deutschen Musikers in Paris,*"
in which I made the unhappy hero die with this creed
upon his lips : " I believe in God, Mozart, and Beet-

hovén." It was a good thing for me that my opera was finished, for I found myself compelled for a long time after this to abandon every attempt at true artistic work. I had to set myself to making for Schlesinger instrumental arrangements of every imaginable kind down to those for the *cornet-à-piston*—the only means by which I could better my situation. I spent the winter of 1840-'41 in the dreariest fashion, and in the spring I went into the country at Meudon.

As the summer came I longed for intellectual work again, and the opportunity for it came sooner than I thought. I learned that my scheme of a libretto for the "Flying Dutchman" had already been put into the hands of a writer (Paul Fouché), and I saw that unless I finally consented to part with it, I should be cheated out of it altogether under one pretext or another. So I at last agreed, for a specified sum, to give up my scheme altogether.

This left me with nothing more pressing to do than to put my subject into German verse myself. But to compose it I needed a piano—for, after a nine months' interruption of any kind of musical production, I had to work myself back into the musical atmosphere. I hired a piano, but when it had come I walked about it in an agony of anxiety ; I feared to find that I was no longer a musician.

I began with the sailors' chorus and the spinning-song ; everything went easily, fluently, and I fairly shouted for joy as I felt through my whole being that I was still an artist. In seven weeks the opera was finished.

But at the end of this time petty wants and necessi-

his later career to others at the very moment when his first
marked success brought his name most prominently before
the world.

The translator believes that he may venture, without passing
beyond the proper limits of his undertaking, to briefly supply
the record of Wagner's later work ; endeavoring to continue
the plan followed in the autobiography itself—to give rather
those facts which bear upon the art-life of the composer than
to enter into ordinary biographical details.

* * * * * * *

In October, 1842, Wagner's " Rienzi " was at last produced
at Dresden, and met with a success that secured his appointment, almost immediately, to the post of Kapellmeister at the
Dresden Opera House. During the three years following
his acceptance of this office, he composed Tannhäuser, which
was first performed in October, 1845. Among his minor
works produced during the same period were the *Gruss seiner
Treuen an Friedrich August den Geliebten* (1844), and the
Liebesmahl der Apostel (1845). "The Flying Dutchman"
was repeatedly and successfully performed under his direction.

We gain from the autobiography some knowledge of Wagner's liberal political opinions. The revolution of 1848, reaching its culminating point in Dresden, engaged his warmest
sympathy. He was an active leader in the political agitation
which led to it, and became so deeply involved with the revolutionary party that he was among the first of those whom
its downfall compelled to save themselves by flight beyond
the German border. On May 7, 1849, just after the insurrection of that month, he left Dresden and escaped to Zurich.

Here he was well received, and became a citizen of the
canton. In 1850 he was appointed director of the Zurich
Musical Society and of the orchestra at the city theatre.
He continued to compose with remarkable rapidity and fer-
tility, and during his residence in Switzerland he completed
" Lohengrin," and the libretto and part of the music of the
" Nibelungen." In 1858 he left Zurich, and resided succes-
sively in Italy, Paris, Vienna and Carlsruhe, spending but a
short time in each city. " Lohengrin " was produced in

Paris during his residence there, but failed to secure public attention and was almost immediately withdrawn.

Soon after his return to Germany, Wagner attracted the attention of the music-loving Ludwig, the young king of Bavaria, with whom his relations have ever since been of the most intimate character. He established himself in Munich, and made it not only his residence but the centre of all his artistic life—producing his works at the royal theatre under his own supervision, and receiving from the king every necessary aid in the execution of his plans.

" Tristan und Isolde" appeared in 1865 ; and in June, 1868, " Die Meistersinger von Nürnberg" was produced, Wagner watching its performance from a seat beside the king. In September, 1869, " Rheingold," the prelude to his great composition of the " Nibelungen," was brought out at the royal theatre, but without the success which had been looked for.

After the close of the Franco-German war, an attempt was made to secure Wagner for Berlin, as " general musical director," the office formerly filled by Meyerbeer. But although he visited Berlin to debate the matter, the project was not carried out, and he returned to Munich.

Here the great project of a Wagner theatre was formed—a theatre which should be devoted exclusively to the production of his own works, and to the carrying out of his own beliefs as to the union of their dramatic and musical elements. Baireuth was selected as the site of the structure ; Wagner societies were formed throughout Germany to aid the plan ; the composer himself, in the summer of 1872, made a journey through Germany, giving concerts in the leading cities of the empire for the purpose of increasing the building-fund. The king of Bavaria has also greatly aided the undertaking. The corner-stone of the Baireuth theatre was laid in May, 1872, and the building is now rapidly approaching completion.

MISCELLANIES.

"*THE LOVE-VETO.*"

(DAS LIEBESVERBOT.)

THE STORY OF THE FIRST PERFORMANCE OF AN OPERA.

ONE beautiful morning I stole away from my associates, to take a solitary breakfast at the Schlackenburg, and to seize the opportunity to write out in my note-book the scheme for the text of a new opera. I had made myself master, for this end, of the story of Shakespeare's "Measure.for Measure," which, in a fashion befitting my mood at the moment, I had freely converted into an opera libretto, and had given it the title of "The Love-Veto." The ideas of the school of "Young Europe," then so prevalent, and the reading of "Ardinghello" worked upon by the mood into which I had fallen, opposed to the German school of operatic music, gave a coloring to my conception—which was in special opposition to the puritanic spirit of hypocrisy, and tended toward the open worship of undisguised sensuousness. I sought to grasp the serious Shakespearean theme only in this construction; I saw only the gloomy, severely righteous Angelo, himself burning with the most fiery passion for the beautiful Novice; while she, as she begs him for the pardon of the brother who has been sentenced to die for a criminal love, kindles the most consuming flame in the rigid puritan by the warmth of her own human feeling. It by no means suited my mood to perceive that these powerful motives had

only been so richly developed in Shakespeare's drama
in order that they might afterwards be all the more
justly weighed in the scales of righteousness; I only
cared to expose the crime of hypocrisy and the sin
against nature in this moral despotism.

And so I let the " Measure for Measure " part of
it pass altogether, and let only the hypocrite be punished through his self-avenging love. I transferred
the story from the fabulous Vienna to the capital of
glowing Sicily, where a German governor, shocked
at the incomprehensibly light morals of the people,
attempts to introduce a puritanical reform—in which
he lamentably fails. Perhaps the " Muet de Portici "
helped a little in this idea, and recollections of " the
Sicilian Vespers " may have had something to do with
it; and when I think, finally, that the gentle Sicilian
Bellini may also be counted among the factors of this
composition, I positively have to laugh at the amazing
quid-pro-quo into which these extraordinary misconceptions shaped themselves.

But it was the winter of 1835-'36 before I completed
the whole score of my opera. It was done among
the distracting influences of my connection with the
little theatre at Magdeburg, where I for two winters
superintended, as musical director, the operatic performances. A certain growing savagery of taste had
arisen from my close association with German operatic
affairs, and this was so preserved in the whole plan
and execution of my work, that the young enthusiast
in Beethoven and Weber would certainly never have
been recognized through this score.

Its fate was as follows.

In spite of royal aid and the interference of the the-
atre-committee in the affairs of the management, our
worthy director remained in a state of perennial bankruptcy, and a continuance of theatrical undertakings
under his superintendence in any form, was not to
be thought of. And so the production of my opera

by the excellent troupe that stood at my service, must
be the starting-point for a thorough change in my decidedly unpromising condition. I had the right to
demand a benefit to cover certain travelling expenses
incurred during the previous summer ; and of course I
fixed upon the production of my own work for this occasion, and took pains to make the favor shown to
me as inexpensive as possible for the management.
Since, in spite of this, they necessarily incurred some
expense for the new opera, I arranged that the receipts of the first performance should pass to them,
while I should only lay claim to those of the second.
The fact that the time for the study of the score would
stretch to the very end of the season, did not seem to
me unfavorable, for I had a right to expect that the
last performances of a troupe that had often been received with unusual favor would meet with more than
the customary approval of the public. Unhappily,
however, we never reached the anticipated favorable
ending of their engagement which was set for the end
of April ; for on account of the delay in the payment
of their salaries, the most admired members of the
troupe, who could find better places elsewhere, gave
notice of their departure before the end of March—
the management having, through lack of funds, no
means whatever at their disposal to counteract this
movement.

I must confess that I was now discouraged ; the
probability of the production of my " Love-Veto "
seemed more than questionable. I owed it only to
my personal popularity among the troupe, that the
singers finally allowed themselves to be persuaded not
only to remain until the end of March, but also to undertake in so short a time the really arduous study of
my opera. The time, indeed, if there were to be two
performances, was cut down so sharply that we had
only ten days before us for all our rehearsals. As we
had not to do with a trifling vaudeville, but (in spite

of the somewhat frivolous character of the music) with
an extended opera abounding in complicated combinations, the undertaking may certainly be called a
foolhardy one.   Still I trusted to the special pains
which the singers took to please me, working all their
mornings and evenings ; and since it was after all absolutely impossible that we could attain to any absolute
safety in the matter, especially as regarded the memory of these persecuted beings, I put my last reliance
on some miracle which I might be able to effect
through the expertness I had acquired as a conductor.
. The remarkable capacity I had for assisting the
singers and keeping them to a certain deceptive fluency in spite of the most perfect uncertainty on their
part, appeared during our few orchestral rehearsals,
where I managed, by constant prompting, joining
loudly in the singing, and sharp directions as to the
necessary action, to keep the whole in such reasonable
running order that one would imagine it was going off
quite respectably.   But alas ! we did not consider the
fact that at the actual performance, and in the presence
of the public, all these vigorous methods of running
the dramatic and musical machinery would be limited
to the signs of my baton and such expression as I
could convey by my manner.

The singers, especially the male element of the *personnel*, were really so extremely uncertain that a certain
constraint arising from this weakened the effectiveness
of their rôles from beginning to end.   The first tenor,
who was gifted with one of the feeblest of memories,
did his very best to fill out the vivacious and exciting
character of his part—that of the scapegrace Lucio—
by bringing into play the regular routine he had acquired in Zampa and Fra Diavolo,—and especially by
the introduction of an immeasurably thick, fluttering,
and brilliant plume.   In spite of this, however, it was
not to be concealed that the public (more especially as
the management had not provided for the printing of

libretti) remained in the densest ignorance of the progress and purport of what was sung. With the exception of some of the female rôles (which met with considerable applause) the whole affair, which I had based
on vigorous, energetic action and dialogue, became a
kind of musical game of shadows on the scene ; to
which the orchestra, often with superfluous noise, gave
inexplicable solutions. As a characteristic illustration
of the way my shades of tone were rendered, I must
mention that the director of a Prussian band, who had
been pleased with the matter in all other respects,
thought it necessary to give me, for use in future.
work, a little benevolent instruction on the treatment
of the Turkish drum.

But before I sketch the further fate of this extraordinary youthful effort, I pause for a moment to give
some little detail of its character, especially in the matter of its plot. The Shakespearean drama, a thoroughly serious one in its nature, was converted in my
scheme into the following conception :

A King of Sicily leaves his kingdom, to make a
journey to Naples ; and gives over to the governor
whom he appoints—who is named simply " Friedrich "
to sufficiently characterize him as a German—the
absolute power to use every means within the royal
prerogative, in the attempt to effect a thorough reform in the morals of the capital, at which the severe
and rigid councillor had been much scandalized. At
the beginning of the piece, the public officials are
discovered hard at work, closing or tearing down
houses of popular resort in a suburb of Palermo, and
carrying their occupants, landlords and servants away
to prison. The people resist this initiative ; terrific
tumult ; the chief of the Sbirri, *Brighella* (basso buffo),
in the midst of the press, and after a drum-roll to call
the attention of the people, reads aloud the order
of the governor, in accordance with which these forcible measures for the moral improvement of the city

had been taken. He is interrupted by general jeering and a chorus of abuse; Lucio, a young nobleman and jovial ne'er-do-weel (tenor), seems about to place himself at the head of the mob, and finds a new motive to connect himself with the cause of the persecuted people when he sees his friend Claudio (also tenor), led by on his way to prison, and discovers that according to some old and forgotten law which Friedrich had hunted out, he is to be punished by death for an illicit love affair. His mistress, his marriage with whom has been prevented by the opposition of her parents, has become a mother; Friedrich's puritanic fanaticism is now added to the hatred of her relatives against him; he has every reason to fear the worst, and puts his only hope of safety in the mercy of the governor, if the pleading of his sister Isabella can' succeed in softening the heart of the stubborn ruler. Lucio answers his friend, that he will at once visit Isabella at the Elizabethan convent, which she had entered as a novice only a little while before.

There, within the silent walls of the convent, we soon make closer acquaintance with this sister, as she is engaged in conversation with her friend Marianna, who, like herself, has entered the place as a novice. Marianna reveals to her friend, from whom she has long been separated, the sad fate that has brought her here. She was enticed by promises of good faith and constancy, into a secret liaison with a man of high position; but it was not long before she found herself betrayed and left in want, and even persecuted by him; for her betrayer proved to be the most powerful personage in the state—none less than the present governor appointed by the king. Isabella gives furious vent to her indignation at this, and is only quieted by her decision to retire from a world in which such a villanous crime can be committed. When Lucio brings her the news of the fate of her own brother, her condemnation of the latter's deed is lost in her rage at the vileness of the hypocritical governor, who can take it upon himself to punish so cruelly the unspeakably smaller fault of one who at least has not been guilty of the sin of a betrayal. Her violent excitement appears to Lucio in a false light ; suddenly kindled into passionate love, he beseeches her to abandon the convent forever and to accept his hand. She promptly and with dignity checks this audacious suitor ; but resolves without a moment's hesitation to accompany him to the judgment hall of the governor.

Here the trial scene is preparing, which I introduced with a burlesque hearing of various violators of the moral code, by Brighella, the chief of the Sbirri. The serious side of the situation thus becomes all the more impressive when the gloomy figure of Friedrich enters among the turbulent people, commanding silence ; and the trial of Claudio is begun by him in the severest form. The implacable governor is about to pronounce sentence, when Isabella enters, and demands a private interview with him. In this interview she controls her emotion before the man so dreaded and yet so despised by her, and appeals at first only to his generosity and mercy. His objections only add to her passionate appeal ; she places her brother's crime before him in the most touching light, and begs him to pardon the human and by no means unpardonable fault. As she sees the impression made by her warm presentation of the case, she continues with increasing ardor to work upon the feelings of the heart of the ruler that is now so harshly closed against her—a heart which cannot have failed to have sometimes experienced like emotions to those by which her brother had been carried away, and to whose own experience she now appealed for aid in her agonized prayer for mercy. And now at last the ice of this hardened heart is broken ; Friedrich, excited to the last degree by Isa-

2*

bella's beauty, is no longer master of himself; he
promises her all that she asks, at the price of—her
love.   She no sooner comprehends this result, than,
roused to fury by such incomprehensible villany, she
rushes to the door and windows, and summons the
people to her that she may expose the hypocrite before all the world.   But as the crowd pours into the
room, Friedrich summons all the energy of desperation, and in a few convincing sentences points out to
her how impossible is the success of her design ; that
it would only be necessary for him to boldly deny her
accusation, say that the proposal was an attempt at a
bribe, and that he would undoubtedly be believed if it
came to the question of disproving the imputation of a
frivolous love affair.   Isabella, herself ashamed and
confused, recognizes the madness of her course, and
gives herself up to silent despair.   But as Friedrich
again announces to the people his intended measures of
extreme severity, and gives the condemned man
notice of his sentence, Isabella, whose thoughts have
been turned to Marianna by this painful reminder of
her history, all at once conceives with lightning-like
rapidity a means of accomplishing by deceit what
is impossible by force.   Her manner passes in an instant from the deepest grief into wantonness ; she turns
to her stricken brother, his despairing friend and the
helpless people, with the assurance that the merriest
of festivals is in store for all,—that the carnival
festivities that the governor has just sternly forbidden,
are to go on with more riotous jollity than ever ; for
that the dreaded ruler had only put on the pretence of
all this cruelty, in order to surprise them all the more
agreeably by himself taking the jolliest part in what he
had before forbidden.   Everyone believes her mad ;
and Friedrich especially reproves her with bitter harsh-
ness for her incomprehensible folly.   But a few words
from her suffice to excite the governor himself to an
ecstasy of joy ; for she promises him in a secret, trust-

ing whisper, the fulfilment of all his wishes, and that she will send him on the following night a message to give him full assurance of his bliss.

Thus ends the first act, in the midst of the wildest excitement. What the quickly-conceived plan of the heroine really is, we ascertain at the beginning of the second act, when she visits her brother's prison, determined first to put him to the test and learn if he is really worthy to be saved. She tells him of Friedrich's shameful proposals, and asks him if he desires to regain his ill-spent life at the cost of his sister's honor ? His first expression of outspoken horror, and his willingness to sacrifice himself (manifested in his farewell to his sister, and his committal to her of the most touching messages for the loved one he must leave behind), are at length succeeded by a softer mood, which carries the unhappy man at last from grief to weakness. Isabella, who is about to announce to him his safety, checks herself in amazement as she sees her brother pass from the heights of noble devotion to the murmured confession of his unconquered love of life,—even to the hesitating question, whether the price of his safety really seems to her impossible. She starts up in fury, thrusts her unworthy brother from her, and declares that added to the shame of his death he bears with him from this moment her heartiest contempt.

After she has left him with the keeper, her self-control shows itself again in her sudden change back to a brighter and braver mood ; she decides to punish the pitiable waverer by keeping him in continued uncertainty concerning his fate, but does not turn from her determination to free the world from the vilest hypocrite that ever attempted to impose laws upon it. She instructs Marianna that she must fill the place of the falsely loved Isabella at the meeting promised to Friedrich for the night ; and she sends to the latter the appointment for this meeting, which it is arranged (in order that he may be more completely entrapped), shall take place at a masque, and in one of the very pleasure-resorts which he had himself suppressed. She announces Friedrich's love for her and the pretended necessity for her yielding to it, to the reckless Lucio in such amazingly wanton fashion that he, generally so unscrupulous himself, falls into a stupefaction of astonishment at it, and then into a desperate fury ; he swears that even if the noble maiden herself consents to submit to this unheard of shame, he will keep it from her by every means in his power, and sooner set all. Palermo in flames and uproar than have it succeed.

He arranges that all his friends and acquaintances shall meet him at evening at the end of the corso, as if to begin the forbidden carnival procession. At the coming on of night, when everything is growing wild and riotous, Lucio himself appears, and seeks to rouse the throng to open and forcible insurrection,—singing a reckless carnival song with the refrain,

> " Who in our pleasure finds no zest,
> We've a dagger here for his sullen breast."

As a band of Sbirri under Brighella approaches to disperse the fantastically-dressed crowd, the riot is on the very verge of an outbreak ; but Lucio begs them to submit for the present, and to separate, but remain near at hand ; for he will find and bring to them the true leader of their plan. Close by is the place which Isabella has rashly pointed out to him as the rendezvous for her meeting with the governor. Lucio lies in wait for the latter, and soon perceives him approaching carefully disguised in a mask ; he seizes him, and as he wrests himself away, is about to follow him, with his drawn sword, when he is himself stopped and turned aside at the instigation of Isabella, who is concealed in the shrubbery near by. Isabella appears, rejoicing at the thought that Marianna's faith-

less spouse is now restored to her ; and, as she believes
that she now carries in her hand the promised pardon
for her brother, is about to generously deny herself
any further revenge, when she breaks the seal by the
light of a torch, and to her horror recognizes the death
sentence, which, through her desire to keep back the
news of the pardon from her brother, and her bribe
to the turnkey, chance has thus brought into her
hands. After a hard conflict with the passion that
consumed him, Friedrich, feeling himself powerless
before it, had determined, though he died as a criminal, still to meet his ruin like a man of honor. One
hour on Isabella's breast ;—then his own death by the
same rigid law to the severity of which Claudio's life
must also fall a victim.

Isabella, who sees in this action only a new accumu-
lation of the hypocrite's villanies, again breaks out
with a fury of despair. At her summons to instant
rebellion against the despicable tyrant, the multitude
gathers about her in wild and excited confusion ; but
Lucio, who appears among them, bitterly advises the
people to give no heed to a woman that is only de-
ceiving them as she had deceived him (he, of course,
being under the delusion that she has been shamefully
false). Renewed confusion follows, and Isabella's
desperation increases ; when suddenly there comes
from the background a comic appeal for help from
Brighella, who, himself upon some jealous quest or
other, has seized by mistake upon the masked governor, and so brings about his discovery. Friedrich is
unmasked : Marianna is recognized, clinging trembling to his side ; amazement, disgust, and exultation
spread among the people ; and Friedrich gloomily
demands that he be taken before the court of the king,
whose return they are expecting, to himself receive his
death sentence. But Claudio, who has been set free
by the jubilant people, tells him that capital punishment is not inflicted for love-crimes in all cases.

Messengers now announce the sudden arrival of the King in the harbor ; and it is decided to give the beloved sovereign, who will see with delight what a failure the gloomy puritanism of the German must be in glowing Sicily, a joyous and loyal welcome home. They say of him, "he enjoys a merry festival better than all your melancholy laws." Friedrich, with his bride Marianna, whom he has wedded anew, opens the procession ; and the novice, who has now abandoned the convent forever, follows with Lucio, in the second couple.

*　　*　　*　　*　　*　　*　　*　　*

I had elaborated these bright and in some respects boldly-planned scenes, in an appropriate and rather careful versification. The police authorities at first objected to the title of my work, which, if it had not been changed, would have been to blame for the utter failure of all my plans for the performance. It was the week before Easter, and performances of light or frivolous pieces were forbidden during this period. Fortunately the magistrate who had the matter in charge had not examined the text with any care, and as I assured him that it was modeled on a very serious Shakespearean work, he contented himself with altering the title ; this certainly had something exciting about it, while the name, "The Novice of Palermo" seemed to have no objectionable features, and no scruples were raised about its incorrectness.

Quite the opposite of this happened to me in Leipzig a short time afterward, where I endeavored to procure the production of my new work instead of the sacrificed "Fairies." The director of the theatre here, whom I hoped to gain over to my plan by flatteringly giving the part of Marianna to his daughter, who was about to make her début,—found in the tendency which he thought he discovered in the subject, a very specious excuse for declining my opera. He considered that even if the magistrates of Leipzig

would permit the performance of it, of which he, in
his esteem for those personages, was very doubtful,—
he certainly could not, in the character of a conscientious father, permit his daughter to appear in it.

As I have said, I had nothing to suffer on account of
this questionable peculiarity of my libretto at the Magdeburg performance, for, as has been intimated, the
subject remained entirely incomprehensible to the audience on account of the confused character of the
acting. This circumstance, and the fact that on account of it there was no opposition to the *tendency*
of the work, made a second performance possible,—
not an objection being made to it for the excellent
reason that nobody bothered himself about it at all.
Feeling perfectly conscious that my opera had produced no impression whatever, and had left the audience in an entirely undecided state as to what all
this meant, I nevertheless counted, considering the
fact that this was the last performance of our company,
upon good and even large receipts, and so did not
hesitate to charge the so-called " full " entrance-price.

Whether anybody might have come by the time
the overture began, I am not in a position to decide
with any accuracy; about a quarter of an hour before
the time fixed for beginning I only saw my lodging-
house keeper and her husband, and a Polish Jew in
full dress seated conspicuously in one of the reserved seats of the parquette.

In spite of this fact I was still hoping for an increase
of the audience, when suddenly a most extraordinary
performance took place behind the scenes. All at
once the husband of my prima donna (the impersonator of Isabella) pounced upon the second tenor,
a very young and handsome fellow (the singer of my
Claudio), against whom the injured spouse had long
nourished a secret jealousy. It seemed that the
prima donna's husband, who had from behind the
curtain inspected with me the composition of the

audience, considered that the time had now arrived
when, without damage to the prospects of the theatre,
he could take his revenge on his wife's lover. Claudio
was so pounded and belabored by him that the unhappy individual was compelled to retire to the dress-
ing-room with his face all bleeding. Isabella was
informed of this, and rushing desperately toward her
furious lord received from him a series of such violent
cuffs that she forthwith went into spasms. The confusion among my *personnel* was now quite boundless ;
everybody took sides with one party or the other,
and everything seemed on the point of a general fight.
It seemed as if this unhappy evening appeared to all
of them precisely calculated for a final settling up of·
all sorts of fancied insults. This much was evident—
that the couple who had suffered under the "love-
veto" (*Liebesverbot*) of Isabella's husband were certainly unable to appear on this occasion. The mana·
ger was sent before the curtain, to announce to the
remarkably made-up little company assembled in the
theatre, that on account of "various adverse circumstances that had arisen" the performance of the
opera could not take place.

No further attempt was ever made to rehabilitate
my youthful production.

A PILGRIMAGE TO BEETHOVEN.

O WANT and Misery, protecting deities of the German musician (unless indeed he happens to be the Capellmeister of a court theatre)—Want and Misery—you shall have the first and the most honorable mention at the very beginning of even this reminiscence of my life ! Let me sing your praises, steadfast companions of mine ! ̲You have kept faith with me and never left me ! You have kept from me with your sturdy hands all happy changes of fate, and sheltered me from the oppressive sunbeams of fortune ! You have ever cast a black shadow over the vain goods of this world ; receive my thanks for your most unwearying devotion ! ̖ Yet, if you can so arrange it, I beseech you to seek out by and by some other protégé, for I would fain see, from very curiosity, how I could perhaps get on without you. At the least I beg you to descend with special force on these political dreamers of ours—those madmen who seek to unite Germany under one sceptre :—for then there would be but one court theatre, but one single Capellmeister ! What would become of my prospects then ! Of my only hopes, that even now seem dim and dreary to me,—even now, when there are still many German court theatres ? But—I see that I am growing wickedly audacious ; pardon, O goddesses, the rash wish that I have uttered ! You know my heart, and know how I am devoted to you, and

how I would remain your devotee though there should
be in Germany a thousand court theatres.   Amen.

Before this daily prayer of mine I begin nothing—
not even the story of my Pilgrimage to Beethoven.

In case this important document should be published
after my death, I believe it necessary to explain who
I am, for without such an explanation much that is contained herein might be utterly unintelligible.   Listen
then, all the world, and you, ye executors of testaments.

My native town is a commonplace city of central
Germany.   I hardly know for what I was originally
intended ; I only remember that I heard one evening
a symphony of Beethoven; that I thereupon fell ill of
a fever ; and that when I recovered I was—a musician.   Perhaps it may be a result of this circumstance
that even after I had become acquainted with much
other noble music I still loved, honored, and idolized
Beethoven more than all.   I knew no greater pleasure than to bury myself in the depths of this great
genius, until at length I imagined myself a part
of it ; and began to honor myself as this little part,—
to gain higher conceptions and views ; in brief, to
become that which the wise are wont to call—a fool.
But my madness was of an amiable sort, and injured
no one ; the bread that I ate while I was in this condition was very dry, the drink that I drank was very
thin ; for giving lessons is not a very profitable business with us, O honored world and executors !

So I lived for awhile in my garret, until it suddenly
occurred to me that the man whose creations I most
honored—was still alive !   I did not comprehend why
I had not thought of this before.   It had not for a
moment suggested itself to me that Beethoven still
existed ; that he could eat bread and breathe the air
like one of us ; yet this Beethoven still lived in
Vienna, and was also a poor German musician !

And now my peace of mind was over.   All my
thoughts tended toward one wish,—*to see Beethoven !*

No Mussulman ever longed more faithfully to make his pilgrimage to the grave of the prophet, than I to the room in which Beethoven lived.

But how should I bring about the execution of my purpose? It was a long journey to Vienna, and I should need money to make it ; I, an unfortunate, who hardly made enough to keep life in his body ! I must devise some extraordinary means to gain the necessary sum. I carried to a publisher a few piano sonatas that I had composed after the model of the master, and speedily convinced the man that I was a lunatic. Nevertheless he was good enough to advise me, that if I wanted to earn a few thalers by my compositions I had better set to work to gain a small reputation by galops and potpourris. I shuddered ; but my longing to see Beethoven won the day ; I composed the galops and potpourris, but I could not bring myself to cast a glance at Beethoven during this period—for I feared to alienate him utterly.

To my grief, however, I was not even paid for this first sacrifice of my purity ; for the publisher ex-plained to me that the first thing to be done was to make myself something of a name. I shuddered again, and fell into despair. But this state of mind nevertheless produced several excellent galops. I really received some money for these, and at last believed I had enough to carry out my project. Two years had passed, however, and I had lived in perpet-ual fear that Beethoven might die before I had earned a reputation by galops and potpourris. But, thank God, he has outlived the brilliancy of my renown ! Glorious Beethoven, forgive me this reputation ! It was made solely that I might behold thee !

Ah, what bliss ! my goal was reached. Who was happier than I ? I could pack my bundle, and take up my journey to Beethoven ! A holy awe oppressed me as I passed out at the gate and turned me toward the south. I would gladly have taken a place in the

Ah, what a delight it was! Here, beside the Bohemian highway, under the open sky, the Septuor of Beethoven was performed with a clearness, a precision, and a deep expression, such as one seldom finds among the most masterly of virtuosos! O great Beethoven, we brought to thee a worthy sacrifice!

We were just at the finale, when—for the road passed up a steep hill just here—an elegant travelling-carriage drew near us, slowly and noiselessly, and at last stopped beside us. An amazingly tall and wonderfully fair young man lay stretched out in the vehicle; he listened with considerable attention to our music, took out his pocket-book, and wrote a few words in it. Then he let fall a gold-piece from the carriage, and drove on, speaking a few words of English to his servant—from which I discovered that he must be an Englishman.

This occurrence threw us into a discord; luckily we had finished the performance of the Septuor. I embraced my friends, and would have accompanied them; but they explained that they must leave the highway here and strike into a path across the fields to reach their home. If Beethoven himself had not been waiting for me, I would have gone thither with them. As it was, we separated with no little emotion, and parted. Later it occurred to me that no one had picked up the Englishman's gold-piece.

In the next inn, which I entered to refresh myself, I found the Englishman seated at an excellent repast. He looked at me for a long while, and at last addressed me in passable German.

"Where are your companions?" he asked.

"They have gone home," said I.

"Take your violin," he continued, "and play something. Here is some money."

I was offended at this, and explained that I did not play for money; further, that I had no violin; and I briefly related to him how I had met the musicians.

" They were good musicians," said the Englishman,
" and the Beethoven symphony was also good."

This observation struck me ; I asked whether he
himself was musical.

" Yes," he answered ; " I play the flute twice a
week ; on Thursday I play the French horn ; and on
Sundays I compose."

That was certainly a good deal ; I stood amazed.
I had never in my life heard of travelling English
musicians.   I decided, therefore, that they must be in
a most excellent position if they could make their
wanderings with such fine equipages.   I asked if he
was a musician by profession.

For some time I received no reply ; at last he answered slowly that he was very wealthy.

My error was plain ; I had certainly offended him
by my inquiry.   Somewhat confused, I remained
silent, and went on with my simple meal.

The Englishman, who again took a long look at
me, began again.   " Do you know Beethoven ? " he
asked.

I replied that I had never been in Vienna, but that
I was at this moment on the way thither to satisfy the
keen longing that I felt to see the idolized master.

" Where do you come from ? " he asked.   " From
L—— ?   That is not far.   I come from England, and
also desire to know Beethoven.   We will both make
his acquaintance ; he is a very celebrated composer."

What an extraordinary meeting ! I thought.   Great
master, what different people you attract !   On foot
and in carriages they make their pilgrimages to you !
My Englishman interested me greatly, but I confess
that I envied him very little on account of his fine
carriage.   It seemed to me that my difficult pilgrimage was more holy and loyal, and that its goal must
give me more pleasure than him who went in pride
and splendor.

The postilion blew his horn ; the Englishman drove

on, calling to me that he would see Beethoven sooner
than I.

I had gone but a few miles further when I unexpectedly came upon him again. This time it was on
the road. One of the wheels of his carriage had
broken; but he still sat within in majestic calm, his
servant behind him, in spite of the fact that the wagon
hung far over to one side. I discovered that they
were waiting for the postilion, who had gone on to a
village a considerable distance in advance to bring a
wheelwright. They had waited a long while; and as
the servant only spoke English, I determined to go
forward myself to the village to hurry the postillion
and the wheelwright back. I found the former in a
tavern, where he was sitting over his brandy, not
troubling himself especially about the Englishman;
but I nevertheless succeeded in speedily taking him
back with the mechanic to the broken carriage. The
damage was soon repaired; the Englishman promised
to announce me at Beethoven's, and drove away.

What was my amazement to overtake him the next
day again. This time he had not broken a wheel, but
had halted calmly in the middle of the road, and was
reading a book; and he appeared quite pleased as he
saw me again approaching.

" I have waited some hours," said he, " because it
occurred to me just here that I had done wrong not to
invite you to drive with me to Beethoven's. Driving
is far better than walking. Come into the carriage."

I was amazed. For a moment I hesitated whether
I should not accept his offer; but I remembered the
vow that I had made the day before when I saw the
Englishman drive away;—I had vowed that no matter
what might happen I would make my pilgrimage on
foot. I declared this to be my resolution, and now it
was the Englishman's turn to be astonished. He repeated his offer, and that he had waited hours for me,
in spite of the fact that he had had his wheel tho-

roughly repaired at the place where he had passed the
night, and had been much delayed thereby. I remained firm, however, and he drove away.

To tell the truth I had a secret prejudice against
him, for a peculiar feeling forced itself upon me that
this Englishman would some time or other bring me
into great embarrassment. Besides, his admiration of
Beethoven and his intention to make his acquaintance
impressed me as rather the impertinent mood of a rich
aristocrat than as the deep and earnest yearning of an
enthusiastic soul. For these reasons I felt an inclination
to avoid him, that I might not debase my own pious
longing by his companionship.

But as though my fate were trying to reveal to me
into what a dangerous connection with this man I
should some day come, I met him again on the evening of the same day, stopped before an inn and apparently waiting for me a second time—for he sat back-
wards in his carriage and looked back along the road in
my direction.

" Sir," said he, " I have again been waiting some
hours for you. Will you ride with me to see Beethoven ? "

This time my surprise was joined with a certain disgust. This extraordinary persistency in serving me
could be only interpreted in one way—that the Englishman, perceiving my growing dislike for him, was
endeavoring to force himself upon me for my own
injury. I again refused his offer, with unconcealed
irritation. He cried out haughtily, "Damn it, you
seem to care very little for Beethoven," and drove
rapidly away.

This was, as it turned out, the last time that I met
the islander during the whole of the journey that
remained before reaching Vienna. At last I trod the
streets of the city ; the end of my pilgrimage was
reached. With what emotions I entered this Mecca
of my faith! All the difficulties of the long and weary

journey were forgotten ; I was at my goal—within the walls that surrounded Beethoven.

I was too deeply moved to think of the immediate fulfilment of my project. I at once inquired, it is true, for Beethoven's dwelling, but only to take up my quarters in his neighborhood. Almost opposite the house in which the master lived, there was a hotel, not too expensive for me ; here I hired a little room in the fifth story, and prepared myself for the greatest event of my life—a visit to Beethoven.

After I had rested for two days, and had fasted and prayed, but had not taken a single look at Vienna, I summoned up my courage, left the hotel, and crossed obliquely to the marvellous house. I was told that Beethoven was not at home. This rather pleased me than otherwise, for I gained time to collect myself. But when the same answer was given to me four times before night,—and with a certain heightened tone, —I decided that this was an unlucky day, and gave up my visit in despair.

As I went back to the hotel, who should nod to me with considerable cordiality from a window of the first story but—my Englishman !

" Have you seen Beethoven ? " he called to me.

" Not yet ; he was not in," I answered, surprised at this repeated encounter. He met me on the steps and insisted with remarkable cordiality on my going to his room.

" Sir," said he, " I have seen you go to Beethoven's house five times to-day. I have been here a number of days, and took lodgings in this wretched hotel in order to be near him. Believe me, it is a very difficult task to get at Beethoven ; the gentleman has many caprices. I called on him six times when I was first here, and was always refused. Now I have taken to getting up very early and sitting at the window until late in the evening, to see when he goes out. But the gentleman *never* seems to go out."

3

" You think then that Beethoven was at home to-day, but denied himself to me ? " cried I, excitedly.

" Undoubtedly ; you and I have both been turned away. And it is especially disagreeable to me, for I didn't come to see Vienna, but Beethoven."

This was very sad news for me. Nevertheless I made the experiment again the next day—but again in vain. The gates of heaven were shut against me.

The Englishman, who always watched my attempt with excited attention from his window, had at last received positive information that Beethoven was really not to be approached. He was thoroughly vexed, but immeasurably persevering. My patience, however, was soon exhausted, for I had more reason for it than he. A week had gradually slipped away without the attainment of my object ; and the income from my galops by no means permitted me a long residence in Vienna. I gradually began to despair.

I communicated my sorrows to the landlord of the hotel. He smiled, and promised to tell me the reason of my woes if I would swear not to betray it to the Englishman. Foreseeing disaster, I made the vow demanded of me.

" You see," said the trusty landlord, " hosts of Englishmen come here to see Herr von Beethoven and make his acquaintance. This annoys Herr von Beethoven so much, and he has been in such a rage at the impertinence of these people, that he makes it absolutely impossible for any stranger to get admittance to him. He is a singular man, and this may be pardoned in him. It is an excellent thing for my hotel, however, for it is generally liberally patronized by Englishmen, who are compelled by their anxiety to see Herr Beethoven to remain my guests longer than they otherwise would. Since you promise me, however, not to betray me to these gentlemen, I hope to find a means to secure your admission to Herr Beethoven."

This was refreshing ; so I had not reached the goal, because I—poor devil—passed for an Englishman! My presentiment was justified—the Englishman was my ruin ! I would have left the house at once, for of course every one that lodged there was taken for an Englishman at Beethoven's, and I was already outlawed for this reason ; but the landlord's promise restrained me,—that he would bring about an opportunity to see and speak with the master. The Englishman, whom I detested from my soul, had meanwhile begun all sorts of intrigues and bribes, but without result.

So several more fruitless days slipped away, during which the receipts from my galops visibly diminished ; till at last the landlord confided to me that I could not fail to meet Beethoven if I would go into a particular beer-garden, whither he went almost daily at a certain hour. At the same time I received from my counsellor certain unmistakable descriptions of the personal appearance of the great master, which would enable me to recognize him. I roused myself, and determined not to put off my happiness until to-morrow. It was impossible to catch Beethoven as he went out, for he always left his house by a back way ; so there was nothing left for me but the beer-garden. Unfortunately, however, I looked there for the master both on this and the two following days without success.

At last on the fourth day, as I again directed my steps to the momentous beer-garden at the appointed hour, I perceived to my horror that the Englishman was cautiously and observantly following me at a distance. The wretch, perpetually watching at his window, had not let the fact escape him that I went out every day at the same hour and in the same direction. He had been struck by this, and at once suspecting that I had found some clue by which to trace out Beethoven, he had decided to take advantage of my presumed discovery. He told me all this with the great-

est frankness, and forthwith declared that he proposed
to follow me everywhere. In vain were all my endeavors to deceive him, or to make him believe that I
had no other purpose in view than to visit, for my own
refreshment, a beer-garden that was far too unfashion-
able to be worth the consideration of a gentleman like
him ; he kept steadfastly to his resolution, and I had
my luck to curse for it. At last I tried rudeness, and
sought to rid myself of him by insolence ; far from letting himself be influenced by this, however, he contented himself with a gentle smile. His fixed idea
was—*to see Beethoven ;* nothing else disturbed him in
the least.

In truth, it was to be ; on this day I was for the
first time to behold the great Beethoven. No words
can picture my ecstasy—or at the same time describe
my rage—as, seated beside my " gentleman," I saw
approaching a man whose carriage and appearance
fully bore out the description that the landlord had
given me of the master. The long blue overcoat, the
tangled, bristling grey hair, and more than these the
features, the expression of the face, as they had long
hovered before my imagination, pictured from an excellent portrait. No mistake was possible ; I had recognized him in an instant ! He passed us with short
and hurried steps ; surprise and reverence enchained
my senses.

The Englishman missed none of my movements ;
he looked with curiosity at the new-comer, who withdrew into the most secluded corner of the beer-garden,
—at this hour almost deserted,—ordered wine, and then
remained for a time in an attitude of deep thought.
My beating heart said to me—" It is he ! " For a moment I forgot my neighbor, and looked with curious
eye and unspeakable emotion upon the man whose
genius had alone ruled over all my thoughts and feelings since I had learned to think and feel. Involuntarily
I began to murmur softly to myself, and fell into a

kind of soliloquy that ended with the but too distinctly uttered words—"Beethoven—it is thou, then, whom I see!"

Nothing escaped my accursed neighbor, who, bending close beside me, had listened with bated breath to my murmuring. I was roused in horror from my deep ecstasy by the words—"Yes, this gentleman is Beethoven! Come, let us introduce ourselves at once!"

Filled with anxiety and disgust I held the cursed Englishman back by the arm.

"What are you going to do?" I cried—"do you mean to disgrace us? Here—in such a place—so utterly without regard to common courtesy?"

"Oh," responded he, "it's a capital opportunity; we shan't easily find a better one."

With this he drew a kind of note-book from his pocket, and would have rushed forthwith upon the man in the blue overcoat. Beside myself, I seized the lunatic by the skirts of his coat, and cried out furiously, "Are you stark mad?"

This proceeding had attracted the attention of the stranger. He seemed to guess, with painful annoyance, that he was the subject of our excitement, and after he had hastily emptied his glass he rose to go away. Hardly had the Englishman perceived this than he tore himself from me with such force that he left one of his coat-skirts in my hand, and threw himself in Beethoven's path. The latter sought to avoid him; but the wretch was before him, and making him a marvellous bow according to the latest English fashion, addressed him as follows:

"I have the honor to introduce myself to that very famous composer and most estimable man—Herr Beethoven."

He had no need to add anything further, for with his first words Beethoven, casting a single glance upon me, had turned away with a hasty start to one side, and had vanished from the garden with the speed of lightning. Not the less did the irrepressible Briton show his intention to pursue the fugitive, when I seized, in a fury of rage, on the remnant of his coat skirts. Somewhat astonished, he checked himself, and cried out in a singular tone :

" Damn it ! This gentleman is worthy to be an Englishman, and I shall certainly make no delay in forming his acquaintance ! "

I stood there stupefied ; this terrible adventure put an end to every hope of mine to see the dearest wish of my heart fulfilled !

It was very clear to me that from this time forth every attempt to approach Beethoven in an ordinary fashion must be perfectly vain. In my ruinous circumstances I had only to decide whether I would at once enter upon my homeward journey with my object unaccomplished, or whether I should make one last desperate endeavor to reach my goal. At the first alternative I shuddered to the bottom of my soul. Who, so near as this to the gates of the holy of holies, could see them close upon him without being fairly annihilated ? Before I gave up the salvation of my soul, then, I would make one more desperate attempt. But what step was there for me to take—what way left me to pursue ? For a long time I could think of nothing definite. Alas, all consciousness was benumbed ; nothing presented itself to my imagination but the remembrance of what I had passed through when I held the vile Englishman's coat-skirts in my hands. Beethoven's side glance at my unlucky self during this frightful catastrophe had not escaped me ; I felt what such a glance must mean ; he had—taken me for an Englishman !

What should I do then, to elude the wrath of the master ? Everything depended on informing him that I was a simple German soul, full of worldly poverty, but more than worldly enthusiasm.

So I decided at last to pour out my heart,—to write. I did so ; told him briefly the history of my life ; how I had become a musician ; how I idolized him ; how I had longed to make his acquaintance ; how I had given up two years to gaining a reputation as a composer of galops ; how I had begun and ended my pilgrimage ; what woes the Englishman had brought upon me, and in what a cruel situation I now found myself. As I felt my heart grow consciously lighter during this summary of my griefs, I even passed into a certain degree of confidence, from the pleasure of this feeling ; I mingled in my letter some frank and rather decided complaints of the unjust cruelty with which I, poor devil, had been treated by the master. I closed my letter with positive enthusiasm ; my eyes swam as I wrote the address—" to Herr Ludwig von Beethoven." I uttered a silent prayer, and myself delivered the letter at Beethoven's house.

As I returned to my hotel, full of enthusiasm—great Heaven ! what brought the horrible Englishman again before my eyes ? He had watched this last errand also from his window; he had seen on my features the happiness of hope, and this was enough to deliver me again into his power. He stopped me on the steps with the question, " Good news ? When shall we see Beethoven ? "

" Never ! never ! " cried I in despair—" Beethoven will never in his life see you again ! Let me go, villain ! We have nothing in common ! "

" Most decidedly we have something in common," responded he, coldly ; " where is the skirt of my coat, sir ? Who authorized you to forcibly deprive me of it ? Do you know, sir, that you are to blame for the behavior of Beethoven toward me ? How was he to find it *en régle* to permit the acquaintance of a gentleman with only one coat-skirt ? "

Furious at seeing the fault thus cast upon me, I cried—" You shall have the coat-skirt back, sir !

Treasure it up as a shameful reminder of the way in which you insulted the great Beethoven, and ruined a poor musician !—Farewell ! may we never see each other again ! "

He sought to restrain me, and to pacify me by assuring me that he had still a large number of coats in the best possible condition ; I must tell him when Beethoven would receive us. But I rushed past him up into my fifth story ; and there I locked myself in and waited for Beethoven's answer.

But how shall I describe what passed within me— around me—when I really received within an hour a little piece of note-paper on which was hastily written —" Pardon me, Herr R——, if I ask you to call for the first time to-morrow morning ; for I am at work to get off a packet of music by post. I expect you to-morrow. Beethoven."

First of all I sank upon my knees and thanked Heaven for this marvellous boon ; my eyes were clouded with burning tears. But at length my emotions broke loose in the wildest joy ; I sprang up and danced about my little bedroom like a madman. I hardly know what I danced ; but I remember that to my infinite shame I suddenly became aware that I was accompanying myself by whistling a galop. This unhappy discovery brought me to myself again ; I left my room and the hotel, and rushed into the streets of Vienna fairly drunken with delight.

Heavens ! My woes had made me utterly forget that I was in Vienna ! How the lively stir of the people of the imperial city delighted me ! I was in an enthusiastic mood, and saw everything with enthusiastic eyes. The somewhat superficial sensuousness of the Viennese seemed the fresh warmth of life ; their frivolous and not very fastidious pursuit of pleasure passed for natural and frank appreciation of the beautiful. I looked over the five daily theatre-bills ; on one of

them I saw announced " *Fidelio*,—opera by Beethoven."

I must go to the theatre, be the receipts from my
galops ever so sadly lessened ! As I came into the
parquette the overture began. This was the rearrangement of the opera that had once—to the honor of
the highly critical public of Vienna—failed, under the
title of " Leonore." Even in this later form I had
nowhere been able to produce it ; and the delight
may be imagined, which I experienced as I now heard
for the first time this glorious novelty. A very young
girl rendered the rôle of Leonore ; yet this singer
seemed even in her early youth to have fairly wed
herself to the genius of Beethoven. With what ardor,
poetic feeling, deep emotion did she depict this wonderful woman ! Her name was Wilhelmine Schröder.
She had gained for herself the noble merit of opening
Beethoven's work to the German public ; for I saw
that evening, that even the superficial Viennese were
roused to thorough enthusiasm. For me the very
heavens were opened ; all was illuminated for me, and
I bowed down before the Genius that had led me—
like Florestan—from night and chains to light and
liberty.

That night I could not sleep. What I had just gone
through and what awaited me on the morrow, was too
great and overwhelming to have let me carry it quietly
into my dreams. I lay awake; I wandered ; I prepared myself to appear before Beethoven. At last the
day appeared ; I waited with impatience for a time
suitable for a morning call ; it came, and I started
forth. The most important event of my life stood before me ; I trembled at the thought.

But I was to pass through a terrible trial.

Leaning against Beethoven's door-post there awaited
me with great sang-froid, my demon—the Englishman !
The villain had bribed everybody—finally even the
landlord. The latter had read Beethoven's open·note

3*

before I had seen it myself, and had betrayed its contents to the Briton.

A cold sweat burst from me at the sight. All romance, all divine ecstasy disappeared. I was again in
his power.

"Come," said the wretch, "let us introduce ourselves to Beethoven!"

At first I thought of helping myself out of the difficulty with a lie, and asserting that I was not on the
way to Beethoven at all. But he at once deprived me
of all possibility of refuge, by explaining to me with
the greatest candor that he had discovered my secret;
and declaring that he would not leave me till we had
seen Beethoven. I sought at first to dissuade him
good-humoredly from his design;—in vain. I fell into
a rage;—in vain. Finally I hoped to escape him by
fleetness of foot. I flew up the steps like an arrow, and
jerked at the bell like a madman. But before the door
was opened the man stood beside me, seized the skirt
of my coat and said: "Don't run away from me! I
have a right to your coat-skirts, and I'll hold fast by
them until we stand in Beethoven's presence."

I turned upon him in a fury, and struggled to free
myself; I even felt tempted to defend myself by physical force against the proud son of Albion—when suddenly the door was opened. An old servant appeared,
frowning as she discovered us in our extraordinary position; and seemed about to shut the door again upon
us. In my anxiety I called my name aloud, and affirmed that I had been invited by Herr Beethoven himself.

The old woman was still in doubt, for the sight of the
Englishman seemed to rouse in her a very just suspi-
cion,—when suddenly, as luck would have it, Beethoven himself appeared at the door of his study. Taking advantage of this moment, I rushed quickly in,
and sought to approach the master to excuse myself.
But I dragged in the Englishman with me, for he

clung to me still. He carried out his purpose, and did not let me go until we stood before Beethoven. I bowed, and stammered out my name ; and though he certainly did not understand it, he seemed to know that I was the one who had written to him. He motioned to me to go into his room; and without being in the least disturbed by Beethoven's amazed look, my companion slipped hastily in after me.

Here I was—in the sanctuary ; but the horrible embarrassment into which the villainous Britisher had led me robbed me of all that beneficent mood that was necessary to worthily enjoy my good fortune. Beethoven's appearance was certainly not in itself adapted to have an agreeable and soothing effect. He was in a somewhat disorderly dishabille ; he wore a red woollen belt around his body ; long, stiff, gray hair hung in disorder about his head ; and his gloomy, repellent expression did not tend to allay my confusion. We sat down at a table covered with pens and paper.

There was a decided feeling of awkwardness ; no one spoke. Beethoven was evidently out of temper at having to receive two persons instead of one.

At last he began by saying in a harsh voice—" You come from L—— ? "

I was about to answer, but he interrupted me ; laying a pencil and sheet of paper before me, he added : —" Write ; I cannot hear."

I knew of Beethoven's deafness, and had prepared myself for it. Nevertheless it went through my heart like a pang when I heard his harsh and broken voice say " I cannot hear." To live in the world joyless and in poverty ; to find one's only exalted happiness in the power of music—and to have to say " I cannot hear ! " In one moment there came to me the full understanding of Beethoven's manner, of the deep sorrow in his face, of the gloomy sadness of his glance, of the firm-set haughtiness of his lips :—*he could not hear !*

Confused, and without knowing what I said, I wrote

an entreaty for his pardon and a brief explanation of the circumstances that had forced me to appear in the company of the Englishman. The latter sat silent and contented opposite Beethoven, who, when he had read my words, turned to him rather sharply with the inquiry what he desired from him ?

" I have the honor "—replied the Briton.

" I can't understand you," cried Beethoven, hastily interrupting him. " I cannot hear, and I can speak but little. Write down what you want with me."

The Englishman quietly reflected for a moment, then drew an elegant music-book from his pocket, and said to me " Good.—Write—I request Herr Beethoven to look at this composition of mine ; if he finds a passage that does not please him, he will have the kindness to mark a cross against it."

I wrote down his request literally, in the hope that we might thus get rid of him. And such was really the result. After Beethoven had read it, he laid the Englishman's composition on the table with a peculiar smile, nodded abruptly, and said " I will send it to you."

With this my " gentleman " was content. He rose, made an especially magnificent bow, and took his leave. I drew a long breath ;—he was gone.

Now for the first time I felt myself in the very sanctuary. Even Beethoven's features grew obviously brighter ; he looked quietly at me for a moment, and began :

" The Englishman has caused you no little trouble ? " said he. " Find consolation with me ; these travelling Englishmen have tortured me to death. They come to-day to see a poor musician as they would go to-morrow to look at some rare animal. I am heartily sorry to have confounded you with him.—You wrote me that you were pleased with my compositions. I am glad of that, for I have little confidence now in pleasing people with my productions."

This cordiality in addressing me soon did away with all my embarrassment ; a thrill of joy ran through me at these simple words. I wrote that I was by no means the only one filled with such ardent enthusiasm for every one of his creations, as to have no dearer wish than, for instance, to gain for my native city the happiness of seeing him once in its midst ;—that he might then convince himself what effect his works produced upon the public.

" I can well believe," he answered, " that my compositions are more appreciated in North Germany. The Viennese often provoke me ; they hear too much wretched stuff every day, to be always in the mood to take an earnest interest in anything serious."

I sought to combat this view, and instanced the fact that I had yesterday attended a performance of " Fidelio," which the Viennese public had received with the most obvious enthusiasm.

" Hm ! Hm ! " muttered the master,—" The ' Fidelio' ! But I know that the people only applaud it out of vanity, after all, for they imagine that in my rearrangement of the opera I only followed their advice. So they seek to reward me for my trouble, and cry bravo ! It's a good-natured, uneducated populace ; so I like better to be among it than among wise people. Does ' Fidelio ' please you ? "

I told him of the impression that the performance of the day before had made upon me, and remarked that the whole had gained most gloriously by the additions that had been made to it. ·

" It is vexatious work," said Beethoven ; " I am no composer of operas ; at least I know of no theatre in the world for which I would care to compose an opera again. If I should make an opera according to my own conception, the people would absolutely flee from it ; for there would be no airs, duetts, trios, and all that nonsense to be found in it, with which operas are stitched together nowadays ;—and what I would substitute for these no singer would sing and no audience hear. They all know nothing deeper than brilliant falsehoods, sparkling nonsense, and sugar-coated dulness. The man who created a true musical drama would be looked upon as a fool—and would be one in very truth if he did not keep such a thing to himself, but wanted to bring it before the public."

" And how should one go to work," I asked excitedly, " to produce such a musical drama ? "

" As Shakespeare did when he wrote his plays "— was the almost angry answer. Then he continued: " The man who has to trouble himself with fitting all sorts of brilliant prattle to women with passable voices, so that they may gain applause by it, should make himself a Parisian man-milliner, not a dramatic composer. For myself, I am not made for such trifling. I know very well that certain wiseacres say of me for this reason that though I have some ability in instrumentation I should never be at home in vocal music. They are right—for they understand by vocal music only operatic music; and as for my being at home in that—Heaven forbid ! "

I ventured to ask if he really thought that any one, after hearing his "Adelaide," would dare to deny him the most brilliant genius for vocal music also ?

" Well," he said after a short pause, " ' Adelaide ' and things of that kind are small matters, after all, that soon fall into the hands of the professional virtuosi—to serve them as opportunities to bring out their brilliant art-touches. Why should not vocal music form a great and serious *genre* by itself as well as instrumental,—that should receive as much respect from the frivolous tribe of singers in its execution, as is demanded of an orchestra in the production of a symphony. The human voice exists. It is a far more beautiful and noble organ of tone than any instrument of an orchestra. Ought it not to be brought into as independent use as this latter ? What new results

might not be gained by such a method ! For it is precisely the character of the human voice, utterly different by nature from the peculiarities of an instrument,
that could be brought out and retained, and could be
capable of the most varying combinations. In instruments, the primal organs of creation and nature find
their representation ; they cannot be sharply determined and defined, for they but repeat primal feelings
as they came forth from the chaos of the first creation,
when there were perhaps no human beings in existence to receive them in their hearts. With the genius of the human voice it is entirely otherwise ; this
represents the human heart, and its isolated, individual emotion. Its character is therefore limited, but
fixed and defined. Let these two elements be brought
together, then ; let them be united ! Let those wild
primal emotions that stretch out into the infinite, that
are represented by instruments, be contrasted with the
clear, definite emotions of the human heart, represented
by the human voice. The addition of the second
element will work beneficently and soothingly upon
the conflict of the elemental emotions, and give to
their course a well-defined and united channel ; and
the human heart itself, in receiving these elemental
emotions, will be immeasurably strengthened and
broadened ; and made capable of feeling clearly what
was before an uncertain presage of the highest ideal,
now changed into a divine knowledge."

Beethoven paused here a moment, as if fatigued.
Then, with a light sigh, he continued :—"It is true that
many obstacles are met with in the attempt to solve
this problem ; in order to sing one has need of words.
But what man could put into words the poetry that
must form the basis of such a union of elements ? Poetry
must stand aside here ; for words are too weak things
for this task.—You will soon hear a new composition
of mine which will remind you of what I am now explaining. It is a symphony with choruses. I call

your attention to the difficulty I had in this, in getting
over the obstacle of the inadequacy of the poetry
which I required to help me. Finally I decided to
choose our Schiller's beautiful "Hymn to Joy"; this
is at least a noble and elevating creation, even though
it is far from expressing what in this case, it is true, no
verses in the world *could* express."

Even now I can hardly comprehend the happiness
that I enjoyed in the fact that Beethoven himself
should thus help me by these explanations to the full
understanding of his last giant symphony, which at
that time must have been barely finished, but which
was as yet known to no one. I expressed to him my
enthusiastic thanks for this certainly rare condescension. At the same time I expressed the delighted surprise that he had given me in this news that the appearance of a new and great work of his composition
might soon be looked for. Tears stood stood in my
eyes—I could have kneeled before him.

Beethoven seemed to perceive my emotion. He
looked at me half sorrowfully, half with a mocking
smile, as he said : "You will be able to be my de-
fender when my new work is spoken of—think of me
then ; the wise people will believe me mad—at all events
they will call me so. Yet you see, Herr R——, that
I am not exactly a madman,—though I might be unhappy enough to be one. People demand of me that
I shall write according to their conception of what is
beautiful and good ; but they do not reflect that I, the
poor deaf man, must have thoughts that are all
my own,—that it is impossible for me to compose
otherwise than as I feel. And that I cannot think and
feel the things that *they* deem beautiful," he added
ironically, "that is my misfortune ! "

With this he rose and strode up and down the
room with short, quick strides. Deeply moved as I
was, I also rose—I felt myself trembling. It would
have been impossible for me to continue the conversa-

tion either by pantomime or writing. I perceived that the time had come when my visit might grow burdensome to the master. To *write* my deep-felt thanks and my farewell, seemed cold; I contented myself by taking my hat, standing before Beethoven, and letting him read in my eyes what was passing within me.

He seemed to understand me. " You are going ? " he asked. " Do you remain any time longer in Vienna ? "

I wrote that I had no other aim in this journey than to become acquainted with him; that as he had deemed me worthy of such an unusual reception, I was more than happy to find my goal reached, and should start the next day on my return.

He answered, smiling, " You wrote to me how you furnished yourself with money for this journey. You should stay here in Vienna and make galops—they are popular wares here."

I declared that all that was over for me, for that I knew nothing that could ever again seem to me to deserve such a sacrifice.

" Well, well," he said, " perhaps something will yet be found ! I—fool that I am—should be far better off if I made galops ; if I go on as I have hitherto, I shall always be in want. *Bon voyage !* " he went on ; " bear me in mind, and console yourself with me in all your trials ! "

Deeply moved, and with tears in my eyes, I was about to take my leave, when he called to me—" Wait ! Let us finish up the musical Englishman. Let us see where the crosses come in."

With this he seized the Englishman's music-book, and smilingly looked through it ; then he carefully folded it up again, wrapped it in paper, took up a heavy music-pen, and drew a gigantic cross across the whole wrapper. And then he handed it to me with the remark, " Kindly return the fortunate being his

masterpiece.   He is an ass—and yet I envy him his
long ears.   Farewell, mein Lieber, and remember me
in kindness."

With this he dismissed me.   Deeply agitated, I
passed out of the room and from the house.

*   *   *   *   *   *   *   *

At the hotel I met the Englishman's servant, as he
was arranging his master's trunk in the travelling carriage.   His goal, too, had been reached ; I was compelled to confess that he too had shown persistency.
I hurried to my room and made my preparations to
begin, the next day, my pedestrian journey back again.
I had to laugh, as I looked at the cross on the wrapper
of the Englishman's composition.   Yet the cross was a
memorial of Beethoven, and I begrudged it to the evil
demon of my pilgrimage.   My decision was quickly
made.   I took the wrapper off, took out my gallops, and
wrapped *them* instead in this condemnatory covering.   I
returned the Englishman his composition without a
wrapper, and accompanied it with a note in which I
informed him that Beethoven envied him, and that he
declared he did not know where to put a cross on such
a work.

As I left the hotel I saw my wretched companion
getting into his carriage.

" Good-by "—he shouted :—" You have done me a
great service.   I am delighted to have made Herr
Beethoven's acquaintance.   Will you go to Italy with
me ? "

" What are you after there ? " asked I in reply.

" I want to make the acquaintance of Rossini—he is
a very celebrated composer."

" Good luck ! " I called.   "*I* know Beethoven ; and
with that I have enough for all my life."

We parted.   I cast one longing look towards
Beethoven's house, and turned to the northward—exalted and ennobled in heart.

AN END IN PARIS.

——————•••——————

WE have just buried him. It was cold and cloudy weather, and there were but few of us. The Englishman was there ; he is going to erect a monument to him ; it would be better if he paid his debts.

It was a dreary business. The first biting air of winter checked one's breath ; no one could speak, and the funeral sermon was dispensed with.

Yet nevertheless you must know that he whom we buried was a good man and an honest German musician. He had a soft heart, and always wept when they whipped the wretched horses in the Paris streets. He was of gentle nature, and never went into a rage when the *gamins* pushed him off the narrow sidewalk. But unhappily he had a tender artist's conscience, was ambitious, and without a talent for intrigue ; and he had once in his youth seen Beethoven, which had so turned his head that he could never truly find his bearings in Paris.

It was a good deal more than a year ago that I saw a large and remarkably beautiful Newfoundland dog bathing in the fountain basin of the Palais Royal. Lover of dogs as I am, I stood and watched the beautiful animal, which at last left the basin, and followed the call of a man who at first attracted my attention only as the owner of the dog. The man was by no means so beautiful to look upon as his dog. He was clean, but dressed according to Heaven knows what

provincial fashion.   Yet his features impressed me ; I
soon remembered that I had known them before ;—my
interest in the dog vanished—I rushed into the arms of
my old friend R——.

We were happy over our reunion; he was fairly
overcome by emotion.   I took him to the Café de la
Rotonde ; I drank tea with rum ; he, coffee—with
tears.

" But what in the world," I began at last, " brings
you to Paris ?   You, the insignificant musician from
your fifth story in the side street of a provincial
town ? "

" My friend," said he, " call it the preternatural curiosity to see how people lived au sixième in Paris ; or
the human curiosity to discover whether I might not
get down to the deuxième or even to the premier—I
am not very clear about it myself.   Before all things,
however, I could not help tearing myself away from
the misery of the German provinces ; and without
tasting the unquestionably greater comfort of the German capitals, rushing into the very capital of the world,
—where the art of all nations comes to a focus, where
the artists of all nations find recognition,—where I also
hope to see satisfied that little portion of ambition that
Heaven—doubtless by mistake—has put into my
heart.".

"Your ambition is natural," said I, " and I can
pardon it, even though it surprises me a little, in you
particularly.   But let us see with what means you propose to nourish your ambitious efforts.   How much
money do you make a year ?   Don't be alarmed !   I
know you were a poor devil, and that there's no question of rents in this case—that's a matter of course.
Still, I must assume that you must have either won
money in a lottery, or that you enjoy the protection
of a rich patron or relative to such an extent as to provide you with a passable annual income for at least
ten years."

"That's the way you ridiculous people look at things," said my friend with a good-natured smile, after he had recovered from his first alarm. "Such prosaic adjuncts appear to you at once as the chief things concerned. Nothing of all these, my dearest friend! I am poor ; in a few weeks I shall even be without a sou ; but what of that ? I have been assured that I have talent. Have I then chosen Tunis to use it in ? No ; I have come to Paris ! Here I shall see if they deceived me when they attributed talent to me—or if I really have it. In the first case, I shall be quickly and willingly undeceived, and shall go quietly home again to my little room, with a clear understanding of myself. In the second case, I shall find my talent paid for quicker and better in Paris than anywhere else in the world.—Ah, don't smile ;—try rather to bring up some worthy argument against me."

"My dear fellow," I said, "I smile no longer ; for at this moment a certain sorrowful feeling thrills through me, that gives me a deep anxiety for you and your magnificent dog. I know that even if you are economical, your excellent animal will still consume a good deal. Are you going to feed yourself and him with your talent?—That is praiseworthy, for self-preservation is the first duty, but humanity towards animals a second and more beautiful one.—But tell me, how are you going to bring your talent into play ? What are your plans ? Tell me them."

"It's a good thing that you ask me about plans," was the answer ; "you shall hear a good quantity of them, for you must know that I am especially rich in plans. First, I am thinking of an opera ; I am provided with completed works, with half-finished ones, and with a large number of schemes of all kinds—for the grand opera and the comic.—Don't answer !—I am prepared to find that this will not be a matter to be arranged all at once, and so I count it only as the basis of my efforts. But even if I can't hope to see

an opera of mine produced immediately, at least I can
count upon being speedily informed whether the management will accept my compositions or not.—My
friend, you are smiling again—but say nothing ! I know
what objection you mean to make, and I will at once
reply to it.   I am convinced that in this respect, too, I
shall have to contend with all sorts of obstacles.   But
in what will these consist ?   Assuredly in nothing but
competition.   The greatest talent of the world assem-
bles here, and offers its productions ; the management
are therefore bound to make a severe trial of what is
submitted ;   the   path   must   be   forever   closed   to
bunglers ;   only   works   of   special   distinction   must
enjoy the honor of selection.—Good !—I have prepared
myself for this examination, and desire no distinction
without deserving it.   What should I have to fear beside this competition ?   Shall I believe that here also
the customary servile tricks are in vogue ?   Here, in
Paris, the capital of free France, where there is a press
that exposes every abuse and corruption and makes it
impossible ?—where it is possible for merit alone to
gain applause from the great public that cannot be
bribed ? ”

“ The   public ? ”   interrupted   I ;—“ you   are   right
there.   I believe too that with your talent you might
count upon success as soon as you had to deal with
the *public* only.   But you are sadly in error, my poor
friend, as to the ease of the means for getting before
it !   It is not the competition of talent, among which
you will have to fight, but the competition of repu-
tations and personal interests.   If you are certain of
a decided and influential protection, venture upon the
conflict ; but without this and without money—stand
off, for you must fail without even having gained consideration.   There will be no question of estimating
your talents or your labor (even that would be a favor
without   precedent) ;—but   there   will   only   be   taken
into consideration what name you bear.   Since there's

no reputation attaching to this name, and it is not to be found on any list of *rentiers*, you and your talent remain unnoticed."

But my reply failed to produce the intended result upon my enthusiastic friend. He was out of humor, but he put no faith in what I said. I went on and asked him what he could think of to do so that he might make a little reputation in some other way, that could be of assistance to him in afterward undertaking, with more prospect of success, the execution of the decisive plan he had communicated to me?

This suggestion seemed to drive away his ill-humor. " Listen," he said. " You know I have always had a great partiality for instrumental music. Here in Paris, where a kind of *cultus* of Beethoven seems to be established, I can certainly hope that his coutryman and most ardent admirer will have no difficulty in gaining a hearing, when he endeavors to bring before the public his own attempts to approach the unattainable model—be these attempts ever so feeble."

" Permit me to interrupt you there," said I ; " Beethoven *is* fairly deified—so far you are right. But remember that it is his *name*, his *reputation* that is worshipped. That name, placed before any work that is worthy of the great master, is sufficient to make people see the beauties of it at once. But put any other name before the same composition, and it wouldn't induce even the management of a concert-room to notice even the most brilliant part of it."

" That is false ! " exclaimed my friend rather angrily. " It is plain that you mean to systematically discourage me and frighten me away from the path to fame. But you shall not succeed ! "

" I know you, and can pardon you," I returned. " But I must add, that in pursuing this latter plan also, you will encounter precisely the same difficulties that are always in the way of an artist without a reputation—be his talents what they may—here where people have far too little time to trouble themselves about hidden treasures. Both plans must be regarded as means for strengthening and taking advantage of a reputation that is already made—but not in the least as methods of obtaining one. Your efforts for the production of your instrumental compositions will either be altogether neglected, or, if your works are conceived in that bold and original fashion that you admire in Beethoven, they will be considered bombastic and heavy, and sent back to you with this opinion."

"But," interrupted my friend, "how if I have already provided against such a judgment? What if, foreseeing this, I have composed works which, for the very purpose of producing them before a merely superficial audience, I have arranged in that favorite modern fashion which, it is true, I detest from the bottom of my heart, but which even the greatest artists have not shrunk from using as a first means of attracting?"

"Then people will tell you that your work is too light and shallow to catch the public ear, between the works of Beethoven and Musard!"

"O my dear fellow," cried my dear friend—"now I see clearly that you are only chaffing me! You are and always will be a droll *farceur!*"

And my friend stamped his foot laughingly, and brought it down so hard on his dog's beautiful paw, that the latter howled aloud; but a moment after, licking his master's hand, seemed to beseech him no longer to take my objections in jest.

"You see," said I, "that it isn't always a good thing to take earnest for jest. But apart from this, pray tell me what other plans could induce you to exchange your modest home for vast Paris. Tell me in what other way,—if you should for my sake abandon the two schemes already mentioned,—you would propose to try making the necessary reputation for yourself?"

" Merely out of spite toward your extraordinary spirit of contradiction," said he in reply, " I will go on in the enumeration of my plans. I know that nothing is more affected nowadays in Paris salons, than those spirited and sympathetic romances and ballads that are precisely to the taste of the French people, and that have been transplanted hither from our own home. Think of Franz Schubert's songs and the reputation they have here ! This is a kind of composition that thoroughly suits my fancy, and I feel that I am capable of doing something really meritorious in it. I will bring my songs before the public, and perhaps I shall have the luck that so many others have had— to attract the attention of one of the directors of the opera here, by such unassuming compositions, to such a degree that he will honor me by an order for an opera."

The dog gave another loud yelp; but this time it was I who, in a convulsion of laughter, had trod upon the excellent beast's paw.

" What "—I shouted—" is it possible that you seriously hold such mad notions ? What in all the world can justify you—"

" Good God "—interrupted the enthusiast—" haven't such cases happened often enough before ? Shall I show you the papers in which I have repeatedly read how such and such a director was so carried away by hearing a *romanza*—how such and such a famous poet was so attracted by the hitherto unrecognized talent of a composer, that both instantly united in declaring—the one that he would forthwith furnish him a libretto—the other that he would produce the opera that should be thus ordered ?"

" Oh," said I, all at once filled with sorrow, " is that the way things stand ? Newspaper notices have turned your honest, childlike brain ? Dear friend, if you would only read a third, and only believe a quarter, of everything that comes to you through that

4

channel !   Our directors have much else to do beside
listening to the singing of *romanzas*, and going into
enthusiasm over them !   And even granting that this
could be a possible means of getting a reputation, by
whom would you have your *romanzas* sung ? "

" By whom but by the same famous singers and
prime donne who so often, with the kindest readiness,
undertake the task of bringing for the first time favorably before the public the productions of unknown or
repressed talent ?   Or perhaps I have been deceived
in this too by false newspaper notices ? "

" My friend," I replied, " God knows how far I am
from denying that noble hearts of this sort beat below
the throats of our famous singers and songstresses.
But to attain the honor of such protection, some
other requisites are necessary ; you can easily imagine
what a competition there must be in this also ; and
that it requires a decidedly influential introduction to
make it clear to the noble hearts aforesaid that one
really *is* an unrecognized genius.—My poor friend,
have you any other plans ? "

At this he was fairly beside himself.   He turned
sharply and angrily away—though not without some
consideration for his dog.

" And if I had plans as numerous as the sands of
the sea," he cried, " you should not hear another one !
Go ! You are my enemy ! Inexorable !—but you shall
not triumph !   Tell me—I will ask you only one thing
more—tell me, unhappy man ! how have the innum-
erable people made their beginning who have become
first well known in Paris, and then famous? "

" Ask them "—I answered, my coolness somewhat
disturbed ; " perhaps you can find out.   For me—I
do not know ! ' "

" Here, here ! " called the deluded man excitedly
to his magnificent dog.   " You are no longer a friend
of mine," said he, turning hastily to me.   " But your
cold scorn shall not see me blench ! *In one year you*

shall either be able to learn from every street gamin
where my house is, or you shall receive directions
where to come—to see me die ! Farewell ! ''
He whistled shrilly to his dog—a discord—and he
and his companion were gone like lightning. I could
not overtake them.

* * * * * * *

For the next few days,—in which all my efforts to
find out the lodging of my friend proved in vain,—I
could not help feeling keenly how wrong I had been
not to have more consideration for the characteristics of
so deep and enthusiastic a spirit, than I had shown in
my harsh and perhaps exaggerated replies to such in-
nocently told plans. In my creditable purpose of fright-
ening him as much as possible from his intentions,—
because I did not believe him to be the man, either in
his outward situation or inward character, to follow
out such a complicated path to his ambitions as that
which formed the object of his plans,—in this creditable purpose of mine, I say, I had not remembered
that I was not dealing with an easily convinced, yielding
being, but with a man whose inmost belief in the
divine and indisputable truth of his art had reached
such a point of fanaticism, that it had imparted an
inexorable and obstinate cast to his otherwise mild
and gentle nature.

Undoubtedly—I thought to myself—he is at this
moment wandering through the Paris streets, with the
firm conviction that he need only come to a decision
as to which of his plans he shall first adopt,—in order
to shine at once upon that theatre-placard which represents to a certain extent the end of the perspective
of his schemes. Undoubtedly he is at this moment
giving some old beggar a sou, with perfect confidence
that in a few months he can hand him a napoleon.

The longer our separation lasted,—the vainer were
my efforts to discover my friend,—the more (for I confess my weakness) the confidence he had expressed

gained upon me ; until I allowed myself.to be so far
led astray by it as to now and then cast a glance at
this or that placard of a musical performance, to see if
I could not discover in some corner the name of my
credulous enthusiast.   And the more this exploration
proved in vain, so much the more did an increasing
faith—strange to say—become associated with my
friendly sympathy,—a faith that after all it was not impossible that my friend might succeed ;—that perhaps
even now, while I was anxiously seeking him, his
peculiar talent had been already discovered and recognized by some important personage ;—that perhaps
one of those very commissions had already been given
to him, the successful execution of which would bring
to him happiness, fame—and Heaven knows what besides.   Why not ?   Does not every deeply enthusiastic soul pursue a star ?   And may not his be a lucky
star ?   May not miracles happen, to reveal the richness of a hidden treasure ?

The very fact that I nowhere saw a romance, an
overture, or anything of that nature advertised under
my friend's name, led me to believe that he had tried
his most ambitious plan first, and with success ; and
that, despising the narrower ways to public recognition, he was now fully occupied in the composition of
an opera of at least five acts.   It is true, it struck me
that I never found him at any of the centres of artistic
activity, or met anybody that knew anything of him ;
but at the same time, as I frequented these sanctuaries
but little myself, I decided that it was only *I* that was
so unfortunate as not to penetrate into those regions
where his fame was already shining in brilliant beams.

It may be imagined, however, that it took a long
time to change what was at first only pitying sympathy for my friend, into a full confidence in his happy
star.   I only reached this point after passing through
all the various phases of fear, doubt, and hope.   It
took a long time ; and for this reason it was, that al-

most a year-had passed, since the day when I had met
in the Palais Royal a beautiful dog and an enthusiastic friend. During this time wonderfully successful
speculations had brought me to such a point of good
fortune, that, like Polycrates, I feared I should shortly
meet with some considerable piece of ill-luck. I
thought, in fact, that I could already forsee this ill-
fortune distinctly; and it was in rather a gloomy
mood that I one day started out, as my custom was,
for a walk in the Champs Elysées.

It was autumn ; the faded leaves were falling from
the trees, and the sky hung gray, as with age, above
the various elysian splendors. But not the less did
Punchinello continue to renew his time-honored furies
of rage ; in his blind wrath the rash being continued to
set at naught the principles of human justice, until at
last the demoniac principle so strikingly represented
by the chained cat, overcomes with superhuman claws
the audacious defiance of the presumptuous mortal.

Suddenly I heard close by me, but a short distance
from the modest theatre of Punchinello's cruel deeds,
the following strangely accented soliloquy in German :
" Capital ! Capital ! Where in the world have I
let myself be led to look for what I might have found
so near at home ! What ! Shall I despise *this* stage,
on which the most striking political and poetic truths
are so clearly and intelligibly set forth—presented
with such sensible taste to the most receptive and least
assuming of audiences ? Isn't this rash being Don
Juan ? Isn't this horribly beautiful white cat the
Commendatore on horseback as he lived and looked ?
How the artistic meaning of this drama will be heightened and made clear when my music contributes its
part to it ! What sonorous voices those actors have !
And the cat—ah ! the cat ! What undiscovered fasci-
nations lie hidden in her beauteous throat ! Now she
utters no sound ;—now she is utterly and entirely
demoniac ; but what an expression she will make

when she sings the *fioriture* that I will compose exclusively for her ! What an exquisite *portamento* she
will bring to the execution of that preternatural chro-
matic scale ! With what terrible fascination she will
smile when she sings the passage that is destined to
be so famous in the future— ' O Punchinello, thou art
lost.' —What a scheme ! And what an opportunity
Punchinello's continual beatings will give me to bring
the *tam-tam* into play ! Why do I hesitate ! I must
get the director's favor at once. Here I can proceed
directly—there's no antechamber here ! With a single
step I am in the very sanctuary—before the man
whose divinely prescient eye will recognize genius in
me. Or—what if I should meet with rivalry ? What
if the cat—quick, before it is too late ! "

With these words the soliloquizer would have
rushed upon the Punch-and-Judy booth. But I had
quickly recognized my friend, and decided to prevent
a scandal. I seized him, and, embracing him, turned
him with his face toward me.

" Who is it ? " he cried out angrily. But in a
moment he recognized me, quickly drew away from
me, and added coldly—" I might have known that you
would hold me back from this step also—the last that
I can take to save myself. Let me go, or I may be
too late ! "

Again I seized him ; but though I this time succeeded in restraining him from advancing toward the
theatre, I could not move him from the spot where he
stood. I gained time, however, to look at him more
thoroughly.

Good God ! In what a state did I find him ! I do
not speak of his dress, but of his features ;—the
former was poor and neglected, but the latter were terrible. His frank and hearty courage had disappeared.
His eyes wandered in a lifeless, rigid way ; his blanched
and sunken cheeks told not of trouble only—the dark
spots upon them told also of the pangs—of hunger !

As I looked at him with the bitterest feelings of anguish, he too seemed touched, for he tried less forcibly to tear himself away.

"How are you, dear R——?" I asked in a broken voice. Smiling sadly, I added "Where is that noble dog of yours?"

He looked up gloomily. "Stolen!" was his abrupt answer.

"Not sold?" I asked.

"Wretch!" cried he fiercely, "are you too like the Englishman?"

I did not understand what he was talking about. "Come," said I in a shaken voice,—"Come! Take me to your lodging; I have a great deal to talk over with you."

"You will soon find out my lodgings without my help," said he. "The year is not gone yet! At this moment I am on the road to recognition—to fortune. But leave me!—You have no faith in it! Why should one preach to the deaf? You must needs *see* to believe. Good! Very soon you *shall* see! But let me go, if you would not have me hold you my sworn enemy."

I held his hands tighter. "Where is your lodging?" I asked. "Come—lead me there. We will have a friendly, hearty talk—if it must be—over your schemes."

"You shall know them as soon as they are carried out," said he. "Quadrilles—galops—those are my forte! You shall see and hear! Do you see that cat? She shall help me to some valuable. copyright! See how smooth she is—how prettily she licks her lips! Think how it will be when the most spirited chromatics, accompanied by the most delicate groans and sobs in the world, issue from that mouth! Think of that, my good fellow! Oh, you have no fancy— you! Let me go—let me go! *You* have no imagination!"

I held him fast again and most urgently renewed my
request that he would take me to his house; but without effect. His eyes were fixed with an excited glare
upon the cat.

"How everything depends on her!" said he:—
"Fortune, honor, fame lie in her soft paws. Heaven
direct her heart and grant me her favor! She looks
kindly at me; yes, that is the feline character. She
is kind—courteous—immeasurably courteous! But she
is a cat—a perjured, faithless cat! Wait—I can *compel*
thee—I have a noble dog—he'll inspire respect in thee.
Victory! I have won! Where is my dog?"

In his delirous excitement he had shouted these last
words in a shrill shriek. He looked hurriedly about,
seeming to seek his dog. His searching glance fell
upon the broad roadway. Just then there rode past,
on a beautiful horse, a man of elegant appearance—an
Englishman, to judge by his physiognomy and the
peculiar cut of his clothes; beside him ran a large and
beautiful Newfoundland dog, barking gayly.

"Ha! My presentiment—" shrieked my friend
furiously at the sight:—"Curse him! My dog! My
dog!"

All my strength was vain against the overwhelming
force with which the unhappy man tore himself away
like lightning. He shot like an arrow after the horseman, who at this moment chanced to spur his horse
into a full gallop which the dog accompanied with
merry gambols. I ran after him in vain. What exer-
tion can equal the effort of a madman?—I saw the
horseman and the dog, with my friend, turn into a side
street leading to the Faubourg du Roule; but when I
reached the street all were out of sight.

Let it suffice to say that all my efforts to discover a
trace of the lost ones were utterly in vain.

Greatly shaken, and myself excited almost to madness, I was at length forced to give up my search.
But it will be readily conceived that I did not on that

account cease to make daily efforts to find some guide
which could lead me to the dwelling of my unhappy
friend. I inquired in every place that had any connection whatever with music—but nowhere could I find
the slightest information. Only in the sacred antechamber of the opera, some of the lowest of the officials remembered a melancholy, wretched being, who
had often been there and waited for an audience ;—but
of whose name and residence, of course, no one knew
anything. Every other means—even that of the
police—led to just as little trustworthy traces ; even
these guardians of the public safety did not seem to
have thought it necessary to trouble themselves about
the unfortunate man.

I fell into despair : when one day, about two months
after the occurrence in the Champs Elysées, a letter
was handed to me in an indirect way, through one of
my acquaintances. I opened it with a feeling of coming trouble, and read these brief words :—

" *My dear friend, come—to see me die.*" The address given indicated a narrow alley on Montmartre.

I could not weep—I hastened to Montmartre. Following the address I reached one of those wretched
and miserable houses that are to be found in the side
streets of this quarter of the city. In spite of its squalid
exterior this building did not fail to rise to a fifth
story ; my friend seemed to have regarded this circumstance with pleasure; and I was also compelled to
mount by the same dizzy path. But it was worth the
trouble ; for on asking after my friend I was directed
to a room in the rear. On this side of the house, it
is true, one was denied the out-look into the giant
street (some four feet wide) ; but was rewarded for
this by a far more beautiful prospect of all Paris.

I found my unhappy enthusiast sitting up in his sick-
bed, enjoying this glorious view. His face and his
whole body were far more meagre and haggard than
on that day in the Champs Elysées ; yet his expression

4*

was more satisfactory than at that time. The frighted, wild, almost maddened look, the terrible brightness of his eyes, had disappeared; his eyes were dim and almost lustreless; the ghastly dark spots upon his cheeks seemed to have changed into a general wasting away.

Trembling, but with a quiet expression, he extended his hand to me with the words—" Pardon me, dear friend; and thank you for coming."

The singularly gentle and sonorous tone in which he spoke these few words, made a deeply affecting impression upon me—as indeed his very look had already done. I pressed his hand; but I wept and could not speak.

" I think," continued my friend after a moment of emotion, "it must be a good deal more than a year since we met in that bright Palais Royal ;—I haven't entirely kept my word; it was impossible, with my best efforts, to become famous within a year; and on the other hand it is not my fault that I could not write to you punctually at the termination of the year whither you should come to see me die; in spite of all my pains I had not got so far.—Do not weep, my friend ;—there was a time when I had to beg you not to laugh."

I would have spoken, but speech failed me. " Let me go on," said the dying man. " It is easy for me, and I owe you an account of many things. I am certain that I shall not be alive to-morrow; so hear my history to-day. It is a simple one, my friend; very simple. There are no extraordinary complications in it.; no surprising chances of fortune; no interesting details. Don't be afraid that your patience shall be exhausted by the ease of speech that is now vouchsafed to me and that might perhaps tempt me into garrulity—for there have been days, mein Lieber, when I could not utter a single syllable.—Listen ! When I think of it, and consider the circumstances in

which you now find me, I feel it unnecessary to assure
you that my fate has not been a brilliant one. Indeed
I hardly need to tell you the details of those events
among which my enthusiastic credulity met its ruin.
Let it suffice to say that it was not upon the *rocks*
that I was shattered. Ah, the shipwrecked man is
very happy who goes down in a storm! No, they
were bogs and sloughs in which I sank! Such a slough,
mein Theuerer, surrounds all those proud and shining
temples of art toward which we poor fools make our
pilgrimages, with an enthusiasm as though the very
salvation of our souls was to be gained within ·them.
Happy is the trifler! With a single successful *en-
trechat* he is in a position to dash past the slough at
once. Happy the rich man! His well-trained steed
needs but one touch of the golden spurs to bear him
quickly over. But woe to the enthusiast who, believing the morass to be but a flowery meadow, sinks into
it beyond the power of saving, and becomes the ·food
of frogs and toads! See, my friend, these vile vermin
have fed on *me;* there is not left in me one drop of
blood! Shall I tell you how it happened? Why?—
You see me succumb; let it suffice me to say that I
was not conquered on the field of battle—but—how
vile it is to tell!—I died of hunger in the antechamber!
They are terrible—these antechambers:—and do you
know, there are many of them—very many of them,
in Paris—with benches of velvet as well as of wood,
heated and unheated, paved and unpaved!"

"In these antechambers," continued my friend,
"I have dreamed away a bright year of my life. I
dreamed much and strangely ;—wild, fabulous things
out of the Arabian Nights—of men and cattle, gold
and dross. I dreamed of gods and contrabassi, of
diamond snuff-boxes and prime donne, of satin coats
and admiring lords, of songstresses and five-franc
pieces. Between my dreams it often seemed to me as
though I heard the complaining, ghostly tones of the

hautbois ; the sound stirred through all my nerves and
penetrated my heart.   One day when I dreamed most
wildly, and this hautbois tone thrilled through me
most painfully, I suddenly awoke and found that I was
mad.   I remember, at least, that I forgot what I had
so often done,—to make a deep reverence to the servant as I left the antechamber,—the reason, by the
bye, that I never dared to go back to that one,—for
how would the servant have received me ?

   " So I left the asylum of my dreams with an uncertain step ; on the threshold of the building I suddenly
fell.   I had fallen over my poor dog, who made *his* antechamber in the street according to his custom, and
waited for his fortunate master, to whom it was permitted to have his antechamber among human beings.
This dog, I must tell you, was of the greatest service
to me, for I had to thank him and his beauty that the
servant at the antechambers now and then cast a glance
of consideration upon me.   Unfortunately he lost his
beauty with every day, for hunger raged in his vitals
as well.   This gave me great anxiety, for I saw that it
would soon be all over with the servant's favor ; already a scornful smile played about his lips.—As I
said, I fell over my dog.   I do not know how long I
lay there ; I did not notice the kicks that I perhaps
received from the passers-by ; but at last the gentlest
kisses awakened me—the warm tongue of the poor animal.   I rose ; and in a lucid moment I saw what was
the most important duty before me—the feeding of
my dog.   A discriminating old-clothes merchant gave
a few sous for my wretched waistcoat.   My dog was
fed, and what he left—I ate.   This agreed thoroughly
with him, but I could no longer digest.   The revenue
derived from one of my treasures, an old ring of my
grandmother's, was sufficient to give the dog all his lost
beauty back again.   He flourished again—destructive
prosperity !

   In my own brain it grew worse and worse ;—I hardly

know what went on there, but I remember that one day I was seized with an irresistible desire to discover the devil. My dog accompanied me, bright with beauty, to the doors of the concert Musard. Did I hope to meet the devil there? I hardly know. I watched the people going in—and whom should I see among them? The vile *Englishman*,—the same, just as he used to look, quite unchanged,—just as he was when he so nearly ruined me with Beethoven, as I have told you.

" I was horrified; I was prepared, it is true, to meet a spirit of the under-world—but not to see this earthly spectre. What were my feelings when the wretch at once recognized me! I could not avoid him, the crowd pressed us together. Involuntarily and in decided opposition to the custom of his own country, he was forced to sink into the arms that I had raised to force my way through the press. There he lay, pressed fast to my breast, that thrilled with a thousand horrible emotions. It was a fearful moment! But we were soon more at liberty, and he freed himself from my embrace with a certain disgust. I would have fled, but it was impossible.

" ' Welcome, mein Herr!' said the Briton; ' It is charming to find you always in the path of art! Let us go this time to Musard.'

" Furious with rage, I could say nothing in reply but 'To the Devil!'

" ' Yes,' he replied, ' they say it is rather devilish there. I made a composition last Sunday that I want to present to Musard. Do you know him? Will you introduce me to him?'

" My detestation of this spectre changed into a terrible anxiety; urged on by this, I succeeded in escaping and fled to the boulevard; my noble dog sprang barking after.

" In an instant the Englishman was again at my side;

he arrested me, and said excitedly 'Sir, does that splendid dog belong to you ? '

" ' Yes.'

" ' Ah—but he is a fine one ! Sir, I will give you fifty guineas for that dog. You know it's the proper thing for a gentleman to have a dog of that sort, and I have already had a good many in my possession. But, unhappily, the beasts were all unmusical ; they could not endure to have me play the flute or the horn, and so they all ran away. But now I must assume that since you are so fortunate as to be a musician, your dog must be musical also.

" ' I venture to hope, therefore, that he will stay with me, too. So I offer you fifty guineas for the beast.'

" ' Wretch,' I cried, 'my friend is not for sale for all Britain ! '

" With this I ran hurriedly away, my dog before me. I turned into the side streets leading to the place where I generally passed the night. It was bright moonlight ; now and then I looked fearfully around ; to my horror I fancied that I saw the lank figure of the Englishman following me. I redoubled my speed, and looked around still more anxiously ; sometimes I saw the spectre—sometimes not. Panting, I reached my asylum, gave my dog his food, and stretched myself hungry upon my hard bed.

" I slept long, and had frightful dreams. When I awoke—my noble dog was gone. How he got away from me, or how he was seduced away through the door —albeit this was but badly locked—is still incomprehensible to me. I called, searched for him, until I sank down with a groan.

" You remember that I saw the villain again one day in the Champs Elysées,—you know what exertions I made to regain possession of him ; but you do *not* know that the animal knew me, but fled from me and from my call like a wild beast of the wilderness ! Yet I followed him and the satanic rider till the latter rode into a

gateway which shut clanging behind him and the dog.
In my rage I thundered at the gate ; a furious barking
was the answer. Stunned, and as though utterly annihilated, I leaned against the gate, until at last a horribly
executed scale on the French horn, that reached my
ears from the lower story of the elegant hotel, and was
followed by a subdued, complaining howl,—aroused
me from my stupor. I laughed aloud, and went my
way."

Deeply moved, my friend paused ; however easy it
was for him to talk, his excitement was a terrible strain
upon him. He could no longer sit erect in bed,—he
sank back with a light groan. There was a long pause ;
I looked at the poor fellow with the keenest distress ;
that soft flush appeared upon his cheeks, that is peculiar to the consumptive. He had closed his eyes ; his
breath came in light and almost ethereal motion.

I waited anxiously for the moment when I might
venture to ask him in what possible way I could help
him. At last he opened his eyes again ; a soft, singular brilliancy was in the look he turned upon me.

" My poor friend," I began ; "you see me beside
you with the sad request that you will let me serve
you in some way. If you have a single wish—tell it
to me, I beseech you."

He answered smiling—" So impatient for my will,
my friend ? Give yourself no anxiety ; you are remembered in it.—But will you not hear how it happened that your poor brother came to die ? You see,
I want my story to be known to one single soul, at
least ; but I know of no one who troubles himself
about me—unless it be you.

" Don't be afraid that I shall exert myself too much.
I feel better—easier. I have no difficulty in breathing
—it is easy for me to talk. Besides, you see I have
but little more to tell.

" You can imagine that after that point at which I
left off in my story, I had nothing more to do with

outward experiences.	From that time the history of
my inner life begins—for from that time I knew that I
must die.

"That terrible scale on the French horn in the Englishman's hotel, filled me with such an irresistible hatred
of life, that I decided to die quickly.	I ought not to
take any credit to myself for this decision, it is true,
for it was no longer a matter of choice whether I lived
or died.	Something had broken in my breast, that
left behind it what seemed like a long-drawn whirring
sound ; and as this died away, I felt light and well, as
I had never felt before,—and I knew that my end was
near.	How happy I was at the thought !	How the
prospect of a speedy dissolution cheered me,—the feeling that I suddenly experienced in every portion of
my wasted frame !	Unconscious of all outward sur-
roundings, and not knowing where my uncertain steps
were leading me, I had reached the heights of Mont-
martre.	I bid the "hill of martyrs" welcome, and
decided that I would die there.	I, too, die for the
purity of my faith—and so I also can call myself a mar-
tyr, even though this belief of mine be opposed by
nothing—but hunger.

"Here then I, the homeless one, took up my dwelling, asking nothing but this bed, and that the scores
and papers I had left in a wretched nook in the city,
should be brought to me ; for unfortunately I had not
succeeded in making use of them anywhere as a pawn-
pledge.	You see, I lie here, and have decided to die
in God and pure music.	A friend will close my eyes ;
the little that I leave behind me will suffice to pay my
debts, and I shall not want for an honorable grave.—
Tell me, what could I wish for more ? "

At last I gave expression to my pent-up emotion.
"What "— I cried—"could you only make use of me
for this last sad service ?	Could your friend—be he
ever so powerless—serve you in no other way than
this ?	I beseech you, tell me one thing—was it mis-

trust of my friendship that kept you from asking of me
—from telling me sooner of your fate ? "

" Ah, do not reproach me," said he soothingly ;
" don't reproach me if I confess to you that I had fallen .
into the insane idea that you were my enemy. When
I found that you were not, my brain was in such a
condition as deprived me of all responsibility for my
own will. I felt as though I had no right to any communication with sensible beings. Pardon me, and be
kinder to me than I was to you ! Give me your hand,
and let this debt of my life be paid."

I could not refuse ; I seized his hand and burst into
tears. I saw that my friend's strength was fast ebbing
away. He could no longer raise himself in bed ; the
changing flush grew dimmer on his pallid cheeks.

" One little matter of business, my dear friend,"—
he said ; " call it my last testament !--I desire, first—
that my debts be paid. The poor people who took
me in have nursed me willingly and dunned me but
little ; they must be paid. A few other creditors, too,
whose names you will find put down on this paper. I
devote to these payments all my property—my compositions there, and here my note-book, in which I
have entered my musical memoranda and fancies. I
leave it to your skill, my experienced friend, to have
as much of this legacy as possible sold, and to devote
the receipts to the payment of my worldly debts.—

" I desire, secondly—that you will not beat my dog
if you happen to come across him. I take it for
granted that he has already suffered fearfully through
the Englishman's French horn, as a punishment for
his faithlessness.—I forgive him !—

" Thirdly, I desire that the story of my life in Paris
shall be published (my name being suppressed), that
it may serve as a wholesome warning to every fool
that is like me.—

" Fourthly, I ask for an honorable grave, but without ornament or excessive show. A few persons only

will serve me as mourners; you will find their names
and addresses in my note-book. The costs of the burial
are to be contributed by you and them.—Amen !

" And now"— continued the dying man after a
pause caused by his increasing weakness ;—" now one
word concerning my beliefs.—I believe in God, Mozart,
and Beethoven, and in their disciples and apostles ; I
believe in the Holy Ghost and the truth of Art—one
and indivisible ; I believe that this art proceeds from
God and dwells in the hearts of all enlightened men ;
I believe that whoever has revelled in the glorious joys
of this high art must be forever devoted to it and can
never repudiate it ; I believe that all may become
blessed through this art, and that therefore it is permitted to any one to die of hunger for its sake ; I believe that I shall become most happy through death ;
I believe that I have been on earth a discordant chord,
that shall be made harmonious and clear by death. I
believe in a last judgment, that shall fearfully damn
all those who have dared on this earth to make profit
out of this chaste and holy art—who have disgraced
it and dishonored it through badness of heart and the
coarse instincts of sensuality ; I believe that such men
will be condemned to hear their own music through
all eternity. I believe, on the other hand, that the
true disciples of pure art will be glorified in a divine
atmosphere of sun-illumined, fragrant concords, and
united eternally with the divine source of all harmony.
And may a merciful lot be granted me ! Amen ! "—

I almost thought that my friend's ardent prayer was
already fulfilled, so divinely clear was his eye—he lay
so entranced in breathless stillness. But his exces-.
sively feeble breath—almost imperceptible—convinced
me that he was still alive. Softly, but very distinctly,
he whispered " Rejoice, ye Faithful, for the bliss to
which you go is great ! "

He was silent ; the brightness in his eyes died

away; his lips wore a happy smile. I closed his eyes, and prayed God that my death might be like his.

Who knows what passed away in this human being, and left no trace? Was it a Mozart—a Beethoven? Who can tell; and who can dispute me when I say that in him there died an artist who would have blessed the whole world with his creations, had he not been driven to starvation? I ask—who can prove the contrary?

None of those that followed his body to the grave dared to dispute it; there were only two besides myself,—a philologist and a painter; one person had been kept away by a cold—others had no time.

As we quietly approached the cemetery of Montmartre, we noticed a beautiful dog, who snuffed at the bier and the coffin. I recognized the animal and looked around; I perceived the Englishman on horseback. He did not seem to understand the restless behavior of his dog, and dismounting, gave his horse to his groom and joined us in the cemetery.

"Whom are you burying, sir?" he asked.

"That dog's master," said I in reply.

"Damn it!" he cried, "I am sorry to hear that the gentleman is dead, without receiving the money for his beast. I meant it for him, and have tried to get an opportunity to send it to him—in spite of the fact that the dog howls during my practising. But I will make good my error, and devote the fifty guineas for the dog to a monument to be erected over the grave of this excellent gentleman."

He went and mounted his horse. The dog remained beside the grave; the Englishman rode away.

DER FREISCHÜTZ IN PARIS.

I.

DER FREISCHÜTZ; AN ADDRESS TO THE PARISIAN PUBLIC.

IN the midst of the Bohemian forests, as old as the world, lies the Wolfsschlucht,—the wolf's ravine,—the legend of which lived among the people up to the time of the Thirty Years' War, which put an end to the last traces of German glory. Then, however, like so many mystic memories, it died away. Even at that time the majority only knew of the mysterious ravine through hearsay; it was said that this or that hunter, wandering sometime through wild and trackless forest solitudes, on unknown trails and in directions which he could not define, had suddenly chanced, he knew not how, upon the edge of the Wolfsschlucht. Such a hunter would tell of the horrible things that he had seen on gazing down into it—things that made his hearer cross himself and commend himself to his patron saint with the prayer that he might never be lost in that region. Even while approaching the hunter had heard a singular sound; stifled sobs and groans swept through the broad branches of the old fir-trees, which of themselves moved their dark tops hither and thither; and all this while the wind was perfectly still. Reaching the edge, he peered down into an abyss, into whose depths his eye could not penetrate. Rocky fragments raised themselves in the shape of human limbs and ghastly, distorted faces ; beside them heaps of black stones took the forms of frogs and lizards ; farther down in the depths these forms appeared to be alive ; they moved, crawled, and rolled away in clumsy, chaotic masses ; the ground beneath them could not be distinguished. Only pale mists rose constantly up from it, and spread abroad pestilential odors ; here and there they separated and stretched themselves out into great sheets that took on the forms of human beings with convulsively distorted features. In the midst of all this horror there sat upon a rotten stump an enormous owl, stupid with the torpor of the daytime ; and opposite to this was a dark cavern in the rocks, the entrance to which was watched by two monsters horribly formed of serpents, toads, and lizards. These, apparently endowed with life, like all that the abyss concealed, lay in a sleep like death ; and whatever moved seemed only the movement of one who dreamed ; so that the frightful thought occurred to the hunter—how all this brood would come to life when midnight came !

But what he heard filled him with more horror than what he saw. A stormy wind, that moved nothing, and the breath of which he could not feel, howled across the chasm—then ceased suddenly, as though listening to itself, only to break forth again with more furious rage than ever. Frightful shrieks rose from below ; and then a flock of countless birds of prey flew about the depths of the abyss, raised itself like a black covering above the ravine, and sank back again into the darkness. Their croakings sounded to the hunter like the groans of the damned, and pierced his heart with an anguish never felt before. He had never heard such a shriek—beside which all the croaking of the ravens seemed to him like the songs of nightingales,—and now again all was silent. Every motion

startled him ; there only seemed to be a heavy crawl-
ing in the abyss below, and the owl flapped his wings
once heavily, as though in a dream.

The most fearless hunter—the one best acquainted
with the midnight terrors of the woods,—fled away
aghast, like a timid deer ; and without minding the
path, rushed directly for the nearest loiterer—the
nearest hut—only to meet a human being to whom he
could narrate the horrors he had seen—which, nevertheless, he never could find language to describe.
How could he rid himself of such a recollection ?

Happy is the youth who bears in his heart a pure,
true love ! That alone can drive away any terrors
that he can imagine befalling him. Is not his beloved
his sheltering spirit, his guardian angel, that follows
him everywhere, shines within him, and diffuses peace
and warmth throughout his inner life ? Since he has
loved, he is no longer the rough, harsh hunter, revel-
ling in blood and the slaughter of game. His beloved
has taught him to see the diviner part of the creation,
and to hear the voices that speak to him from the mysterious silence of the woods. He feels himself seized
with pity now, when the deer springs through the un-
derbrush ; he fulfils the duties of his calling with
reluctant trembling, and could weep when he sees the
tears in the eyes of the noble prey lying at his feet.

And yet he cannot but love the rough labor of the
woods ; for he has to thank his skill as a hunter and
his prowess as a marksman, for the privilege of striving for the hand of his sweetheart. The forester's
daughter must only belong to her father's successor in
the office ; and to gain this inheritance of forestry he
must succeed in the trial of marksmanship on the day
of his marriage ; if he does not show then that he is a
thoroughly sure shot, he fails of his reward—he loses
both forestership and bride ! His heart must be firm
and strong, his sight unwavering ; his hand must not
tremble.

But the nearer the decisive moment approaches, the more his good fortune seems to abandon him. Heretofore the most skilful marksman, it often happens to him now to rove all day through the woods without bringing home the most trifling booty. What ill luck pursues him? If it be sympathy with the game that has grown so confiding, why should he miss when he aims at some bird of prey, for whom he has *no* sympathy? Why should he miss even in shooting at a mark, when his object is to carry home to his sweetheart some ribbon he has won, to drive away her anxiety? The old forester shakes his head; his betrothed grows more anxious with every day; our hunter wanders through the woods a prey to gloomy thoughts. He ponders on his ill-luck, and seeks to find a reason for it.

Then there rises in his memory the day when his fate led him to the edge of the Wolfsschlucht; the groaning and sobbing in the pine-branches, the horrible croaking of the flock of night-birds, again confuse his brain. He believes himself a prey to some hellish power, that, jealous of his happiness, has sworn his ruin. And all that he has heard of the Wild Huntsman and his hunt comes back into his memory. This was a hellish confusion of huntsmen, horses, hounds, and stags, that swept by above the forest in the unholy hours of midnight. Woe to him who was in its path! The human heart was too weak to withstand the effect of this chaos of clanging weapons, horrible hunting-calls, horn-blasts, barking of dogs and neighing of horses;—he who had seen the wild hunt was almost sure to die soon after.

The young hunter remembered having heard of the leader of this wild tumult; a godless hunter-prince among the damned, who now as the evil spirit Samiel arose to take his part among his faithful hunters in these nightly forays. It is true, his companion laughs at him, when our hunter is with him, calling this legend of the Wild Huntsman a mere old wives' tale;

yet it is this very wild and audacious comrade that
inspires him with the greatest horror. In truth, he is
already a recruit of Samiel ; he knows of secret means
—of magic spells—through which one can be certain
of his shot. He tells him that if one appears at a certain hour at an appointed place, one may banish evil
spirits by the aid of a few trifling vows, and make
them obedient to one's self; if he will but follow him, he
promises to make him bullets that shall hit the most
distant mark according to his wishes ;—these are
called '' Freikugeln,'' and he who uses them is a
'' Freischütz.''

The youth listens in amazement. Shall he not believe
in invisible spirits, when he remembers how he—once
the best marksman of them all—can no longer trust
his gun that has hitherto never missed its mark ? His
peace of mind is gone ; faith and hope waver within
him. The decisive day approaches ; his fate—once in
his own hands—now seems controlled by hostile powers ; he must conquer these with their own weapons.
He has decided. Where shall he appear to cast the
magic bullets ? In the Wolfsschlucht. In the Wolfsschlucht, and at midnight? His hair stands on end—
for now he understands it all. But he understands
also that there is no longer any retreat. Hell has
gained him, even if he does not win his bride to-morrow. Shall he give her up ? Impossible. Only his
courage can save him—and he is brave. And so he
consents.

Once more, late in the evening, he visits the forester's house ; pale and with gloomy look, he approaches
his beloved. The sight of the sweet, pure girl no
longer soothes him ; her faith in God oppresses him
like mockery ; who is it that helps *him* to win his
bride ?

The leaves rustle gently around the lonely house ;
the girl's companion seeks to cheer the saddened pair ;
but he sits brooding and staring out into the night.

His sweetheart throws her arm around him ; but her gentle whispers are drowned in the harsh creakings of the dark fir-trees—that he hears ever and anon, recalling him to himself as though with the voice of the deadly terror that is in his heart. Suddenly he tears himself from the arms of the terrified and anxious bride :—to possess her he is ready to risk the salvation of his soul.

He rushes out and away. With wonderful accuracy he follows the unknown path. The way seems to clear before him, that leads him to the abyss of horror where his companion has already made his preparations for the gloomy work. In vain the spirit of his mother appears, warning him away. The memory of the maiden that he.must lose if he hesitates, urges him onward. He descends into the ravine and enters the circle of the hellish conjuror. And hell responds to him ; that which the hunter foresaw as he approached the chasm by day, is now fulfilled at midnight. All around him awakes from its death-like sleep ; becomes alive, turns and stretches itself ; the howling increases to a roar,—the groaning to a raging bellow ; a thousand monsters surround the magic circle. No shrinking now—or we are lost ! Suddenly the Wild Hunt thunders past above his head ; his senses reel ; he falls unconscious to the ground—and when he wakes again— ?

During the night seven magic bullets are cast. Six of them must infallibly hit any mark that may be chosen ; but the seventh belongs to him that gave the rest their fortune—and this one will turn as pleases him. The two hunters divide them—the caster of the bullets taking three ; the candidate for the maiden's hand takes four.

The prince arrives in person to superintend the arrangements for the trial of the marksman's skill. The hunters waste their bullets in the strife for his favor in the preliminary hunt ; it is the seventh bullet which the

5

would-be bridegroom, who now begins again to make
constant misses, treasures up for the last decisive shot.
For this trial, a white dove that suddenly starts up is
pointed out as the mark ; he pulls the trigger, and his
beloved, who is just approaching with her bridesmaids
through the shrubbery, falls wounded, bathed in blood.

Samiel has secured his payment ; will he gain the
young hunter for his wild hunt—the young hunter
whom the darkness of madness has encompassed ?

* * * * * *

Such is the legend of the Freischütz.   It seems to be
the very poem for those Bohemian forests, whose dark
and gloomy aspect makes it easily conceivable that the
isolated beings that live among them think themselves
—if not positively the prey of some demoniac power of
nature—at least hopelessly under its control.   And in
this very characteristic is to be found the specifically
German character of this and similar traditions ; it is
so sharply defined by natural surroundings, that to it
alone is to be attributed the origin of that demoniac
imagery, which, among other peoples, not equally
subject to the influence of nature, rather takes on
forms derived from human society, or from ruling
religions and metaphysical ideas.   Though it may not
be wanting in the elements of horror, such imagery is
not in the latter case *altogether* horrible ; pathos appears through its horror ; and regret for the lost para-
dise of a purely natural life somewhat mitigates the
dread of the deserted mother nature's vengeance.

What we have described is purely German.   Everywhere else we find the devil going about among mankind ; forcing witches and enchanters to obey his will
and then arbitrarily giving them over to the stake or
saving them from death.   We even see him appear
as a *paterfamilias*, and guard his son with suspicious
scrupulousness.   But even the roughest peasant no
longer believes all this nowadays, for such proceedings are pictured too bluntly as taking place in every-

day life—in which he knows they no longer happen ; while the secret, mysterious relations of the human heart to the strange nature around it, have not yet come to an end. In its eloquent silence, this latter still speaks to the heart just as it did a thousand years ago ; and what was told in the very gray of antiquity is understood to-day as easily as then. For this reason it is that the legend of *nature* ever remains the inexhaustible resource of the poet in his intercourse with his people.

But only from this very people that invented the legend of the Freischütz, and feels itself to-day under its influence, could come a musical poet of true genius, who could hit upon the idea of creating a great musical work upon a dramatic basis derived from that legend. If he understood truly the fundamental spirit of the popular poem here presented to him, and felt himself able to call by his music into full and mystic life what was indicated in this characteristic creation,—he knew that he should be fully understood in turn by his people, from the mystic sounds of his overture to the childlike and simple fashioning of the " Jungfernkranz."

And indeed, in glorifying the old folks-legend of his home, the artist assured himself an unprecedented success. His countrymen both from north and south, from the disciple of Kant's " Kritik der reinen Vernunft " to the readers of the Viennese fashionable journals, united in admiration of the melodies of this pure and deep elegy. The Berlin philosopher stammered out " We twine for thee the maiden's wreath " (Jungfernkranz) ; the police director repeated enthusiastically " Through the forest, through the meadows " ; while the court lackey sang, in hoarser voice, " What is fitting on earth." And I can remember how I studied as a boy, to get the demon-like expression in gesture and voice necessary for the proper harsh performance of " Here in this earthly vale of woes." The Austrian grenadiers marched to the hunter's chorus ;

Prince Metternich danced to the music of the Bohemian
peasants' " Landler " ; and the students of Jena sung
the scoffing chorus after their professors.   The most
opposing tendencies of political life met here in a single
point of union ; " Der Freischütz " was heard, sung,
and danced from one end of Germany to the other.

And you too, promenaders of the Bois de Boulogne,
—you too have hummed the melodies of the " Freischütz " ; the hand-organs played the Hunter's Chorus
in the streets ; the *opéra comique* did not scorn the
" Jungfernkranz " ; and the delicious air " How did
slumber come upon me ?" has repeatedly enchanted
the audiences of your salons.   But do you understand
what you sing ?   I doubt it greatly.   On what my
doubt rests, however, it is difficult to say ;—not less difficult, certainly, than to explain to you that thoroughly
foreign German nature, from which those melodies proceeded.   I should almost think myself compelled to
begin at the forest—which, by the way, is just what
you don't understand.   The Bois is something quite
different ; as different as your " rêverie" is from our
" Empfindsamkeit."

We are truly a singular people !   " Through the forests, through the meadows," moves us to tears ; while
we look with dry eyes on thirty-four principalities
around us, instead of on one united fatherland !   You
who only go into enthusiasm when " la France " is
concerned, must look on this as a decided weakness ;
but it is precisely this weakness that you must share
if you would rightly understand " Through the forests,
through the meadows " ; for it is this very weakness
that you have to thank for the wonderful score of the
Freischütz, which you are about to have performed
before you with the greatest accuracy—unquestionably
for the purpose of learning to understand it in just the
way in which it is *impossible* for you to understand it.

You will not forsake Paris and its customs by one
hair's-breadth for this purpose ; the Freischütz must

come *there* and exhibit himself to you ; you encourage
him to make himself at ease, to do precisely as though
he were at home ; for you want to hear and see him
as he *is*,—no longer in the costume of "Robin des
Bois," but honest and open-hearted—something like
the "Postillon de Longjumeau." So you say. But
all this is to be done in the "Academie royale de
musique," and that worthy establishment has ordi-
nances which must make the feeling of unembarrassed
ease decidedly difficult for the poor Freischütz.

It is written there :—Thou shalt dance ! But that
he does not do ; he is far too heavy-spirited for that,
and he lets the peasants and maidens do it for him at
the tavern. It is written also :—Thou shalt not speak,
but shalt sing recitative ! But here is a dialogue of
the most complete naïveté. It's all very well ; but
you can't free him from ballet-dancing and singing
recitative,—for he is to present himself at the grand
opera !

There might be, it is true, a simple method of getting out of the difficulty ; and this would be to make
an exception for once for the sake of this glorious
work. But you will not adopt this means ;—for you
are only free when you want to be ; and in this case,
unfortunately, you *don't* want to be. You have heard
of the Wolfsschlucht and of a devil, Samiel ; and forthwith the machinery of the grand opera comes into
your minds ; the rest is of no consequence to you.
You want ballet and recitative, and you have chosen
the most remarkable of your composers to make the
music for it. That you have chosen such a one does
you honor, and shows that you know how to value
our masterpiece. I know no one of the contemporary
French musicians who could understand the score of
the Freischütz so well as the author of the *Symphonie
fantastique*, and would be so capable as he of com-
pleting it, if that were necessary. He is a man of
genius, and no one recognizes more fully than I the

irresistible strength of his poetic force.   He has conscientious principles, that permit him to follow the
strong bent of his talent, and in every one of his symphonies there is revealed the inner compulsion which
the author could not escape.   But precisely because of
the distinguished capabilities of M. Berlioz, I lay before him with confidence my remarks upon his work.

The score of Der Freischütz is a finished whole, perfectly rounded in every part, as well in thought as in
form.   Would not the omission of the smallest part be
to maim or distort the master's work ?   Have we to
deal here with the re-construction, to suit the needs of
our time, of a score that had its origin in the child-
hood of art ?   The re-arrangement of a work which
its author failed to develop sufficiently, through his
ignorance of the technical means that are to-day at
our disposal ?   Every one knows that there is nothing
of this kind to be done ; M. Berlioz would repel with
indignation a proposition of this character.—No.
What is in question now, is to bring perfect and
original work into concord, with conditions that are
exterior to it—foreign to it.   And how shall this be
done ?

A score sanctified by twenty years of success, in
favor of which the royal academy of music proposes
for once to deviate from the strict rules that exclude
foreign music from its repertoire, in order to take its
part in the most brilliant triumph that any piece ever
won in any theatre,—such a score cannot control a
few rules of precedent and routine ?   May it not be
demanded that it shall be produced in that primal form
that makes up so great a part of its originality ?—Yet
this is the sacrifice that is asked of us, is it not ?   Or
do you think I am mistaken ?   Do you think that the
ballet and recitative introduced by you would *not* distort the physiognomy of Weber's work ?   If you replace a simple—often times witty and lively dialogue,
by a recitative which always becomes heavy in the

mouths of the singers, do you not believe that the characteristic of cordial heartiness will altogether disappear from it—that characteristic that makes the very soul of the Bohemian peasant-scenes ? Must not the confidential chat of the two girls in the lovely forest-house necessarily lose its freshness and truth? And however well these recitatives might be arranged, however artistically they might harmonize with the general coloring of the work, they would not the less destroy its symmetry. It is plain that the German composer constantly had regard to the dialogue. The song-pieces embrace but little ; and, if utterly overwhelmed by the gigantic recitative that is added, they would lose in sense and consequently in effect.

In this drama, where the *song* has so deep a significance and so important a meaning, you will find none of those noisy combination passages, of those deafening finales, to which the grand opera has accustomed you. In the " Muet de Portici," in the " Huguenots," in the " Jewess," it is necessary that the intermediate passages between the pieces, on account of the considerable dimensions of the latter, should be filled out by recitative ; in this case dialogue would seem petty, ridiculous, and exactly like a parody. How extraordinary it would be, for instance, if between the grand duet and the finale of the second act of the " Muet," Masaniello should suddenly begin to talk ; or if, after the combination passages of the fourth act of the " Huguenots," Raoul and Valentine should prepare the way for the grand duet that follows, by a dialogue, even though it were in the most carefully chosen phraseology ! Of course this would jar upon you ; and rightly.

Very good. But what is an æsthetic necessity for these operas of greater extent, would be, for precisely the contrary reasons, ruinous for the Freischütz, in which the song passages embrace so much less.

·In regard to this matter, I foresee that where the

scenes conveyed by the dialogue need a dramatic accent, M. Berlioz will give the reins to his fertile fancy ; I can imagine the expression of gloomy energy which he will give to the scene in which Kaspar tries to weave his devilish web about his friend, as he presses him to test the magic bullet, and that he may further win him over to the standard of hell, asks him the fearful question—"Coward, dost thou believe the sin is not already upon thee? Dost think this eagle has been *given* to thee?"—I am certain that at this passage deafening applause will reward the excellent additions of M. Berlioz ; but I am not less certain, that after this recitative Kaspar's energetic, short aria at the close of the act, will pass for a piece of music unworthy of any particular consideration.

Thus you will have something entirely new—something remarkable, if you will; and we, who know the Freischütz, and need no recitative to complete it, shall with pleasure see the works of M. Berlioz enriched by a new creation ; but we shall still doubt whether you can be taught by this means to *understand* our Freischütz. You will delight yourselves with varying music, now cheerful, now wild and spirit-like, that will please your ears, yet at the same time affect you with a sense of horror ; you will hear songs performed with wonderful perfection, that up to this time have only been sung moderately well for you ; a well arranged dramatic declamation will lead you smoothly from one vocal passage to another ; and yet you will feel with annoyance the absence of many things to which you are accustomed, and which you can with difficulty do without. The anticipations which will have been nourished with regard to Weber's work, can and must only awaken in you the desire for some new excitement of the senses—just such a desire as the works generally brought before you with such a preparation really fulfil. But your expectations will find themselves disappointed ; for this work was created by its author with quite another purpose, and by no means to satisfy the demands of the Royal Academy of Music.

In the passage where, upon our stage, five musicians take up their fiddles and horns at the door of a tavern, and a few sturdy peasant lads whirl their ungraceful sweethearts in the circle of the dance—in this passage *you* will suddenly behold the choregraphic celebrities of the day appear before you ; you will see that smiling cutter of capers who but yesterday strutted in his fine gold-colored costume, receiving the graceful sylphs one after the other in his arms. The latter will do their best to show you Bohemian peasant dances,—but in vain ; you will continually miss their pirouettes and artistic caperings. Yet they will still give you enough of this sort of thing to transport you, in fancy, to the sphere of your customary enjoyments ; they will recall to you the brilliant works of your own famous authors, in which you have so often revelled, and you will demand at least a piece like " William Tell " in which also hunters, shepherds, and various other charming things appropriate to country life, appear.

But after these dances you will have nothing more of that kind ; in the first act you have nothing but the air " Through the forests, through the meadows," a drinking song of twenty to eighty bars, and, instead of a noisy finale, the singular musical outpourings of a hellish rascal, which you certainly will not receive as an aria.

Yet no !—I am mistaken. You will have whole scenes of recitative of such strong musical originality as (I am convinced) few have had before ; for I know how the brilliant invention of your distinguished composer will feel itself stimulated to add nothing but beautiful and strong passages to the masterpiece that he so honors and admires. It is precisely for this reason that you will not learn to understand the Freischütz ; and—who knows ?—perhaps what you do hear

5*

of it will destroy in you the wish to make acquaintance with it in its simple and primitive form.

If it could really appear before you in its purity and simplicity; if, instead of the complicated, intricate dances that on your stage will accompany the modest bridal procession, you could only hear the little song that, as I said, the Berlin philosophical student hums as he goes ; if, instead of the exquisite recitative, you could hear the simple dialogue that every German student knows by heart—would you even then gain a *true* comprehension of the Freischütz ?   Would it excite among you the unanimous applause which the " Muet de Portici " called forth with us ? Ah—I doubt it greatly ; and perhaps the same doubt passed like a dark cloud over M. Berlioz's spirit when the director of your grand opera commissioned him to provide the Freischütz with ballet and recitative.   .

It is a great piece of good fortune that it was precisely M. Berlioz, who was entrusted with this task ; certainly no German musician would have ventured, out of regard for the work and the master, to undertake such a matter ; and in France no one but M. Berlioz is capable of such an attempt.   At least we have the certainty that everything down to the seemingly least important note, will be respected ; that nothing will be struck out, and only exactly so much added as is necessary to satisfy the demands of the Grand Opera's regulations—rules which you think you must not dare to violate, even in a single instance.

And it is precisely this that gives me such gloomy presentiments with regard to our beloved " Freischütz."—Ah !—if you would and could but hear and see our *true* Freischütz,—you might feel the anxiety that now oppresses me, in the form of a friendly appreciation on your own part of the peculiarity of that spiritual life, which belongs to the German nation as a birthright; you would look kindly upon the silent attraction that draws the German away from the life of his large cities,—wretchedly and clumsily imitative of foreign influences, as it is,—and takes him back to nature ; attracts him to the solitude of the forests, that he may there reawaken those emotions for which your language has not even a word,—but which those mystic, clear tones of our Weber explain to us as thoroughly as your exquisite decorations and enervating music must make them lifeless and irrecognizable for you.

And yet—attempt it ! Try to breathe the fresh air of our forests through this strange and heavy atmosphere. I only fear that, even at the best, the unnatural mixture that results will disagree with you.

DER FREISCHÜTZ IN PARIS.

II.

"LE FREISCHÜTZ;" A REPORT TO GERMANY.

O MY glorious German Fatherland! How I must love thee—how I must glorify thee—if only because Der Freischütz was born upon thy soil! How I must needs love the German people who love the Freischütz, who even to-day believe in that simple legend; who still in their manhood feel the sweet and mystic awe that filled them in their youth!—Ah, blessed German Träumerei! Fantasy that surrounds the forest, the evening, the stars, the moon, the village clock when it strikes seven! How happy is he that understands you,—that can feel with you, dream and wander with you! It is bliss to feel that I am a German!

This, and much else that is beyond expression, thrilled through my heart like a blissful dagger-stroke; I felt the burning wound, that penetrated even to my brain,—but made delicious tears to flow instead of blood. What it was—on what occasion it was, that I received this blessed wound, I can tell no one here in this great and brilliant Paris; for here there are few but Frenchmen,—and the French are a merry people, full of wit and jest; they would of a certainty grow merrier still, make still better jokes and fun, if I should tell them what it was that gave me that blessed wound.

But you, my gifted German countrymen,—you will not laugh ; you will understand me, when I tell you that it came at a certain passage in the Freischütz.   It was the place where the peasants had taken their sweethearts by the hand, and waltzed with them in the inn ; the hunter bridegroom remained alone at his table in the open air; he brooded over his ill-fortune ; the evening grew darker, and far away sounded the horns accompanying the dance.

I wept, as I saw and heard this, and my neighbors at the Paris opera imagined some great misfortune must have happened to me.   As I dried my tears, I rubbed my eye-glasses, and planned that I would write something about this Freischütz.   The French took care, in the course of the performance, that a vast quantity of material should be furnished me for my projected essay ;—but to get proper control of it all, permit me, I beg you, to do what the French are so fond of doing—to proceed logically ; and so—to begin at the beginning.

You know well enough undoubtedly, my fortunate German countrymen, that no people in the world is so perfect that it will not now and then appropriate the appreciable advantages of another ; you know it and can speak of it from your own experience.   And in this way it happened that the most perfect nation of the earth—for all the world knows that the French at least think themselves such—one day took a fancy to follow this universal peculiarity of nations, that they might see for once what their worthy neighbors had to offer in exchange for the thousand glorious things which they themselves had the generous habit of presenting to them, year after year.   The French had heard that Der Freischütz was really an excellent thing, and they decided to see, for once, what there was in it, after all. They remembered, it is true, a piece full of charming music, that had been played somewhere about three hundred times, and of which it was said that it had been composed after the model of this same Freischütz.

This was called " Robin des Bois ! " and they were assured that in the composition of it French culture had done all it could to make the matter logical and enjoyable. Of course they could not but believe that all that was good in this " Robin des Bois, " especially as the piece had been decidedly successful, was owing to French art; that they had seen and heard in it only a French piece in which a few innocent foreign couplets had been mingled; and that for this reason they had still to hear and make their acquaintance with the real German national production. On the whole, they were right in this belief. The director of the grand opera, as the highest representative of the French popular intelligence in art, decided, therefore, to have his singers study and perform the *real* Freischütz, in its true form, ostensibly for the purpose of proving to the Germans that even in Paris one understood how to be really just.

There is, it is true, still another tradition about this Parisian Freischütz-legend. It has been surmised that a simple music-dealers' speculation supplied the poetic stimulus for it, and that the cautious director had followed this stimulus all the more willingly because the treasury of the theatre had fallen into such a state, owing to the perpetual failure of the most trusted musical banking-firms, that it was thought best to negotiate a safe loan with a house so well known and in such good credit as the German " Freischütz."

However all this may be, fine phrases were not to be wanting at such an opportunity. Much must be said about a brilliant tribute that it been thought proper to pay to a foreign master-piece—that is a matter of course. And since we must always put unconditional faith in a Frenchman wherever he boasts of his unselfish sentiments—we will not think otherwise than that it was all as it was represented.

So it was decided—this Freischütz should be represented *as it is ;*—principally because the grand opera
could not give the Robin des Bois arrangement (that
being the property of the Opera Comique), and partly
because that arrangement had shown by its remarkable success that there must be something *behind* this
Freischütz—that is to say silver, gold and bank-notes.
The director had decided to undertake an exploring
expedition in search of these excellent little matters,
and so he appointed the chief men of his realm a
grand council, that should help him to discover the
treasure.

The council held a sitting ; but its first discoveries
were only the difficulties that lay in the way of making
the unshapely, foreign Freischütz capable of collecting
an audience for the immense grand opera.

There was one great evil :—there was no *logic* in
the text ; and furthermore, it was German,—so that
no human being, least of all a Frenchman, could understand it. Both these disagreeable peculiarities, it was
finally decided, should be disposed of in this way :—
that an Italian should be selected, who should translate the illogical German libretto into the French
language.

This was certainly a most brilliant idea ; but neither
Italian nor Frenchman could come to a decision as to
the principal point at issue—namely, what should the
piece be called ! " Il franco Arciero " was too Italian ;
" Franc-tireur " might have been understood by a German perhaps, but certainly not by a Frenchman. And
so at last the only means of solving the question was
hit upon ; they would call it " *Le Freischutz*," and thus
have the advantage of all possibility of misconcep-
tion.

After this question of this title had been settled, and
M. Pacini had been commissioned to translate the libretto into French and supply it as far as possible with
logic,—the regulations of the grand opera came for-

ward in all their majesty. A graceful giant appeared
and commanded—"*there must be dancing!*"

There was universal alarm;—for so far as could be
gathered from the score of the Freischütz, there was
not a single *air de danse* to be found in the whole of
it! Here was a terrible business; no human being
could tell after what passage of this accursed music the
man in the gold-colored satin costume and the two
ladies with the long legs and short skirts, should be
allowed—to *dance!* certainly not after the measure
of the vulgar "Landler," that slipped in just before
Max's aria?—Possibly after the hunter's chorus,—or
after the aria "How slumber comes?"

It was desperate. But one must dance at least once!
and the Freischütz must receive the addition of a Ballet passage—even though it had been designed to perform it only in its true form. All scruples of conscience
were, indeed, overcome when it was remembered that
Weber had himself written an "Invitation to the
Dance." Who could object then, if, according to the
master's own invitation—one danced? they embraced
each other; the matter appeared righteously decided.

But now there suddenly appeared another mighty
law and spake—"*ye shall not* SPEAK!"—the unhappy
council of discovery had clean forgotten that the singers of this Freischütz had just as much to say as to sing;
and they fell anew into despair. All looked brood-
ingly before them; the director asked the fates what
had become of the *original* performance of the Freischütz?—Here there was no solution. The recitative
to "Euryanthe" could not be made to fit,—else they
might have helped themselves with that, as they had
before done with the "Invitation to the Dance." Some
act of violence must be committed—the dialogue must
be made into a recitative!

As there was no Italian to be found who could compose this recitative, as the Spaniards just now do very
little in the musical way, and the English were too

much occupied with the Corn Law, to busy themselves
with the composition of a recitative to the German
Freischütz,—they had of necessity to choose a Frenchman for the task;—and as M. Berlioz had already
written so much foolish and eccentric music, therefore
—according to the council of discovery—no one could
be so well-fitted as he for adding something to this
mad, original Freischütz.

M. Berlioz congratulated the Freischütz on having
fallen into his hands,—for he knew it and loved it, and
knew that it would be least distorted through his work.
With truly artistic conscientiousness, he undertook not
to change a note of Weber's score—not to leave out
anything, and not to add anything but what the director
and the council of discovery held to be necessary to
satisfy the tyrannous laws of the opera. He felt that,
so far as possible, the same respect must be shown to
this opera that we show in Germany to "Fra Diavolo,"
for example, and the "Black Domino," which we
produce precisely in their original form, without
adding ·Bach's fugues or eight-voiced motettes,—or
without leaving out spirited couplets like "si brave, si
beau, Postillon de Longjumeau."

Despite the fact that I now knew our beloved
Freischütz to be in the very best French hands, I
could not help giving place, in my German heart, to
some dark misgivings as to the success of the undertaking. It was impossible for me to believe that the
same Frenchmen, who knew no possible way to
procure the entry of our Freischütz upon their stage in
its original shape, could comprehend and understand
it if it came to their sight and hearing with a distorted exterior. I decided therefore, in my patriotic
zeal, to give the Parisian public my view of their plan,
and ·so I had an essay printed in which I expressed
them freely and without embarrassment.

First of all, I thought it necessary to make the
French better acquainted with the nature and the

legend of the Freischütz ; I made them comprehend, so far as I could, what was to be understood by a *Franc-tireur*, what was meant by a *balle-franche*, what were the conditions of a " Jungfernkranz "—in brief, I told them everything that every school-boy understands with us. At the same time I advised them with regard to the Bohemian forests and the German love of dreaming ;—it is impossible for a Frenchman to think of a German without woods and Träumerei, a circumstance which decidedly came to my aid just here.

Furthermore, I expressed my misgivings, called the attention of the public to the injurious effect upon the simple form of the original work, of the dancer with the golden-satin costume and the two ladies with long legs and short skirts ; and above all things prepared them for the evil result that would arise from this fact, that the many small and brief musical pieces of the original opera would lose themselves among the recitative, which would necessarily have a most disproportionate length, and thus injure the impression made by the *arie* and ballads, not to speak of the disadvantage that in any case the fresh and often naïve dialogue of the German libretto would lose its meaning and life even through the most skilful musical arrangement.

In this way I did what I thought necessary to defend our national property, in advance, from the almost unavoidable event of the failure of the experiment about to be made with it.

Everything opposed my purpose ; I was told that I was wrong, and assured that I exaggerated the claims of Der Freischütz to originality. But unhappily my prophecy was almost literally fulfilled. After the performance many admitted that I had been right ; but others declared that our Freischütz amounted to nothing. I am convinced that these latter are wrong ; but to give a motive to their horrible declaration—to

make it possible to imagine how such an idea as that
the Freischütz amounted to nothing could possibly
occur to these people—one must have heard and seen
the performance of it at the theatre of the *Academie
Royale de Musique.*

It had not been possible for M. Berlioz to secure
the first singers of the opera for the rôles of the
Freischütz. The public and the opera itself had to
content themselves with the second rank of these
creatures, and suffice it to say that even the *first* rank
were of little account. The singers and songstresses
of the second rank are children of darkness, and are
very often positively ridiculed.—Every one knows,
however, that this does not benefit the *ensemble*, even
in French operas ; and in the performance of our glorious Freischütz, in which so much appears ridiculous to
the French on account of their national character, this
second class of singers had certainly an enlivening, if
not an elevating effect. I for my part laughed a great
deal even when the Frenchmen remained sober ; for
as I finally came to the conclusion that I was looking
at—God knows what—but certainly not my beloved
Freischütz, I let all my pious scruples go by the
board, and laughed more furiously than anybody—
except at the beginning, at the passage where I have
already stated that I wept.

On the whole it may be assumed that the entire
personnel of the Paris grand opera was in a dreamy
state—in which effect I may have been partly at fault
through my essay, in which I pointed out to the
public the matter of forests and revery. It seemed to
me that my directions had been understood and
carried out with frightful punctiliousness. The scene-
painters had naturally not suffered the scene to be
lacking in forests, and so nothing seemed to remain
for the singers to do but to undertake the Träumerei
for their part. They also wept copiously, and Samiel
went so far as to tremble. This trembling of his I

must especially describe, and at once; for it was a point at which all my scruples dissolved into cheerful merriment.

Samiel was a slim fellow of some twenty-five years of age; he wore a handsome Spanish costume, over which he had casually thrown a black, flower-embroidered mantle. The expression of his face was highly interesting—to which effect his elegant side-whiskers undoubtedly contributed. For the rest, he was a merry fellow, and of lively temperament, and played most skilfully with Max the-rôle of a Parisian police-spy. With his body stretched forward, his finger on his lips, he often, during Max's aria, approached the unhappy young hunter with delicate caution, in order, as it appeared, to understand what he was singing— which was in very truth a difficult matter to discover, as even the audience (in spite of the libretto) were not unfrequently in doubt as to whether Max was singing Italian or French.—Once, at the passage where Max, in order to address to the fates his rash inquiry, had placed himself close to the foot-lights, Samiel had gotten so close to him that the word " Dieu " (enunciated with overwhelming force) reached his comprehension. But this word appeared to have an extremely disagreeable effect upon him; for he hardly understood it, when he felt it incumbent upon him to execute a trembling-scene such as had never taken place in my presence even on the French stage. All the world knows what perfection the French actors and actresses have gained in the execution of trembling; but what Samiel accomplished in this respect reduced everything else to the merest child's play.

The stage of the grand opera is, as may be conceived, very deep and broad. And therefore it can be pictured what a distance it was that Samiel traversed from Max's position near the lamps on the extreme left, to the background at the extreme right— accompanied by continual trembling of hands, legs, head and body—after he had heard that word that was so disagreeable to him. He had already trembled away for some little time, when he had reached the middle of the stage ; and it was therefore sadly to be feared that with the amazing effort that this manœuvre must have cost him, he would give out before he reached his goal in the background.

But nothing happens without calculation in French theatres. Even in this case the manager had calculated Samiel's strength, and had given the machinist orders to withdraw the wild huntsman down into a trap-door. This happened punctually, and indeed exactly at the right moment ; a flash of lightning that for an instant took the place of Samiel did its part toward the completion of the whole ; and we had the consolation of being able to believe that the godless trembler in his subterranean refuge would find time and nursing to refresh himself after his unheard of fatigues.

Max gave the dreamy portion of his character decidedly the most prominence ; and however well-fitted this was, in general, to his rôle, he nevertheless carried his dreamy forgetfulness somewhat too far. Often, for instance, he forget even the key in which the orchestra was playing, according to Weber's copy, and in the obstinacy of his revery, struck a somewhat lower one,—through which his performance produced a singular but by no means pleasing effect. In his aria he wandered thus in sad perplexity between " forests and meadows ; "— it may be said that he exaggerated his dreamy perplexity as well as the lowness of his spirits.*

His comrade Kaspar, on the contrary, was merry

---

* A pun is confessedly untranslatable ; but that which Wagner makes here upon the lowering of his voice from the key and the lowering of his spirits, is too good for any reader of German to miss. " Man kann sagen," says Wagner, " er übertrieb die träumerische Verwirrung so wie seine *Herabgestimmtheit.*"—TRANSLATOR.

and ingenuous, in spite of the fact that his appearance had a most mystic effect. His especially dreary face by no means coincided well with his well-assumed behavior ; and besides, nothing could be more melancholy to think of than his walk. The singer of Kaspar had hitherto been in the habit (so excellent a one for contributing to one's public spirit) of singing in the chorus ; as he was of unusually tall figure, he had always (on account of the aforesaid estimable feeling for general equality) endeavored to keep this conspicuous trait of his limbs in better harmony with the bodily *ensemble* of his colleagues. But he could not make his *head* shorter without extreme inconvenience, and therefore preferred to accomplish the salutary shortening of his body by a peculiarly bent and contracted use of his legs. By means of this self-denying endeavor, the ensemble of the chorus, except where it was altogether wretched, had always been successful ; and also in the part of Kaspar the unselfish habit of our singer, resulting from this, was of great service ; for, as I have already remarked, it preserved (with the melancholy hue of his features), when opposed to the natural good-natured bonhommie of the impersonator, the balance so extremely to be desired in the character of this deep-dyed rascal. At least, it seemed so to the Frenchmen, for however droll and ludicrous the effect of Kaspar's walk and manner was upon them, they were convinced that this was all as it should be, and that the singer was in this way doing his best to give expression to his rôle.

Toward the end of the opera it became clear to them also that Kaspar was in league with the devil :—who could have had any doubt of it, indeed, when he witnessed the extraordinary and singular manner of death, or rather of burial, that befel the godless fellow ? For after Kaspar had been struck by the shot that (on account of logic) was so perplexing to the Frenchmen, he still had, as everybody knows, to receive a visit

from Samiel. The wretch cursed (as it is traditional
to do in this situation) God and all the world; but
when he forgot himself so much as to honor Samiel
himself with a curse, the latter received it so ill that
he instantly carried him away with him under the
theatre; by which performance not only the chorus,
who all at once lost sight of Kaspar, and the prince,
who had, as is well-known, undertaken to have the
villain hurled into the Wolfsschlucht, were placed in
painful perplexity. Both chorus and prince, however,
with the presénce of mind of Frenchmen, withdrew
from the affair by assuming an attitude as if nothing
particular had happened after all; they let the matter
take its own course, and avenged themselves for the
over-hasty disappearance of Kaspar by conferring on
him, as a funeral sermon, some well-deserved epithets.

Besides all this, the Prince and his court were well
calculated to inspire respect. Both were dressed in
oriental costume, and their attire betrayed the fact
that the Prince must rule over an extraordinarily
extended kingdom. He himself, with some of the
grandees of his realm, wore a Turkish dress; from
which it could be seen that he must be either sultan
or, at least, pacha of Egypt. The remainder of his
court, as also his remarkably numerous body-guard,
were, however, dressed in Chinese costume; from
which fact it distinctly appeared that the empire of
their ruler extended at least from Constantinople to
Peking. But as all the remaining *personnel* were
dressed with conspicuous faithfulness in *Bohemian*
costume, nothing remained to be assumed but that
the powerful sultan had extended his boundaries also
to the north-west from Constantinople as far as Prague
and Töplitz. All the world knows, however, that
the Turks, even in their most brilliant period of con-
quest, never penetrated farther than to before Vienna;
and so we must come to the conclusion that the cos-
tume-tailor of the grand opera is either in possession

of special historical documents that place him in a
position to know the record of the Turkish people
better than we do, or that he, voluntarily or involuntarily, transferred the history of our Freischütz
from Bohemia to Húngary; in favor of which conjec-
ture, it is true, the unmistakably Bohemian and not
Hungarian costume of the peasants and hunters cannot be cited ; but the historical fact favors it, that
Hungary was once under the dominion of the Turkish sultan. At all events the idea was romantic—to
a certain extent oriental ; and beside, it made a good
moral impression, when one saw the ruler of all Mus-
selmans entering with such unprejudiced cordiality into
strictly christian negotiations with a hermit; he thus
gave to all christian powers the excellent lesson, that
they should also conduct themselves humanely toward
Mohammedans and Jews.

But let us leave the details of the performance ; if I
should relate everything that happened in the course of
it, to turn my patriotic mood into convulsive merriment, I should have a hard and tedious task. Permit me then only to express my opinion as to the
effect of the scheme and execution of our Parisian
Freischütz.

I had feared beforehand that M. Berlioz's recitative,
besides producing an injurious effect its too great
protraction, would especially damage the general
result by the fact that the composer would often permit himself to be tempted by some favorable opportunity to follow the force of his own creative faculty,
and so give his recitative a too great independence.
But I found at the performance (and, oddly enough,
I found to my *sorrow*), that M. Berlioz, in the composition of his recitative, had entirely refrained from
all ambitious effort, and had even taken pains to
throw his own work into the background. I say
that I found this out *to my sorrow;* for he had not
only *distorted* the Freischütz in this endeavor, but

had made it hopelessly tedious. This unfortunate trait was evident in the impression it produced on the French themselves, for whom M. Berlioz's work was especially calculated. It would, it is true, often have produced a disagreeable and painful feeling in us Germans, to hear the bursts of applause that would undoubtedly have accompanied M. Berlioz's recitative if the latter had laid aside his modesty and given himself up to his own ambitious inspiration; but these bursts of applause would still have been tributes to the Freischütz, as far as its Parisian performance was concerned;—the French would have been enlivened by them, and at length would not have found even our own countryman tedious.

But the precisely opposite effect was produced; this recitative gave nothing in return for that of which it robbed the true and fresh aspect of the romantic opera; and it contributed its part to the fullest extent toward driving the audience to desperation, by imposing upon it the worst of all evils—unlimited ennui.

The way in which the recitative was sung not a little increased the fault already resting upon its shoulders; all the singers thought they must represent Norma or Moses; they constantly introduced portamenti, *tremolo* effects, and similar elevating accompaniments.

This appeared most painfully in the scene between the two girls, Agathe and Annchen. Agathe, who appeared to constantly imagine that she was Donizetti's " Favorita," with her murdered innocence, wept without intermission, constantly wore a sad aspect, and occasionally experienced a spasm of terror. She was dressed in a (certainly original) Bohemian peasant's costume of satin and point-lace; while Annchen appeared in a coquettish ball-dress. Annchen appeared to have some glimmering idea that she was intended to represent a lively character; but simple merriment is as entirely unknown to French ladies as

coquetry is to ours. The foolish Annchen whom we
see on the German stage, as she sings "If there
should come a shapely lad," seizes the corners of her
apron and skips toward Agathe; she nods her head
when propriety demands it, and casts down her eyes
when it is proper to do so. But this was purely
impossible for the Parisian Annchen. She preferred
to stand in one spot from the beginning to the end
of her aria, and to cast coquettish glances toward
the "lions'" box,—by which means she was convinced that she gave a most satisfactory characterization
of a German maiden. The French did not seem to
notice anything remarkable about this—nor, indeed,
did I.

But the scene in which the accursed law which
forbids the singers to speak showed its most destructive influence, was the scene at the Wolfsschlucht.
Everything that Weber has Kaspar and Max *speak*
during this melodrama, must of course be sung in the
present case—and in this way stretched out in a fashion that was positively unbearable. The Frenchmen
were especially indignant at this; the whole "hell's-
kitchen" as they called it seemed to them an incomprehensibly ridiculous thing; and to waste so much time
over it entirely exhausted their patience. If they could
only have had some noises or amusing apparitions in
connection with it,—if only, instead of the tedious
death's-heads, a chain of imps and sylphs had formed
the circle;—if, instead of a nasty owl raising his
wings, a wanton dancer had only flourished her petti-
coats and her legs,—or if, at least, certain unprejudiced nuns had devoted themselves to the seduction
of the phlegmatic young hunter,—then the Parisians
would have known where they were. But nothing
of all this happened; and even Kaspar, who should
have been entirely occupied with his bullet-casting,
experienced a painful impatience at the extraordinary
lack of apparitions. With me it was not much bet-

ter; for as I perceived the ill-humor of the audience around me, I uttered a silent prayer to all the saints that they would induce the manager to produce some few of his devices.

Kaspar and I had perceived with unconcealed joy, that after the casting of the first bullet an unexpected noise broke from one of the bushes, ceased again upon the instant, but unfortunately left a very disagreeable smell behind it. This beginning was certainly calculated to awaken hopes, which nevertheless remained unfulfilled upon the casting of the *second* bullet. Full of expectancy, therefore, Kaspar cried out the *third* bullet; I shared his eagerness—but again nothing happened;—we were covered with shame at this inefficiency on Samiel's part, and hid our faces. But the *fourth* bullet must be cast; and now to our great satisfaction, we saw, besides two bats which flew above the circle, several will-o'-the-wisps dancing in the air, which unfortunately put the melancholy Max in great perplexity by their persistency in approaching too near him. The *fifth* bullet was therefore cast amid the most brilliant prospects—for now or never the Wild Hunt must make its appearance. And as a fact it did not keep us waiting longer;—upon a mountain, six feet above the heads of the two hunters, four naked boys appeared, mystically illuminated; they carried bows and arrows, for which reason they were generally considered to be cupids; they made a few gestures, as though dancing the can-can, and hurried behind the scenes. Very much the same feats were performed by a lion, a wolf and a bear, as well as by four other boys, who, also naked and with bows and arrows, followed the Wild Hunt upon its way.

Terrible as had been the effect of these apparitions, Kaspar and I could have wished that the terror might be continued after the *sixth* bullet; but here the manager considered a pause necessary—probably to give the terrified ladies in the boxes an opportunity to in some degree recover themselves. But when I saw what happened after the *seventh* bullet, I perceived that this pause had been a pause of preparation,—for without it what followed could not possibly have produced its intended mysterious effect.

Upon the bridge that led over the waterfall, there appeared three men with cloaks of striking blackness ; the same thing happened in the foreground, and precisely where Max was standing. The latter must certainly have taken these guests for funeral mutes,—for their appearance made so disagreeable an impression upon him that he could not refrain from dashing himself at full length upon the ground.—With this ended the horrors of the Wolfsschlucht.

But I see that I am again falling into the relation of details ; and in order to cut off this tempting path once for all, I now undertake to say nothing more about the performance of the Parisian Freischütz, but to occupy myself entirely with the audience and its judgment of our national work.

The Parisians in general are wont to look upon the performances of the grand opera as fairly faultless; for they know of no establishment where they can see an opera better given. And so they could not be of any other opinion, than that they had also seen the Freischütz perfectly well performed, and certainly better than they could have seen it at any of the theatres of Germany. Everything which seemed to them tedious and foolish about the Freischütz, they were therefore not disposed to attribute to the faults of the performer ; but at once adopted the conviction that what might be a masterpiece for Germans, was for *them* mere twaddle. The remembrance of " Robin des Bois " confirmed them in this belief; for this re-arrangement of Der Freischütz had made, as I had already sufficiently explained, an unheard-of success ; and since this honor was not conferred upon the original also, the universal impression was naturally that the re-arrangement must be infinitely better. And in truth, it did have the advantage that M. Berlioz's terribly long recitative did not counteract the effect of the airs from Weber; and besides, the author of "Robin des Bois" had ·been so fortunate as to introduce *Logic* into the proceedings of his drama.

There is something very extraordinary about this Logic. As the French have arranged their language according to its strictest rules, they demand that these rules must be respected in all that is spoken in that language. I have heard Frenchmen who were otherwise greatly pleased with the performance of the Freischütz, who nevertheless came back to this one point of objection—*there was nothing logical in it.* Now it had never occurred to me in my life to make logical researches into the Freischütz, and I therefore asked precisely what one was to understand by the term in this case? I learned that the number of the magic bullets gave special offence to the logical natures of the Frenchmen. Why—they said—*seven* bullets? Why this unheard-of luxury? Were not *three* enough? three is a number that can be easily looked after and used, under all circumstances. How is it possible to bring about the sensible employment of seven bullets in one short act? there ought to be at least five entire acts, to give the proper opportunity for solving this problem correctly,—and even then one would encounter the difficulty of disposing of several bullets in one act. For in truth it is no joke—that appeared evident —to have to do with such magic bullets; and how opposed it is to all common sense, to imagine that two hunters could so thoughtlessly and without reason mould *six* such bullets on some fine morning—knowing, too, as they must have done, that there was something uncanny about the seventh !

A similar opinion was expressed, with undisguised dissatisfaction, about the catastrophe of the piece. "How was it possible," they said "that a shot aimed

at a dove could apparently kill a maiden and really put
to death a worthless hunter? We grant that there is
a possibility of a shot's missing a dove and killing a
human being,—such accidents unfortunately occasionally occur;—but how a bride and all those who are
present could imagine for five full minutes that they
too were hit—that surpasses all belief! Besides, this
shot is wanting in all dramatic probability. How
much more logical it would be if the young hunter, in
despair at missing his shot, should shoot himself
through the head with the last bullet! the bride
rushes toward him and tries to seize the pistol from
his hand—it goes off during the struggle, the bullet
flies past the hunter—thanks to the efforts of the bride
—and shoots down the godless comrade, placed in a
direct range behind him! There *would* be some logic
in that!"

My brain whirled; I had not thought of this kind of
constructed truths, and had accepted the Freischütz
with all its lack of logic—just as it was. Thus it may
be seen what extraordinary brains these Frenchmen
have! They see the Freischütz but once, and are at
once in a position to prove that we Germans have
labored under a frightful error with regard to its logi-
calness for five-and-twenty years! Unhappy people
that we are—who have always believed that a shot
fired at seven o'clock at a mountain eagle, can bring it
about that the picture of one's great grandfather can
fall from the wall in a hunting castle a mile and a half
away! *

Logic is the consuming passion of the French, and
they pass their judgment in accordance with it. No
one of the newspaper critics, be he ever so opposed to
another, fails at this opportunity to place himself upon
the most logical basis, no matter how difficult the

---

* A popular superstition illustrated in many German legends of forest
life.—TRANSLATOR.

proof of his opinion must oftentimes be—when, for
example, one journal expresses the opinion that the
Freischütz is gray—another, that it is undeniably
green. M. Berlioz arranged it best in the *Journal des
Débats ;* in his article on Der Freischütz, he did not
neglect to say a few favorable words of Weber and his
masterpiece, which received not a little admiration
from the fact that he also spoke in the same favorable
terms of the performance. This was natural, for we
know that the critic himself had arranged the musical
mise en scène ; and he was on that account bound to
pay a compliment to those performers who had taken
the pains, under his leadership, to study an opera so
disagreeable to them. But M. Berlioz showed his
true modesty by not saying a word in his article of
the value of his recitative. And everyone was touched
when, in the next number of the same journal, M.
Berlioz's colleague, M. Jules Janin, undertook the
friendly task of also speaking of the Freischütz, — but
found an opportunity while doing so to say only a decisive word of praise with reference to the recitative of
his friend and companion-journalist. There was no
one who did not find this arrangement of the two colleagues a very sensible one, in accordance with all the
rules of Parisian logic.

Other journals took other courses, according to
their specific logical laws ; those which are in opposition to the management of the grand opera naturally
could not refrain from giving a candid opinion of
the unsuccessful performance, which they sought to
strengthen by not leaving a single good trait in our
Freischütz.

But most logically of all was their opinion expressed
by the *Charivari* in its article :—the author of the article heartily congratulated the management of the
grand opera upon having *offered an asylum to the
masterpiece of German art, after it had received no*

recognition from the composer's own countrymen, and had been banished from its native soil!

And when I come to this passage, my patience is at last exhausted. Till now I have laughed,—and I have even reason to do the same at the article in the *Charivari;* but there are points at which laughter ceases, however much material for it may remain. Shall I tell you, my German countrymen, what has decided me not to laugh at the above-mentioned article? You must know, then, that it is anger at the impossibility, in this great capital of this amazingly free France, of finding acceptance in a single journal for a powerful reply to that stupid insult—as well as for any representation whatever of the failures of the Paris Freischütz.

The French only allow attacks and denials between *Parties;* in such cases they have no conscience as to denying each other the last spark of honor or sense. But the quietest and most sensible statement or explanation, as soon as it is directed at *all* parties alike, must never be allowed to reach their eyes. They lie to each other in such cases as to what they know and what they don't know, make use of their absurd logic, and are proud of the fact that they know nothing in the world but what they *want* to know.

This is the true state of the case. These *spirituel* Frenchmen are wanting not only in the capacity but also in the desire—though it be only out of curiosity— to go beyond the limits of their traditional beliefs about the good and the beautiful. I am saying nothing new in saying this, of course—for there *isn't* anything new to say about them, since they never, in spite of their annual changes of fashion, can *become new.* But I must again call to mind what has been said so often, because the idea has recently obtained among us that there was a growing resemblance between Germans and Frenchmen in artistic taste. This impression has undoubtedly been caused by our learning that the French translated Goethe, and played Beethoven's symphonies with masterly skill. Both have been done, and are done, it is true. But I have also announced to you to-day that they have performed the Freischütz. As much as this has done to a growing rapport between the two nations, Goethe and Beethoven have also done;—but not more ; and this is less than a little ; for the Freischütz especially has contributed of late to alienate the French from the Germans.

We must not nourish any illusions on this point ; in many ways the French will always remain strangers to us, even though they wear dress-coats and cravats similar to our own.

If we should desire to approach nearer to them, for a thousand reasons that we might have for doing so, we should have to reject a good portion of our best property ;—we cannot deceive the French, and make them believe by pretences that—for example— we compose French music, unless the whole inner nature of it is modelled after what they call their Logic. This would be a difficult piece of work, and any one who speaks from experience can give assurance that a double dose of national feeling and patriotism is necessary to keep one's heart from being fairly eaten out by all the French demands. But for this very reason there can be no greater pleasure than when one succeeds in getting the advantage of Frenchmen in spite of their extraordinary logic ; it is not easy to do, however, for they are as watchful as possible, and their custom-houses are ordered to forbid foreign importations with all possible severity,—or at least the duties on imports are very high and it costs a great deal to raise them.

We Germans, on the contrary,—how over-honest and amiable we are, to seek with such industrious complacency after tasteful bits in the masterpieces of neighboring nations ! Yes—even to accept the most tasteless parts of them as something wonder-

6*

ful and foreign, and carry them to our chemists to
make remedies of with which to cure those portions
of our own frames that have been injured by too much
sedentary life ! You ought to know that these remedies are only valuable as protections against vermin ;
and that the Parisian knows his own wares so well that
he does not even attribute this virtue to them—for
which reason it is, by the way, that so many vermin
flourish in the glorious French capital.

Ah ! how kindly and complacent you are toward all
those meannesses that disgust even the French themselves ! Do you know that on account of this very
angelic virtue you make yourselves still more a subject
of jest for this laughter-loving people ? They tell how
one of them visited the theatre of Berlin or Vienna in
April or May, this year, and that " Fra Diavolo" or
" Zampa " was being performed there. Every Frenchman that hears this decides (by his logic) that you are
the most ridiculous people on the face of the earth ;
and he forthwith proceeds to die of laughing.

I heard such a burst of laughter a while ago : and
because I had been laughing at something else, I did
not join in it this time, but doubled my fists, and
swore. Whoever cares to know what it was that I
swore, shall know it some time ; if I were more than I
am—if I were one of those happy beings of whom
Schiller sings in his hexameters—you should know at
once what I swore to myself, when I heard the Frenchmen laughing at our devotion to " Zampa " and " Fra
Diavolo " !

What ! Are we, the gifted nation among whom God
permitted a Mozart and a Beethoven to arise,—are we
made to be the sport of Paris salons ? We serve them
now as such ; and we deserve to ; the shallowest pate
on the Boulevard des Italiens has the right to laugh at
us,—for we act so as to merit it. I do not consider it
matter of blame to us that we are capable of recognizing the merits of French art,—for it is only this trait

that raises us by a heaven's-height above the French themselves ; we are to be congratulated that we are able to estimate at its full value all that foreign countries offer us ; it is a remarkable gift that benevolent Heaven has conferred upon us Germans ; for without it no universal genius, like Mozart, could have been created among us,—and by its means we are capable of forgiving every one that makes sport of us.

.But with all that, it is in the nature of things that there should be times of war as well as times of peace ; and if you desire some time in such a period of strife to avenge yourselves upon the French, you cannot punish them more keenly than by sending back to them by extra post, some fine day, these emissaries of their holy spirit — " Fra Diavolo " — " Zampa " — " The Faithful Shepherd "—and the rest, whatever christian names they have.

Be sure, that if the French are forced to listen again to the preachings of these gifted teachers, they will die of ennui ;—for the French are above all things a spirited people, and hate nothing with such ardent bitterness as this same *ennui.*

This, my German countrymen, would be an excellent and well-deserved punishment for the abuses that our dear, dear Freischütz has suffered here. If you have really banished it from your soil, as the *Charivari* assures us with such perfect confidence, hasten to let it come back again ; for you have many worthless wares to exchange, in return for which the French will gladly give you back your Freischütz.

THE MUSIC OF THE FUTURE.

—————•••—————

.

A LETTER TO A FRENCH FRIEND, FRANÇOIS VIL-
LOT; USED AS A PREFACE TO A PROSE TRANS-
LATION OF WAGNER'S LIBRETTI.

M Y HONORED FRIEND:
You desired to receive from me personally,
some clear definition of those ideas which I published
some years ago in Germany in a series of art essays, and
which excited enough attention, as well as opposition,
to prepare for me a curious and expectant reception
in France also. You considered this to be important
for my own interest as well, as you kindly believed
that you might assume that much error and prejudice
would be dispelled by a well-considered explanation
of my ideas, and that many perplexed critics .would
feel themselves in a better situation, on the intended
production of one of my musical dramas in Paris, to
criticise only the work of art itself, and not at the same
time to give their judgment on an apparently questionable theory.

I confess that it would have been extremely difficult
for me to have complied with your kindly meant request, if you had not at the same time pointed out to
me the only way in which I believed I could do so,
by your expressed wish to lay before the public a
translation of my operatic poems. For it would have
seemed impossible to me to again wander through the
labyrinth of theoretical speculation in purely abstract

fashion ; and I can recognize, from the dislike that now keeps me from even reading over again my theoretical writings, the fact that at the time I wrote those works I was in a thoroughly abnormal state, such as may be experienced once in the life of an artist, but cannot well be repeated.

Allow me first of all to describe this state to you in its principal characteristic features, as far as I can at present recognize them. If you will grant me some space for this purpose, I can then hope, proceeding from the description of a subjective mood, to place before you the concrete contents of artistic theories which it would now be impossible for me to repeat in a purely abstract form,—while this latter would also be a hindrance to the object of my communication.

If we may regard all nature, looked at as a whole, as a process of development from the unconscious to consciousness, and if this process appears most conspicuously in the human individual, the observation of it in the life of the artist is certainly one of the most interesting, because in him and his creations the world represents itself and comes to conscious existence. But in the artist, too, the presenting force is in its very nature unconscious—instinctive ; and even where he requires thought in order to form the outline of his intuition, by the aid of the technical ability with which he is endowed, into an objective work of art, it is not exactly reflection that decides for him the choice of his means of expression, but rather an instinctive impulse, which constitutes, indeed, the character of his peculiar talent. The necessity for continued reflection will only come to him, when he meets with some great obstacle to the application of the means necessary for his expression—that is, where the means for the presentation of his artistic purpose are continually rendered difficult or are even forbidden to him.

That artist will find himself much the most frequently in the latter position, who requires for representation of his object not only lifeless tools, but a union of living artistic forces. Such a union, in the most extended sense, is a necessity to the dramatic poet, in order to give to his poem the most intelligible expression. And for this he has to go to the stage, which, as the exponent or representative, forms of itself, with the laws peculiar to it, a special art-department. The dramatic poet goes to this stage as to a completed art-element; he must mingle himself with it and its peculiar nature, in order to see his artistic purpose realized. If his tendencies are fully in accord with those of the stage, there can be no talk of such a conflict as I have mentioned; and only the character of this accord needs to be mentioned, to determine the worth of the work of art called into being by it. If, on the contrary, those tendencies are entirely divergent, it is easy to understand the sore need of the artist who sees himself forced to employ for the expression of his artistic purpose an art-instrument which in its nature belongs to another purpose than his own.

The consciousness that was forced upon me, that I found *myself* in such a situation, compelled me during a certain period of my life to confine myself to the more or less unconscious methods of artistic production, in order to gain by persistent reflection some knowledge of this problematic situation by the investigation of its reasons. I may assume, that the problem here presented had *never* pressed so hard upon an artist as precisely upon me, because the artistic elements that entered into the matter had certainly never before stood in such manifold and peculiar relations to one another as here, where poetry and music on the one hand, and the modern lyric scene on the other, should unite in the most untrustworthy and equivocal institution of our time—the operatic stage. And here let me at once point out to you the difference—very important in my eyes—which exists between the relation of operatic composers to the operatic stage in France and Italy, and that which prevails in Germany. It is so considerable that you will easily perceive, from the characteristics of this difference, how it is that the problem I have described could so visibly present itself only to a *German* author.

In Italy, where the opera was first elaborated, no other task has ever been set before the musician than to write a number of airs for special singers, in whom dramatic talent was entirely a secondary consideration ;—airs that should give these *virtuosi* an opportunity to bring into play their several specific vocal powers. All that poetry and scenery contributed to this exhibition of the performer's art, was an excuse for time and space for it ; with the singer alternated the dancer, who danced precisely the same that the other sang ; and the composer had no other task than to contribute variations on a certain selected type of tune. Here, therefore, there was complete agreement in purpose, down to the smallest detail, because, while the composer composed for certain fixed voices and their individual characteristics, these, in turn, showed him the character of the variations he must make. In this way the Italian became an *art-genre* by itself, which, while it had nothing to do with the true drama, had also nothing to do with true music ; for, for him who understands art, the decline of Italian music dates from the rise of the opera in Italy—an opinion that will be readily comprehended by anyone who has gained a true conception of the ·dignity, the richness, and the unspeakably expressive depth of the Italian church music of the earlier centuries ; and who, after hearing for example the *Stabat Mater* of Palestrina, can hardly believe it to be possible that the Italian opera is the legitimate daughter of so wonderful a mother. This I only mention in passing ; let us, as far as our present object is concerned, bear chiefly in mind the fact that in Italy, even down to our own day, the most perfect

harmony exists between the purposes of the operatic
stage and those of the composer.

In France, also, this relation has not changed,—
though here the task is increased as well for the singers as for the composer ; for the dramatic poet enters
into the matter to a far more important degree here
than in Italy. Conformably to the national character,
and to the important development of dramatic poetry
and action that had gone before, this branch of art
made demands upon the opera as well. In the establishment of the grand opera, a strict style was gradually formed, borrowed in its main features from the
rules of the Théâtre Français, which included in itself
all the arrangements and requirements of a dramatic
representation. Without characterizing it more particularly at this moment, let us bear in mind the one
fact that there existed here *a theatre that served as a
model*, in which this style was developed, equally de-
termining the course of both performer and author ;
that the author found the exactly-defined frame
all ready prepared, which he was to fill with action
and music ; that he had known and trained singers
and impersonators in mind, with whom he was in perfect accord as to his purpose.

The opera reached Germany, however, as an entirely completed foreign product,—foreign, in its very
nature, to the whole character of the nation. First of
all, German princes brought Italian opera troupes to
their courts ; German composers had to visit Italy to
perfect themselves there in the art of operatic composition. At a later period the theatres themselves took
it up, especially the public production of translations
of French operas. Attempts at German opera consisted in nothing but the recitation of foreign operas
in the German language. No central theatre, to serve
as a model for this purpose, was ever established.
All remained in the greatest anarchy—Italian and
French styles and German imitations side by side.

Endeavors to make from the original, undeveloped, German musical drama, an independent and popular *genre*, were almost always repressed by the influence of formal elaboration, as it came from foreign countries.

A more conspicuous evil which arose among these distracting influences, was the entire absence of style in operatic representations. In cities whose small population only offered a small and· seldom varied audience, French, Italian, and German operas imitated from both or derived from the lowest forms of Vaudeville, tragic or comic, all sung by precisely the same singers, were performed in the most rapid succession, in order to make the repertoire attractive by variety. What had been arranged for the best Italian singers, with special regard to their individual capabilities, was sung by singers without instruction, without vocal flexibility, in a language entirely the opposite of the Italian in character,—and generally sung with laughable distortions.—French operas, dependent upon the pathetic declamation of pointed rhetorical phrases, were produced in translations which had been made by literary penny-a-liners at the lowest price, generally without regard to the· connection between the declamation and the music, and with mistakes in prosody that were calculated to make one's hair stand on end ; a circumstance which put an effectual end to the development of a healthful style in the performances, and made both singers and audience indifferent to the text of the operas. Awkwardness on all sides arose from this ; there was nowhere an operatic theatre to serve as an example and to give the tone ; the education of even the obtainable voices was faulty or entirely wanting ; everywhere artistic anarchy prevailed.

You perceive that there was practically *no* operatic theatre in existence for the true and earnest musician. If his inclination or education inclined him toward the theatre, he was forced to betake himself to writing in

Italy for the Italian, or in France for the French opera ; and while Mozart and Gluck wrote Italian and French works, the really national music of Germany grew up upon an entirely different basis from that of the opera.   Turning away from the opera altogether, and in that very branch of composition from which the Italians had diverged with the first appearance of the opera, a truly characteristic music developed in Germany, from Bach to Beethoven, up to the climax of its marvellous richness,—a school that has led German music to its universally recognized importance.

For the German musician who looked out from his own field of choral and instrumental music upon that of *dramatic* music, there existed no complete and attractive form in the line of opera, which, by its relative perfection, could serve him as an example in such a way as he could be served in those classes of music which were more in his own school.   While a noble, completed form of composition lay before him in the oratorio, and especially in the symphony, the opera merely offered him a disconnected chaos of trifling and undeveloped methods, upon which there rested the burden of a conventionality incomprehensible to him, and subversive of all efforts towards free development.

In order to clearly understand what I mean, compare the broad, rich form of a symphony of Beethoven with the music of his opera of " Fidelio " ; you will feel at once how the master found himself trammelled and confined in this latter field, and how he could hardly ever reach the true development of his proper powers ; for which reason, in order to pour himself out for once in all his fulness, he threw himself with the force of desperation, as it were, upon his overture, — and produced a musical creation of a breadth and importance such as had been before unknown.   He withdrew disheartened from this one attempt at an opera ; without, however, giving up the wish that he might be able to find a poem that would render possible the full exercise of his musical power. It was the *Ideal* that hovered before him.

And in fact there *must* of necessity arise in the German musician some *ideal* aim in regard to the opera— that form of artistic production that is for him so problematical, that continually attracts and as constantly repels him,—that so entirely fails to satisfy him in the way in which it is actually brought before him :—and in this fact lies the peculiar significance of German efforts in art, not only in this but in almost every artistic field. Permit me to point out the characteristics of this significance a little more closely.

The Latin nations of Europe indisputably attained, at an early period, to one great point of advantage over the Germanic—namely, in the development of *Form.* While Italy, Spain, and France made for themselves that pleasing and appropriate form which soon gained a general and proper adoption for all outward expression in life and art, Germany remained in this respect in a state of undeniable anarchy, which could not be concealed, but was rather increased, by the fact that it sought to make use of the already perfect form employed by foreigners. The obvious disadvantage under which the German nation labored on this account in all which concerned outward form (and how much this includes !), retarded the development of German art and literature so long, that it has only been since the latter half of the last century that such a movement showed itself in Germany, as the Latin nations had experienced ever since the beginning of the period of the Renaissance.

This German movement could at first assume little character but that of a reaction against the foreign, distorted, and therefore distorting Latinized forms ; yet as this could not act favorably to a German form that had not been *repressed*, but had in reality *never existed*, the movement tended strongly toward the discovery of some method of expression of a purely ideal *human* nature,—not to one that should belong to this one nation alone. The influence of the two leading German poets, Goethe and Schiller, peculiar, new, and unprecedented as it was in art-history, shows itself in this,—that now for the first time this problem of an ideal, purely human art-form in its fullest meaning became the object of investigation ; and the search· for this form was almost the most important element of their labors. Rebelling against the force of that method of expression that still passed for a law among the Latin nations, they succeeded in looking upon this method objectively, in comprehending its disadvantages as well as its advantages, in going back from it to the origin of all European art-form—the Greek ; and finally, grasping the antique form with the requisite freedom, to proceed from it to an ideal art-expression which, as one purely human and freed from narrow national customs, could develop these customs into a form that should be human in the truest sense, and only obey eternal laws.

The disadvantage under which the German had thus far labored as opposed to the Latin, was thus converted into an advantage. For while the Frenchman, for example, contented himself with an entirely developed, congruous form, and, willingly subjecting himself to its apparently unalterable laws, devoted himself only to continual reproductions of it, and thus felt himself committed to what was, in a higher sense, a stagnation of his productiveness,—the German, with a full recognition of the advantageous elements of such a position, nevertheless saw its disadvantageous elements as well. The lack of freedom in it did not escape him, and the prospect opened to him of an ideal art-form in which what was always valuable in every method of expression should have representation, freed from the fetters of the purely fortuitous and the false. The immeasurable importance of such a

form must consist in this, that, putting aside the lim-
iting factor of narrow national influence, it should be
one universally intelligible and open to every people.

If, in the matter of literature, the differences of the
European languages would act as an obstacle to this,
it must be in music, that language intelligible to all
men, that the great equalizing power is to be found,
which, converting the language of ideas into the
language of the feelings, would bring the deepest
secrets of the artistic conception to general comprehension, especially if this comprehension can be made distinct through the plastic expression of dramatic representation,—can be given such a distinctness as up to
this time painting alone has been able to claim as its
peculiar influence.

You see here, hastily sketched, the plan of that work
of art which always presented itself to me as the ideal
one, and which I at one time felt impelled to describe
in its theoretic features. It was at a period when a
gradually increasing distaste for that school of art
which, when compared with the ideal I had conceived,
had only the repulsive resemblance to it that an.ape
has to a man,—it was at a time when distaste for this
had so gained possession of me that I longed to flee
before it and hide myself in the most complete retirement.

That I may make this period of my life intelligible
to you, permit me, without wearying you with biographical details, to describe to you the peculiar conflict in the midst of which a German musician found
himself placed, who, with Beethoven's symphonies in
his heart, saw himself forced into relations with the
modern opera, as I have described it as existing in
Germany.

In spite of a serious and scientific education, I had
been from my earliest youth in constant and intimate
association with the theatre. This early youth of
mine was passed during the last years of the life of

Karl Maria von Weber, who periodically brought out
his operas in the city where I lived—Dresden. I received my earliest impressions of music from this
master, whose melodies filled me with dreamy serious-
ness, and whose personality fascinated me even to
enthusiasm. His death in a foreign land filled my
childish heart with dismay. I first learned of Beethoven when I was told of his death also, which occurred not long after Weber's ; and I learned his
music, too, attracted to it, as it were, by the enigmatical news that he was dead. Excited by such sad impressions, a love for music developed more and more
strongly within me. But it was only later, and especially after my other studies had introduced me to
the knowledge of classical antiquity and had aroused
in me the impulse to poetic efforts, that I attained to
the deepest musical study. I proposed to compose
the music for a tragedy that I had written.

It is said that Rossini once asked his teacher if it
was necessary to learn counterpoint in order to compose an opera ? And as the latter, having in mind the
modern Italian opera, replied that it was not, his pupil
gladly abandoned it.—After my teacher had taught
me the most difficult portions of counterpoint, he said
to me, " Probably you will never have occasion to
write a fugue ; but the fact that you *can* write one will
give you technical independence and make everything
else easy to you." With this schooling I entered upon
the practical career of a theatrical musical director,
and began to compose after libretti written by myself.

Let this brief biographical sketch suffice you. After
what I have told you of the situation of the opera in
Germany, you will the more easily conceive the course
of my development. The peculiar, gnawing feeling
that oppressed me in conducting our ordinary operas,
was often interrupted by an indescribable, enthusiastic
feeling of happiness, when here and there, in the performance of nobler works, I became thoroughly con-

scious, in the midst of the representation, of the incomparable influence of dramatic-musical combinations ;—an influence of such depth, fervor, and life as
no other art is capable of producing.

That such impressions, which, with the rapidity of
lightning, made clear to me undreamed-of possibilities, could constantly renew themselves for me,—this
was the thing which bound me to the theatre, much as
the typical spirit of our operatic performances filled
me with disgust. Among especially strong impressions of this character, I remember the hearing of an
opera by Spontini in Berlin, under that master's own
direction ; and I felt myself, too, thoroughly elevated
and ennobled for a time, when I was teaching a small
opera company Méhul's noble " Joseph." And
when, twenty years ago, I spent some time in Paris,
the performances at the grand opera could not fail, by
the perfection of their musical and dramatic *mise en
scène*, to exercise a most dazzling and exciting influence upon me. But greatest of all was the effect
produced upon me in early youth by the artistic
efforts of a dramatic singer of (in my eyes) entirely un-
surpassed merit—Schröder-Devrient. Paris, and perhaps you yourself, made, in her time, the acquaintance of that great *artiste*. The incomparable dramatic talent of this woman, the inimitable harmony
and strong individuality of her representations, which
I studied with eyes and ears, filled me with a fascination that had a decisive influence on my whole artistic
career. The possibilities of such a performance were
revealed to me, and with her in view, there grew up
in my mind a legitimate demand, not for musical-dra-
matic representation alone, but for the *poetic-musical
conception* of a work of art to which I could hardly
continue to give the name of " opera."

I was pained to see such an *artiste* compelled, in order to gain material for her dramatic talent, to take up
the most insignificant productions in the field of oper-

atic composition; and when I was repeatedly amazed
to see what fervor and what transporting beauty she
put into her delineation of Romeo in Bellini's feeble
work, I said to myself what an incomparable work of
art that would need to be, that should be fully worthy
in all its parts of the dramatic talent of such an *artiste*,
and of a company of artists equal to her !

The higher my idea of what could be accomplished
in the line of opera aspired, and the more this idea
seemed to me possible to realize by turning the whole
full stream to which Beethoven swelled German music, into the channel of musical drama, so much the
more discouraging and repulsive became for me the
daily intercourse with the kind of opera that actually
existed, that lay so far from the ideal that I inwardly
recognized. Spare me the description of the inward
discontent that at last grew to be unbearable, which
filled the soul of an artist who, while he saw with ever
increasing distinctness the possibility of realizing an
incomparably perfect art-work, at the same time found
himself associated, in a circle of daily duties from
which there was no escape, with a class of art which,
in its ordinary mechanical execution, showed him the
precise contrary of the ideal with which he was himself filled. All my efforts to work toward a reform in
the operatic institution itself, — my propositions to
give this institution, by assuming in it a decided
course, an impulse toward the fulfilment of my ideal
wishes, through the adoption of that degree of excellence that was now rare as the future standard of *all*
performances,—all these endeavors were of no avail.
At last I was compelled to see distinctly what was
really designed in the culture of the modern theatre,
and especially of the opera ; and this unendurable recognition of its true purpose so filled me with detestation and despair, that, giving up every effort at reform, I withdrew entirely from my connection with
the unworthy institution.

I had time to meditate upon this position of the stage toward the public, and to take into account those social relations which would determine the theatre that I had in mind, as surely as this latter proceeded from our modern social status. And as I had found a certain, real ground for the character of my dramatic and musical ideal in what artists of genius rarely and in isolated cases accomplished, so history furnished me with a typical model for the ideal relation I had conceived between the stage and the public. I found this in the theatre of ancient Athens ;—there, where the theatre only opened its doors on special and hallowed festivals ; where there was united with the enjoyment of art a religious celebration, in which the most distinguished men of the state took part as poets and actors, appearing, like priests, before the assembled populace of the city and country, which was so imbued with high anticipations of the dignity of the work to be performed, that an Æschylus and a Sophocles could bring the most sublime of all poetic creations before the people, certain of their full understanding of it.

The reasons for the decline of this incomparable work of art, into which I sorrowfully saw myself forced to inquire, appeared to me at once. The *social* causes of this decline first attracted my attention, and I thought that I saw in these at the same time the reasons of the decline of the ancient state itself. Consequently I sought to fix upon the social basis of such a political arrangement of the human race, as, while it improved upon the errors of the ancient state, could bring about a state of affairs in which the relation of art to public concerns, as it once subsisted in Athens, could be restored in a fashion if possible even nobler —at all events more lasting.

I published my ideas bearing upon this point in a paper entitled " Art and Revolution." I abandoned my original wish to publish this among a series of

7

articles in a French political journal, when I was assured that that particular period (it was in the year
1848) was not suitable for gaining the attention of the
Parisians for such a subject.   At present I think 'it
would be an exceedingly great digression, if I should
acquaint you more in detail with the contents of that
publication; and you will certainly thank me for sparing
you any attempt to do so.   It is enough that I should
point out to you, in what I have said above, the apparently divergent thoughts in which I was absorbed,
to gain for my artistic ideal some ground in a reality,
even if it should be, so to speak, merely an ideal one.

   But the investigation into the character of the
lamentable destruction of the great Greek art-work attracted me still more strongly.   Here I was first struck
by the remarkable phenomenon of the division and
separation of those individual branches of art which
had formerly been united in the perfect and complete
drama.   The special art-ingredients detached themselves
from that omnipotent union in which they, working for
a single object, had rendered it possible to make intelligible to the whole people the noblest and deepest purposes of humanity,—detached themselves from it to
become no longer the inspired teachers of the public,
but the consoling.pastime of special art-lovers ; so
that while gladiatorial combats and battles of wild
beasts were exhibited to the populace, the educated
man occupied himself in solitude with literature and
painting.   It was important for me, above all things,
that I thought myself forced to recognize that the
special, separately developed branches of art, however much their capabilities of expression might finally
be brought out and heightened by great geniuses,
nevertheless, without falling into unnaturalness and
decided error, could never aim to supply in any way
the place of that all-powerful work of art which was
only possible through a union of their forces.

   Having at hand the opinions of the greatest critics,

—the investigations, for instance, of a Lessing into the limits of painting and poetry,—I believed that I might form the theory that every *individual* branch of art follows out a development of its powers that finally leads it to their limits ; and that it cannot pass these limits without the danger of losing itself in the unintelligible and absolutely fantastic—even in the absurd. I thought that I saw in this point the necessity for it to join companionship at this stage with another class of art, related to it, and the only one capable of going on from this position. And as I was of necessity keenly interested (having regard to my own ideal) in following out this tendency in each special kind of art, I finally believed that I could recognize it most distinctly in the relation of poetry to music,—especially considering the remarkable importance modern music has assumed. And as I thus endeavored to imagine that work of art in which all branches of art could unite in their highest perfection, I came as a matter of course to the *conscious* contemplation of that ideal which had *unconsciously* gradually formed within me, and had hovered before the seeking artist. As I could not, especially when I remembered the entirely erroneous position of the theatre toward the public, which I had recognized,—as I could not bring about the possibility of a complete appearance of this ideal art-work in the present, I called my ideal the " Art-work of the Future " (*Kunstwerk der Zukunft*). Under this title I published a more detailed essay, in which I described more closely the ideas just indicated ; and it is to this title that we owe, by the bye, the invention of a spectre of a " Music of the Future," which plays its pranks in such a popular fashion 'even in French art publications, and in relation to which you will now easily guess from what misunderstanding it arose, and with what object it was invented.

I spare you also, my honored friend, the repetition of the details of this essay. I myself attach no other value to it than what it may have for those to whom it does not appear uninteresting, to know how and through what methods of expression a creative artist took pains to find *for himself* solutions to problems that generally only occupy the professional critic, but that can hardly press upon him in the same peculiar way in which they present themselves to the other.

And I will give you also only a general sketch of a third and more elaborate work, which I published soon after the one last mentioned, under the title "Opera and Drama"; for I cannot but believe that the extremely detailed presentation of my chief theories to be found therein, has more interest for myself than it either has now or will have in the future for others. They were personal reflections which I published, and sometimes brought forward in a somewhat polemic manner, urged on by an unusually ardent interest in the subject of them. This subject was a closer investigation of the relations of poetry and music to one another,—and this time with special regard to dramatic art.

Here I thought it necessary, first of all, to combat the erroneous opinion of those who saw in the opera as it existed, if not a perfected ideal, at least the immediate preparation for one. In Italy, and still more in France and Germany, this problem had occupied the leading minds in literature. The conflict between the adherents of Gluck and those of Piccini, in Paris, was nothing but a controversy (from its vary nature indecisive) on the question whether the ideal of the drama was attainable through the opera. Those who believed they could sustain successfully the affirmative side of this question were, in spite of their apparent victories, held in serious check by their opponents as soon as these latter treated music as predominating in opera to such an extent that the result was to be attributed to *it*, and not to poetry. Voltaire, who in the abstract inclined to the affirmative opinion, saw himself forced, as far as the *concrete* state of the case was concerned, to the condemnatory remark " *Ce qui est trop sot pour être dit—on le chante.*"

In Germany, where the same problem, first raised by Lessing, was discussed by Goethe and Schiller, and ·with a decided tendency toward the anticipation of favorable results from the opera—Goethe confirmed involuntarily, in most striking opposition to his *theoretical* belief, the saying of Voltaire. He himself was the author of several opera libretti, and, in order to place himself upon the level of this class of work, he thought it necessary to be as trivial as possible in conception as well as execution—so much so that we only see with regret these very shallow pieces placed among the number of his poetical works.

This favorable opinion of brilliant minds, that has been so often accepted, but could never be fulfilled, showed me on the one hand how seemingly near the possibility lay of attaining the highest results through a complete union of poetry and music in the drama,—but on the other hand the fundamentally erroneous nature of the existing type of opera,—a faultiness of which the musician could not be the first to be conscious, and which might also escape the knowledge of the literary poet. The poet, not himself a musician, found in the opera a securely constructed scaffolding of musical forms, which gave him from the very beginning fixed laws for the conception and execution of the dramatic lining that he must furnish. *He* could not change anything in these forms— it was only the musician who could do so. Of whatever kind their contents might be, the poet, called in to aid, could only cover it, without wish on his part, in such a way that he saw himself compelled, in the conception of the subject and in the versification, to a noticeable lowering of his poetic powers,—even to the open triviality so castigated by·Voltaire. In fact there is no need of calling attention to the wretchedness and shallow-

ness—even the laughable character of the class of
opera libretti; even in France the best attempts of
this character consist rather in the effort to conceal
this evil than to do away with it.   The structure of the
opera, therefore, remained for the poet an untouched,
foreign matter from which he kept himself aloof, but to
which he was obedient; and for this reason real poets,
with rare and unfortunate exceptions, have never had
to do with the opera at all.

The question is now only how it could have been
possible for the *musician* to give to the opera its ideal
importance, if the poet, in his practical relations to it,
could not even fulfil the demand which we make in regard to every sensible play?   For the musician, who,
constantly absorbed in the development of precisely
those purely musical forms, saw nothing before him
but a field for the practice of his specific musical talent?

I consider that I explained successfully in the first
part of my last-mentioned work " Opera and Drama,"
what is contradictory and erroneous in what is here expected from the musician.   While expressing my highest admiration of the beautiful and ennobling work
accomplished by great masters in this field, I was under
no necessity of diminishing their acknowledged reputation in pointing out the weaknesses of their creations, because I could at once refer the cause of these
weaknesses to the erroneous nature of the school of
art.   But what was incumbent upon me after this certainly discouraging representation, was to give some
proof that the ideal perfecting of the opera that had
hovered before many brilliant minds, could only be
conditional upon an entire change in the character of
the poet's part in this art-product.

In order to gain a proper conception of this part to
be taken by the poet—a part so important for the influence of the whole; in order to conceive of it as a
voluntary one, and as wished for by the poet himself,
I considered first of all those repeated and earnestly

expressed hopes and wishes of great poets, such as I have already mentioned, to see in the opera an ideal branch of art. I sought to explain to myself the motive of this wish, and thought I found it in that natural desire of the poet, which decides him, in conception as well as in form, to use language, the materialization of abstract ideas, in such a way as to work immediately upon the feelings themselves. As this tendency is a controlling one even in the *invention* of the poetic subject, and only that life-picture of humanity is called poetic in which all motives attributable to abstract reason disappear in favor of the representation of motives of pure human feeling, so it is also the only criterion for the *form* and *expression* of the poetic recital. The poet seeks, in his language, to make the abstract, conventional meaning of words subordinate to their original, sensible one; and to secure, by rhythmic order, as well as by the almost musical dressing of words in versification, an effect for his phraseology which shall gain possession of and influence the feelings as though by enchantment.

In this course of the poet, so necessary to his very nature, we see him finally come to the limits of his branch of art, where it already seems to touch music; and thus the most successful work of the poet must be, for us, that which should be, in its perfection, entirely musical.

I considered that the mythos, or myth, must be looked upon as the ideal subject for the poet;—that originally nameless poem of the people, that we find in all ages treated in ever new methods by the poets of periods of finished culture. For in it the conventional disappears, and such forms of human relations as are only explicable to the abstract reason vanish almost entirely,—and there appears instead only the always intelligible, the purely human, but in that inimitable concrete form which gives to every genuine myth the individual features that are so easily recognizable. I devoted the second part of my book to the investigations connected with this subject, and carried my presentation of it as far as the question, which must be the most perfect form for the *presentation* of this ideal poetic matter.

In the third part I absorbed myself in the investigation of the technical possibilities in the matter of form, here alluded to; and I gained as the result of this research, the belief that *only the wonderfully rich development* (unknown to earlier centuries) *to which music has attained in our time*, could bring about the realization of these possibilities.

I feel the importance of this opinion too much not to regret that I cannot consider this the place in which I can be permitted a more comprehensive proof of my thesis. I considered that in the third part mentioned above, I established such a proof, sufficiently at least to convince myself; and if I undertake here to give you my views of the matter in a few of its features, I beg of you to take my word for it, that what may seem paradoxical to you was at least explained with more completeness in that paper.

It is undeniable, that since the renaissance of the fine arts among the Christian people of Europe, two species of art have received a new development, and one far more complete than they enjoyed in classical antiquity; —I refer to painting and music. The wonderful and ideal importance which painting gained in the first century of the Renaissance is so entirely beyond doubt, and it has been so well proved what were the characteristics of this art influence, that we will here refer only to the novelty of this phenomenon in the general field of art-history, and to the fact that it belongs entirely to *modern* art; and we may affirm the same in a still higher and (I believe) more important degree, of modern music. Harmony, utterly unknown to antiquity, and its endlessly rich development and employment

in polyphonism, are the discoveries and the peculiar
work of recent centuries.

Among the Greeks we only know music as accompanying the dance. The movements of the dance
gave to it, as to the poems which the singer sang to a
dancing measure, the rules of rhythm, which so entirely
regulated verse and melody that the Greek music
(with which the poetry was almost always understood
as included) can only be looked upon as the dance expressing itself in tones and words. It was these dancing
tunes, maintained among the people and originally be
longing to the worship of the heathen gods, which
(as they originally constituted the chief part of all antique
music) were also used by the earliest Christian congrega-
tions in the celebration of their gradually developing
worship. But this serious celebration, which entirely
excluded the dance as worldly and godless, of course
abandoned also the chief part of the ancient melody,
the very lively and varied rhythm; and through this
means the melody took on the entirely unaccented
character of the choral that is still used in our churches
to-day.

But it is plain that with the withdrawal of the rhythmic movement of this melody, it was robbed of the
motive of expression which was peculiar to it; and
even to-day, we should have an opportunity to convince ourselves of the wonderfully limited expression
of ancient melody after this dress of rhythm was removed,—if we could only imagine how it would be
without the harmony that has been made its basis.
But to increase the expressive power of melody in accordance with its inmost meaning, the Christian spirit
discovered many-voiced harmony on the basis of the
four-voiced accord, which, by its characteristic changes,
from this time gave a motive to the expression of
the melody, such as had been before decided by the
rhythm. We see to what wonderfully fervent expression, hitherto unknown, the melodic phrase attained

7*

through this means,—we see it with ever new conviction, from the perfectly incomparable masterpieces
of Italian church music. The different voices, originally only intended to bring the harmonic chord forming the basis to the ear at the same time with the
note of the melody, finally *themselves* received a free,
expressive, and progressive development, so that with
the help of the so-called art of counterpoint each one
of these voices, while subject to the melody (the *canto
fermo*), moved with independent expression. By this
means, in the works of the greatest masters, such a
church choral produced by its performance an effect so
wonderful, so arousing the heart to its very depths,
that no similar influence of any other art can be compared with it. ·

The decline of this art in Italy, and the simultane-
ous introduction of the development of operatic melody
among the Italians, I can only term a lapse into pagan-
ism. When, with the decline of the church, the
demand for the secular employment of music began
to gain the upper hand among the Italians, the easiest
method of procedure was found to be this—to give
back to melody its original rhythmic feature, and
employ it for song just as it had once been employed
for the dance. The striking incongruity between
modern verse (which had its development in unison
with the Christian melody) and the dancing melody
thus imposed upon it, I need not here point out ; and
I would only call your attention to the fact that the
melody became entirely indifferent to the verse, and
that finally its varying movements were left entirely to
the direction of the singer.

What especially induces us, however, to speak of
the development of this melody as a retrograde and
not as a progressive movement, is, that it undeniably
did not understand the employment of that wonderfully
important invention of christian music,—*harmony*, and
the polyphonism which embodies it. . Upon a basis

of harmony of such barrenness that it can suitably dispense with accompaniment altogether, Italian operatic melody, so far as any fitness or connection of its parts is concerned, has been content to erect such a miserable, temporary structure that the cultured musician of to-day stands in sorrowful amazement before this petty and almost childish art-form, the narrow boundaries of which must condemn even the greatest genius among composers to a perfectly formal conventionality, if ever he has any relations with it.

On the other hand, the same impulse toward the secular employment of the Christian church music, took on a peculiarly novel signification in Germany. German masters, too, went back to the original rhythmic melody, as it had been sustained, with the church-music, uninterruptedly among the people. But instead of *neglecting* the rich harmony of the Christian church-music, these masters sought rather to elaborate this harmony anew, *in unison* with the bright movement of rhythmic melody, in such fashion that rhythm and harmony should join in the expression of the melody. In conjunction with this the independent polyphonism was not only retained, but was developed to such an extent that each one of the voices, by means of the science of counterpoint, took an independent part in the performance of the rhythmic melody, so that this latter was no longer confined to the original *canto fermo*, but appeared in each of the accompanying voices. How it was possible, in this way, to attain even in the church choral an effect unprecedented in variety, only possible to music, and of the most transporting power,—how it was possible to attain this, may be readily conceived by any one who has had the privilege of listening to a fine performance of Bach's vocal compositions ; and I instance here especially a motette of Sebastian Bach's for eight voices— " Sing .unto the Lord a new song "—in which the lyric swing of the rhythmic melody rushes, as it were, through a sea of waves of harmony.

But the elaboration of this rhythmic melody, on the basis of Christian choral harmony, was to gain a still freer development, carried to the finest and most varied points of expression, by means of instrumental music. Without considering at this moment the extreme importance of the orchestra, I take the liberty of first directing your attention, in this connection, only to the amplification of the original dancing air in point of form. By means of the formation of quartettes of stringed instruments, the polyphonic method was enabled to gain the independent control of the different parts of the orchestra also, as it had done of the vocal parts in church music ; and thus freed the orchestra from the subordinate place in which it had hitherto been employed (as it is to-day in the Italian opera), only for the purpose of rhythmic and harmonic accompaniment. It is extremely interesting, and the only thing fairly explanatory of the nature of all musical form, to observe how all the efforts of German masters were directed toward giving to the simple dance-air, performed independently by instruments, a gradually richer and broader development. This air consisted originally only of a short movement, necessarily of four bars, which were doubled or quadrupled ; it seems to have been the fundamental plan of our masters to give to this a greater amplification, and thus to attain to a broader form in which harmony should also be more richly developed.

The peculiar form of the fugue, applied to the dance-melody, gave an opportunity also for extending its duration, by making it possible to present this melody in all the parts in turn, sometimes abbreviated, sometimes in paraphrase, exhibited in various lights by harmonic modulation, and kept in interesting movement by contrapuntal secondary themes.

A second step in this process consisted in the com-

bination of several dance-airs, in arranging them so as
to alternate according to the character of their expression, and in establishing a connection between them
by modulations, in which the science of counterpoint
proved especially useful.

Upon this simple basis was gradually developed
that remarkable art-product, the symphony. Haydn
was the brilliant master who first developed this form
in its broader sense ; and gave to it a deep and expressive meaning, by inexhaustible variety in his
motifs, and in their connection and elaboration.
While the Italian operatic air had kept to its scanty
and conventional structure, as far as form was concerned, it had nevertheless attained, in the mouths of
the most talented and appreciative singers, and borne
upon the breath of the noblest musical organ, to a
sensuous brilliancy which had hitherto been unknown
to the German composers, and the sweet melody of
which was wanting in their instrumental airs.

It was Mozart who first comprehended the nature
of this fascination, and while he added to the Italian
opera the richer developments of German instrumental composition, gave in turn to orchestral melody the full, melodious beauty of the Italian vocal
method.

Beethoven received the rich and promising heritage
of both these masters: He developed the symphonic
form to such a comprehensive breadth, and filled it
with contents of such unprecedentedly various and
ravishing melody, that we stand to-day before the
symphony of Beethoven as before the stone that
marks the boundary of an entirely new period in the
general history of art ; for in it there came into the
world a phenomenon, nothing even approaching
which is to be found in the art of any age or any
nation.

For in this symphony there is spoken by musical
instruments a language of which no one in any pre-

ceding age had any knowledge, inasmuch as the pure
musical expression in it enchains the hearer with a
lasting effect hitherto unknown, in the most incon-
ceivably varied shades of tone, and moves his inmost nature with a strength unattainable by any other
art; revealing to him in its variety so free and audacious a regularity, that it must seem to us more powerful than all logical sequence, yet without in the least
containing in itself the laws of logic. Indeed, that
purely logical mental process which followed the guidance of cause and effect, finds nothing here to cling
to. The symphony must needs appear to us a revelation from another world; and in very truth it does
discover to us a connection between the phenomena
of existence, which differs entirely from the ordinary
logical *nexus*, and in regard to which one thing is undeniable—that it forces itself upon us in the most
overwhelmingly convincing manner, and takes possession of our feelings with such positiveness that the
reasoning faculty is entirely confused and disarmed by
it.

The metaphysical necessity for the discovery of this
entirely new power of language precisely in our own
age, seems to me to lie in the increasingly conventional development of modern tongues. If we look
more closely at the development of these languages,
we shall find in the so-called roots of words an origin which shows us distinctly how in its first beginning the formation of the *idea* from the *thing*, was
almost entirely coincident with the subjective conception with regard to the latter; and the assumption
that the first language of mankind must have had a
great resemblance to singing, need not perhaps appear ridiculous.

Human speech certainly developed from a purely
sensuous, subjectively-felt signification of words, into
a more abstract sense, in such a way that at length
these words had only a conventional meaning left,

which deprived the feelings of all part in the understanding of them, and made their very connection and construction entirely dependent on certain rules that could be learned. Conventionality developed in language, in necessary accord with the moral development of the race ; a conventionality whose laws were no longer comprehensible to the purely natural feelings; but were incorporated in rules of education intelligible only to the reflective powers. And since the modern European languages, further divided into different classes, began to follow their purely conventional development with an increasingly obvious tendency, music has developed, on the other hand, into a hitherto unknown capability of expression.

It seems as though purely human feeling, grown stronger by its very repression on the side of conventional civilization, had sought out a means of bringing into use some laws of language peculiar to itself, by means of which it could express itself intelligibly, freed from the trammels of logical rules of thought. The extraordinary popularity of music in our age, the ever-increasing participation (extending through all classes of society) in the production of music of the deepest character, the growing desire to make of musical culture a necessary part of every education,—all these things which are certainly obvious and undeniable, distinctly prove the justice of the assumption that a deeply-rooted and earnest need of humanity finds expression in modern musical development ; and that music, unintelligible as its language is when tried by the laws of logic, must bear within it a more convincing means of making itself understood, than even those laws contain.

In the light of this unavoidable acknowledgment, there remain but two ways of development open to poetry. Either it must entirely pass over into the field of pure abstraction—of combinations of meanings, and the representation of things by the explanation of the

logical laws of thought;—and this is what. in its guise
as *philosophy*, it already does.   Or it must become in-
timately bound up with music, and with such music as
that whose endless power is revealed to us by the symphony of Beethoven.

Poetry will easily find its way to this, and will recognize its strongest, inmost longing in its final culmina-
tion in music, so soon as it appreciates a want in it,
which only poetry in its turn can supply.   To explain
this want, let us first establish that ineradicable quality
of the human perceptive process, which impelled man
to the discovery of the laws of causality, and because of
which he involuntarily asks himself, in the presence of
every impressive phenomenon—"*Why is this?*"

The hearing of a symphonic musical composition
does not, it is true, entirely silence this question; but
rather, since it cannot answer it, it produces a confusion in the capability of logical presentation, which
may not only disturb it, but can even be the cause of
an entirely erroneous judgment.   To answer this disturbing yet unavoidable question in such a way as to
elude it, in a certain sense, by appeasing it at the beginning—this is something that can only be the work
of the *poet*.   But only that poet can succeed in it, who
fully appreciates the tendency of music, and its inexhaustible power of expression, and therefore so com-
poses his poem that it can penetrate into the finest
fibres of musical texture, and completely dissolve the
spoken idea in feeling.   Obviously, therefore, no poetic
form is fitted for his use but that in which the poet no
longer *describes*, but brings his subject into actual representation, that is convincing to the senses;—and this
form is nothing but—the drama.

The drama, at the moment of its realistic, scenic
presentation, awakens in the spectator real participation in the action presented to him; and this is so
faithfully imitated from real life (or at least from the
possibilities of it), that the sympathetic human feeling

passes through such participation into a state of ecstasy which forgets that momentous question " *Why?* " and willingly yields itself up to the guidance of those new laws through which music makes itself so strangely intelligible, and at the same time—in the deepest sense —gives the only correct answer to that very " Why? "

In the third division of the work I have mentioned, I endeavored finally to present the technical laws in

the philosopher.   He *perceives* all these evils and mistakes, too ; and, disturbed anew by his consciousness
of them, he hurriedly closes his work with a sigh—only
to be understood by those who share with him the
same artistic point of view.

My condition, then, resembled a kind of spasm
(*Krampf*) ; in it I sought to express theoretically
that which the unfavorable relations I have already
described to you as existing between my own artistic
tendencies and the tendencies of our public art exhib-
itions (especially the operatic theatre), seemed to prevent me from expressing in an infallibly convincing way
through direct artistic production.   It was urgently
necessary for me to return from this wretched state to
the normal use of my artistic abilities.   I planned and
carried out a dramatic scheme of such considerable dimensions, that, in merely following the demands of my
subject, I purposely removed myself in this work
from every possibility of incorporating it with our
operatic repertoire as it exists at present.   Only under
the most unusual circumstances could this musical
drama, embracing, as it did, an entirely completed
trilogy, be brought to a public performance.

The ideal possibility thus placed before me, and in
consideration of which I kept myself entirely removed
from the modern opera, flattered my fancy, and raised
the tone of my spirits to such a height that—dispelling
all theoretic caprices by an artistic production henceforth uninterrupted,—I could bring myself back to my
normal and natural condition.   The work of which I
speak, and which I have already in great part carried
out in actual musical composition, is called " the Ring
of the Nibelungen."   If the present endeavor to lay before you others of my operatic poems in a prose translation, does not discourage you, you might perhaps
find me ready to have a similar course pursued with regard to this trilogy also.

While I, entirely resigned to the loss of all further

artistic association with the public, thus refreshed myself by the execution of new art-schemes, after the
pains of my wearisome excursion into the domain of
speculative theory ;—and while no inducement,—not
even the ludicrous misconceptions which were generally applied to my theoretical writings,—could have
persuaded me to return to that field,—I experienced,
on the other hand, a change in my relations to the
public, on which I had not counted in the least.

My operas,—one of which (Lohengrin) I had not
yet produced, while the remainder had only been performed at that theatre with which I was personally
engaged,—spread with growing . success through a
constantly increasing number of the German theatres,
and finally to nearly all ; and attained in them a lasting, undeniable popularity. With this phenomenon,
which in truth surprised me greatly, I renewed such
observations as I had often made in my earlier practical career ;—observations which, if the operatic
stage in one of its aspects repelled me, constantly
attracted me to it in another, by showing me exceptions, and revealing to me, through occasional works
of unusual merit and their influences, such possibilities
as led me, as I mentioned to you above, to lay out
various ideal schemes.

I was not present at any of all these performances
of my operas, and could therefore only decide as to
their nature from the reports of intelligent friends, or
from the peculiar effect of the works among the public. The picture which I draw from the reports of my
friends is not of such a kind as to give me, generally
speaking, a more favorable view of the spirit of these
performances, than I should have gathered from the
nature of most of our operatic representations.

While thus on the whole confirmed in my pessimis-
tic views, I nevertheless enjoyed the advantage of the
pessimist—that of taking all the more pleasure in the
good, the even excellent things, that spring up here

and there, because I had not thought myself justified in expecting or demanding them ; while in my ,earlier days, as an optimist, I had sternly demanded good and excellent results from *everything*,—because they were possible ;—and this had led me into intolerance and ingratitude. The occasional excellent performances, therefore, of which I thus unexpectedly heard, filled me with new zeal as well as with the most earnest gratitude. And whereas I had hitherto only seen the possibility of completely developed artistic accomplishment in a general and fully recognized condition appropriate thereto, this possibility now presented itself as exceptionally attainable.

But what was almost more encouraging for me, was to perceive the unusually strong impression that my operas, even at very questionable and often at most unjust representations of them, produced upon the public. When I think how unfavorably and bitterly the critics expressed themselves with regard to these operas, especially at the beginning—those critics to whom my previously published works had been a horror, and who persisted in taking for granted that my operas, though written at an earlier period, were constructed purposely according to those theories,— when I think of this, I can only see in the expressed pleasure taken by the public in works of precisely my own tendency, a very important and encouraging indication.

Such approval, uninfluenced by criticism on the part of the public at large, was easily comprehensible when the critics said to them, as once happened in Germany, " Turn away from the seductive, siren songs of Rossini; close your ears to his frivolous, melodious trifling ! "—and yet the people continued to take delight in hearing these airs. But here was a case in which the critics persistently warned the public not to spend their money for things which could give them no pleasure ;—for that what they sought in an opera—melodies, melodies—did not exist at all in *my* operas, but that there was nothing in them but the most tedious recitative and the most unintelligible musical hodge-podge ; in short, *" music of the future ! "*

Imagine, then, what an impression it must have made upon me, to receive not only the most irrefutable evidence of the really popular success of my operas among the whole German people, but personal information of a complete reversal of the previous judgment, and of the opinions of such persons as until that time had only found pleasure in the most sensual parts of the opera and ballet, and had repelled with contempt and disgust all persuasion to turn their attention to a more serious direction in dramatic-musical art. Such things frequently happened ; and I take the liberty of briefly explaining to you here, what encouraging and thoroughly consolatory conclusions I thought myself justified in forming from them.

It was plain that the greater or less capability of my own talent had nothing to do with the question here, since even those critics most hostile to me did not pronounce against *this*, but against the direction that I was following; and they sought to explain my final success by saying that my talent was better than my tendencies. I had, therefore, unaffected by the perhaps personally flattering recognition of my abilities, only to take pleasure in the fact that I had proceeded from a correct impulse when I had thought it possible to construct, by the equal and mutual mingling of poetry and music, such a work of art as must produce an irresistibly forcible impression in its scenic production,—and should produce it in such a way that voluntary reflection should disappear before it, passing into purely human emotion. That I saw this result attained, in spite of the great weak points of the performance, on the entire correctness of which so much depended, —this impelled me to still bolder views of the omnipo-

tent influence of music,—opinions concerning which I
will, in closing, endeavor to make myself more completely intelligible to you.

I can only hope to express myself clearly on this
difficult but most important point, if I take nothing but
form into our consideration.   I had endeavored in my
theoretical works to indicate *matter* as well as form ;
but as this, in theoretical writing, could only be done in
a purely abstract and not by a concrete presentation of
it, I necessarily laid myself open here to the danger of
great obscurity of expression, and even to the danger
of being misunderstood.   For this reason, as I said
above, I should not be willing at any price to again
undertake such a method of procedure, even in this
communication to you.   Yet I acknowledge the difficulty of speaking of a *form*, without indicating its *sub-
stance* in any way.   As I confessed to you in the beginning, it was for this reason that your request that I
would submit to you a translation of my operatic
poems was the only thing which could have induced
me to make the attempt to give you any thorough explanation of my theoretical process, as far as it is clear
to myself.   Permit me, therefore, to tell you a little
of these poems ; I hope this will make it possible for
me to speak afterward only of their musical form, to
which so much importance is to be attached in this
connection, and concerning which so many erroneous
ideas have been spread abroad.

First of all I must ask your indulgence because I
cannot lay these poems before you in any other than
a prose translation.   The endless difficulties which the
metrical translation of "Tannhäuser" (which is soon
to be introduced to the Parisian public in a complete
scenic performance) cost us in its preparation, showed
me that works of that kind require a time for their execution, which cannot now be devoted to the translation of my other writings.   I must, therefore, put out
of sight the fact that these poems might make some

impression upon you through the influence of their poetic form, and content myself with only showing you the character of the subjects, their dramatic arrangement, and their tendencies, in order to call your attention to the part which the spirit of music had in their conception and execution. I trust that the translation will be sufficient for this ; it makes no further claim than that of rendering the original text as literally as possible.

The first three of these poems—" The - Flying Dutchman," " Tannhäuser," and " Lohengrin "—were written by me, their music composed, and all (with the exception of " Lohengrin ") performed upon the stage before the composition of my theoretical writings. I might therefore show you in them (if it were entirely possible from the nature of the subject), the course of development of my artistic production up to that point where I saw myself called upon to account to myself theoretically for my method of procedure. But I only mention this to call your attention to the error that has been committed in believing, with regard to these three works, that they were purposely composed according to the abstract rules I had laid down. Let me tell you rather that my boldest conclusions concerning the possible form of the musical drama were forced upon me by the fact that I was, at the very time I made them, carrying in my brain the plan of my great drama of the Nibelungen, for a great part of which I had even written the poetry ; and I had so developed it that my theory was little else than an abstract expression of the productive process that had formulated itself within me. My own peculiar system, if you choose to call it so, was only employed to a very limited extent in those first three poems.

It was otherwise, however, with the latest of the poetic compositions which I submit to you—the " Tristan and Isolde." I projected and executed this after I had entirely composed the music for the

greater part of my Nibelungen drama. The most
urgent inducement to thus break in upon that important work, was the wish to produce a composition that
should be lighter and easier to present, in its scenic
necessities and in its less ambitious extent ; a wish to
the fulfilment of which I was urged partly by the need
of once more hearing something of my own composing ;
while, on the other hand, the encouraging and consolatory experience, which, as I mentioned to you, I
had had in the production of my earlier works in Germany, showed me that my wish was not unattainable.

I am willing that the severest demands, based upon
my theoretical opinions, should be made upon *this*
work : not because I had formed it according to my
system, for I had forgotten all theory in its composition ; but because, in this case, I at length moved with
complete freedom and entire disregard of all theoretic
scruples, in such a way that I myself perceived, at the
performance, that I had passed far *beyond* my system.
Believe me, there is no greater delight than the completely *un*critical frame of mind of the artist while
creating—such as I felt it in the execution of my
" Tristan." It was rendered possible to me, perhaps,
from the fact that a temporary season of reflection had
strengthened me, something in the same fashion in
which my teacher once believed he had strengthened
me by making me learn the most difficult points of
thorough-bass,—not for the writing of fugues, but for
the sake of that which can only be gained for one by
severe discipline—self-reliance, certainty !

Let me briefly allude to an opera which preceded
" The Flying Dutchman "—to " Rienzi," a work full
of youthful ardor, which secured for me my first success in Germany ; and this not only at the theatre
where I first produced it, in Dresden, but constantly,
since then, in many other theatres, and given with my
other compositions. I lay no special stress to-day
upon this work, which had my early impressions of

the heroic operas of Spontini (eminently calculated to arouse the desire of imitation), and the brilliant class of great operas by Auber, Meyerbeer and Halévy (having their origin in Paris), to thank for its conception and form,—I lay no special stress upon it, I say, at this time and in speaking of it to you, because no essential feature of my later views of art was included in it, and because there is no call here to present myself to you as a successful operatic composer, but rather to give you an explanation concerning a problematic tendency of my ideas.

" Rienzi " was completed during my first residence in Paris ; I had the brilliant Grand Opera in view ; and I was foolish enough to flatter myself that I should see my work produced there. If this youthful wish should yet be fulfilled, you would have to think with me that it was an extraordinary fate that permitted so long a time and such utterly different experiences to intervene between the desire and its fulfilment.

This five-act opera, arranged upon the largest scale, was immediately followed by " The Flying Dutchman," which I originally intended to have performed in *one* act only. You see that the splendors of my Parisian ideal had paled for me, and that I began to draw the rules for the form of my conception from another source than from the broad sea of current publicity. The nature of my mood has been explained to you ; it is clearly expressed in my poem. I do not know what poetic value may be attributed to it ; but I know that even in writing the poetic libretto I felt differently than during the composition of my libretto to " Rienzi," where I had nothing in mind but an operatic text which should enable me to fill as richly as possible all the traditional and customary forms peculiar to the Grand Opera,—introductions, finales, choruses, airs, duets, trios, etc.

In this and all succeeding plans I turned, for the

8

selection of my material, once for all from the domain
of history to that of legend. I will refrain here from
describing to you the mental process which directed
me to this decision, and will instead only call attention
to this point :—the *influence* which this choice has exercised on the structure of poetic and especially of
musical form.

All the details necessary for the description and
presentation of the conventionally historic, which a
fixed and limited historical epoch demands in order
to make the action clearly intelligible,—and which are
therefore carried out so circumstantially by the historical novelists and dramatists of to-day,—could be ·here
omitted. And by this means the poetry and especially the music were freed from the necessity of'a
method of treatment entirely foreign to them, and
particularly impossible as far as music was concerned.
The legend, in whatever nation or age it may be
placed, has the advantage that it comprehends only
the purely *human* portion of this age and nation, and
presents this portion in a form peculiar to it, thoroughly concentrated, and therefore easily intelligible.
A ballad, a refrain in the fashion of the people, is sufficient to show us this character with the greatest distinctness. This mythical coloring, in which purely
human action is presented to us, has also the special
merit of greatly facilitating the task which I attributed
above to the poet—that of satisfactorily setting at rest
that question as to the " Why ? "

The spirit is carried by the legendary coloring, just
as by the characteristic scene, into that dreamy condition in which it soon attains to complete clearness of
vision, in which it sees a new connection between the
phenomena of the world,—and such a one as it could
not see with the ordinary eyes of the waking state ;
and it was for this reason that in that state it was continually asking " *Why ?* " as though to overcome its
fear of the mysteries of that world which now becomes

so clear and comprehensible. You will easily understand how music may carry to its fullest completeness
this sight-clearing enchantment.

This legendary character gives a great advantage to
the poetic arrangement of the subject for the reason
already mentioned, that, while the simple process of
the action—easily comprehensible as far as its outward
relations are concerned,—renders unnecessary any
pains-taking for the purpose of explanation of the
course of the story,—the greatest possible portion of
the poem can be devoted to the portrayal of the inner
motives of the action ;—those inmost motives of the
soul which, indeed, the action points out to us as necessary, through the fact that we ourselves feel in our
hearts a sympathy with them.

You will readily perceive, in looking over the poems
submitted to you, that I only gradually became conscious of the advantage here indicated, and only gradually learned to make use of it. Even their outward
volume, increasing with every poem, shows you this.
You will soon observe that the hesitation I manifested
at first in giving a broader development to my poetry,
resulted especially from the fact that I then had too
much in view the traditional form of operatic music,
which had hitherto made any poem impossible that
did not permit the frequent repetition of words. In
the " Flying Dutchman " I first really turned my attention to keeping the action to its simplest features,
to leaving out all useless details such as the intrigues
of everyday life ; and, on the other hand to bringing
out those features more broadly, which, seeming to
me coincident with the peculiarities of the *motives* involved, placed the characteristic coloring of the legendary subject in the right light, in such a way that this
coloring itself became action.

You will perhaps find the action of "Tannhäuser"
far more strongly developed from inner motives. In
this the decisive catastrophe proceeds, without being

in the least forced, from a poetical contest, in which no other influence than that of the most hidden mental mood gives the impulse to the decisive crisis, and in such a way that even the form of this crisis belongs to the purely lyric element.

The whole interest of " Lohengrin " rests upon a process in the heart of Elsa, that touches all the secrets of her soul; the formation of a strangely blissful enchantment, that fills all about her with convincing reality, depends entirely upon her refraining from asking—whence he came? And finally this question forces itself like a cry from the deepest need of her woman's heart, and—the enchantment is gone. You notice how peculiarly this fatal " whence ? " coincides with the theoretical " why ? " to which I have before alluded ?

I too, as I have told you, felt myself forced to this " whence ? " and " why ? "—and in view of these the enchantments of my art long disappeared for me. Yet my period of penance taught me to overcome the questions. Every doubt had passed away, when I finally gave myself up to my " Tristan." I now absorbed myself with complete confidence in the depths of the inmost processes of the soul, and fearlessly drew from this inmost centre of the world their outward forms. A glance at the extent of this poem will show you at once that I now permitted myself to employ, with regard to inner motives, the same detailed accuracy which must be employed by the poet in a historical subject for the explanation of the outward course of events, and which he uses to the disadvantage of the clear explanation of those very motives with which alone I occupied myself. In this case life and death,—the very significance and existence of the outer world—depend upon the inner emotions of the soul alone. The whole effective action is produced by the fact that the inmost soul *demands* it ; and it comes before the observer just as it has been inwardly developed.

Perhaps you will find, in the execution of this poem, much that has been carried too far into the smallest detail, and, though you may acknowledge that this course is permissible to the poet, you may still not understand how he could venture to submit all these delicate details to the musician to be carried out by him. The same timidity would then seize upon you, that decided me, in the conception of the " Flying Dutchman," to give only very general outlines, which should contribute to an entirely musical execution of my plan. But let me here make one reply to your feeling upon this subject ;—that, though the versification was there intended (by constant repetitions of phrases and words, and acting as a basis for the operatic melody), to be extended to the necessary length for this latter,—there is, on the contrary, *no* repetition of words in the musical performance of " Tristan," but, on the contrary, the whole extent of the melody is indicated beforehand in the arrangement of the words and verses,—that is, *the whole melody* is composed poetically.

If my method should succeed in every case, you might bear me witness on this ground alone that a far more intimate commingling of poetry and music can be brought about through this means than through that formerly employed ; and if I may venture to hope at the same time that you will attribute more value to the poetic execution itself of the " Tristan," than was possible in the case of my earlier works, you would decide from this circumstance that a musical form, already thoroughly defined in the poem, was for the advantage of the poetic part of the work at least. But if, according to this, the complete preparation for musical form could give the poem itself an especial value, and do it according to the poet's own wishes, the only question remaining would be whether the musical form of the_ melody itself might not lose by giving up its freedom for the sake of movement and development ?

On this point let the *musician* answer you, and express to you, with the most earnest assurance of its correctness, the opinion that in following this method a richness and inexhaustibleness are added to melody and its form, of which, without this method, one can form no idea.

I believe that I may best conclude my communication by giving the theoretical proof of this opinion. I will endeavor to do this; taking into consideration only the musical form,—*melody*.

I find in the frequent and shrill demands of our superficial musical dilettanti for " Melody, melody ! " a confirmation of the belief that they derive their idea of melody from musical works in which, besides the melody, complete *lack* of melody occurs,—which makes what they think melodious appear so precious. In Italy, an audience assembled at the opera, which occupied its evening with *amusement*. To this entertainment there belonged music, sung upon the stage,—music which was listened to from time to time during the pauses of the conversation ;—during the conversation and the constant exchange of visits between the boxes the music continued, fulfilling the same function for which music is introduced at great dinners,—that is, to encourage by its noise the otherwise timid chat to become louder and more lively. Such music as is played for this purpose fills out the great bulk of Italian opera ; whereas that which is really listened to makes up perhaps a twelfth part of it. An Italian opera must have at least *one* air that people like to listen to ; if it is to succeed, there must be something to interrupt the conversation and be heard with interest at least six times ; and the composer that can draw the attention of the audience a full *dozen* times to his music is celebrated as an inexhaustible musical genius. And what shall we think would become of such an audience, if, suddenly finding itself in the presence of a work which demands a like attention through its

whole duration and for all its parts, it should see itself
torn from all its ordinary customs at musical performances ? And if it could not possibly identify with its
beloved " melody," that which in its most successful
presentation could only pass for an improvement of
that musical noise, which, in its simpler application
only made agreeable conversation easier, while it now
forces itself forward with the pretension that it really
must be *listened to ?* Such an audience would call for
its six or twelve melodies again, that it might gain
opportunity and protection, in the intervals, for its
conversation—which is after all the chief object of an
opera-evening.

In truth, what from a singular narrowness is looked
upon as richness, must needs appear to the more cultured mind as very poverty. The loud demands that
are based upon this error may be pardoned in the
public at large, but not in the art-critic. Let us endeavor, then, to inform ourselves as far as possible,
concerning the reason of this mistaken view.

Let us establish first of all the fact that the *one true
form of music is melody ;* that without melody music
is inconceivable, and that music and melody are inseparable. That a piece of music has *no* melody, can
therefore only mean that the musician has not attained
to the real formation of an effective form, that can
have a decisive influence upon the feelings ; which
simply shows the absence of talent in the composer,—
his want of originality, compelling him to make up his
piece from hackneyed melodic phrases to which the
ear is utterly indifferent. But, in the mouth of the
uncultured frequenter of the opera, and when used
with regard to real music, the expression of this opinion betrays the fact that only a fixed and narrow form
of melody is meant, such as (as we have already seen)
belongs to a very childish stage of musical art ; and
for this reason an exclusive liking for such a form must
also seem childish to us. In this case we have less to

do with *melody* than with the primitive and narrow
form of it,—the *dance* form (*Tanzform*).*

And I do not mean to have expressed myself con-
temptuously with regard to this first origin of melody.
Indeed, I believe that I have proved that it was the
basis of the completed artistic form of the Beethoven
symphony—which certainly gives us a wonderful deal
to thank it for. But one thing must be considered :
that this simple form, which is preserved in its entirely
undeveloped state in the Italian opera, has received an
elaboration in the symphony, which gives it something
such a relation to the original as a full-flowering plant
may be supposed to bear to the shoot from which it
was raised.   I fully accept the importance of the primitive melodic form in the dance-form ; and, following
the rule that every form, however highly developed,
must bear its origin in some recognizable shape within
it if it is at all intelligible, I am prepared to find this
dance-melody in the symphony of Beethoven,—yes,
even to consider that symphony, as a melodious com-
plexity, as nothing else but the idealized dance-form
itself.*

But let us first consider that this form extends
through all the parts of the symphony, and in this is
the very opposite of the Italian opera, in so far as in
that the melody stands entirely alone, and the spaces
between the passages of melody are filled out by an
employment of music which we must set down as
absolutely *un*melodious, because in it music does not
separate itself from the character of mere *noise*.   Even
among the predecessors of Beethoven we find these
doubtful gaps stretching even in symphonies between
the leading melodic passages.   If Haydn, it is true,
could generally give these intervals an interesting significance, Mozart, on the other hand, who, in this re-

---

* The translator makes every apology for the awkward phrase "dance-
form," but finds it the only way of avoiding a long and obscure periphra-
sis.

spect approached far nearer to the Italian idea of melodious form, often—indeed almost habitually—fell
back upon that frivolous phrase-making that often exhibits his symphonic passages in the aspect of the so-
called table music—that is, a music which, between
the presentation of attractive melodies, also presents an
attractive noise for purposes of conversation. To me
at least, the regularly repeated and noisily diffused
modulations of Mozart's symphonies appear as though
I heard the noise of setting and clearing away a royal
banquet, set to music. The original and thoroughly
brilliant method of Beethoven, on the contrary, tended
toward the complete disappearance of these interval
passages, and toward giving the connections between
the principal melodies themselves the character of
melody.

To explain this method more in detail, though it
would be unusually interesting, would occupy too
much space at present. Yet I cannot refrain from
directing your attention especially to the construction
of the opening passages of the Beethoven symphony.
Here we observe the original dancing air, dissected
into its smallest component parts, each one of which,
often consisting of only two notes, seems interesting
and expressive now through its rhythmic, now its
harmonic significance. These parts unite again in
ever renewed groupings, now growing greater, like a
stream, in logical succession,—now parting as though
in a whirl,—but alway sfascinating by such elastic
movements that the listener cannot for an instant free
himself from their influence, but must rather, roused
into keenest sympathy, give to each harmonious tone,
even to each rhythmic pause, its own melodious meaning. The entirely new result of this method was
therefore the development of melody by the most perfect elaboration of all the *motives* contained in it, with
a great and lasting musical work which was, in fine,
nothing else but one single closely connected melody.

8*

It is noticeable that this method, adopted in the domain of instrumental music, was similarly employed
by German masters in mingled orchestral and choral
music,—but has never hitherto been applied completely to the opera. Beethoven, in his grand mass,
used his choir and orchestra almost according to the
same method he had employed in the symphony ; and
this symphonic method was possible for him, because
a form, like the dance-melody itself, was presented to
him in the words of the ecclesiastical text,—universally
known, and almost entirely symbolic as they were,—
a form which he could dissect and unite again by sep-
arations, repetitions, sequences, etc., much as he could
the other. But it would be impossible for a thoughtful musician to proceed in this way with the words of
a dramatic poem, because this does not contain a symbolic signification only, but a definite logical conclusion. This, however, was only to be understood of
those words which, on the other hand, were calculated
only for the traditional forms of the opera ; while it
always must remain possible to find in dramatic poetry
a poetic counterpart of the symphonic form—and one
which, in thoroughly fulfilling this form, should at the
same time comply with the deepest laws of dramatic
structure.

I believe that I can express myself most clearly concerning the problem here encountered—a most difficult
one to handle theoretically—by making use of a metaphor.

I have called the symphony the attained ideal of the
dance-form of melody. But in reality the Beethoven
symphony *contains*, in the part denominated " Min-
uetto " or " Scherzo," a genuine, primitive dancing-
music, to which it would be quite practicable to actually dance. It seems as though an instinctive necessity had impelled the composer to really touch, once
in the course of his work, the *very basis* of it, as though
to feel under his feet the ground that was supporting

him. In the other passages he gets farther and farther away from the possibility of one's actually dancing to his melody,—or if one could, it must needs be such an ideal dance as would hold the same relation to the primitive one that the symphony holds to the original dancing-tune.

And for this reason there is a certain hesitation on the part of the composer in this direction also—a fear to overstep certain limits of musical expression, and especially to push too far the emotional, tragic tendency ; because effects and anticipations would be thus aroused, which awaken in the hearer that disquieting question " *why ?* " which the musician cannot answer to his satisfaction.

The dance which would fully conform to his music —this ideal form of dance—is in reality *dramatic action.* This really stands in the same relation to the primitive dance that the symphony holds toward the primitive dancing tune. Even the original popular dance expresses an action—generally the mutual wooing of a couple ; and this simple act (having to do with the most purely sensuous relations), when carried out in its fullest development, to the presentation of the inmost motives of the soul, is nothing else than *dramatic action.* I trust you will spare me the necessity of showing in more detail that this is not sufficiently accomplished by our ballet. The ballet is the brother of the opera ; of precisely equal birth, proceeding from the same erroneous basis ; and it is for this reason that we like to see them going hand in hand, as though to conceal their mutual defects.

No method, therefore, which rather awakens than soothes the obstructive question " why ? " can express the meaning of the symphony ;—but only dramatic action, with its scenic accompaniments.

In regard to this opinion, which I have already justified, I have only to add in reference to the melodic form, what an enlivening and broadening influence a really appropriate poem can have upon it. The poet, who fully appreciates the inexhaustible capabilities of expression of symphonic melody, will find himself impelled to draw near from his own domain, to the finest and most delicate shades of this melody, which can change its expression so effectually with a single harmonic variation. The former narrow form of operatic melody that was held up to him as a model, will no longer make him anxious to give nothing but an empty, dry scheme. On the other hand, he will reveal to the musicians the secret heretofore concealed from even him, that this form of melody is capable of incalculably richer development than has appeared possible to him, even in the symphony ; and, himself foreseeing this development, he will make his poetic conception with untrammelled freedom.

Where even the symphonist timidly grasped backward at the primitive dance-form, and never dared, even for the sake of gaining in expression, to entirely leave the boundaries which kept him in connection with this form, there *the poet* will say to him :—" dash in boldly into the full waves of the sea of music ; hand-in-hand with me, you can never lose connection with that which is fully intelligible to every man ; for, through me, you stand forever on the basis of dramatic action ; and this action, at the moment of its scenic presentation, is the most directly intelligible of all poems. Extend melody fearlessly, so that it may flow through your whole work like an uninterrupted stream. Do you speak that upon which I keep silence ; for you alone can say it ; and I, though silent, will yet say it all,—for I lead you by the hand."

And indeed the greatness of the poet may be best measured by that concerning which he is silent, in order to let the unspeakable itself speak to us silently. It is only the musician who can bring this that is silent into clear expression ; and the unerring form of *his* loud-resounding silence is endless *melody !*

The symphonist necessarily cannot construct this melody without his own peculiar instrument; and this instrument is *the orchestra.* I do not need to tell you that he will use this instrument in an utterly different fashion from that of the Italian operatic composer, in whose hands the orchestra was nothing else but a monstrous guitar on which to accompany the air.

It will enter into the drama that I have conceived of, much in the same relation that the tragic chorus of the Greeks bore to the dramatic action. It was always present; before its eyes the *motives* of action were displayed; it sought to account for them, and to form from them a judgment of the action itself. But this participation of the chorus was always of a reflective sort and it itself remained isolated from both action and motives; the orchestra of the modern symphonist, on the contrary, will enter into such close sympathy with the motives, that while it on the one hand, as incorporated harmony, makes it possible to give the proper expression to the melody,—on the other hand it keeps the melody itself in the necessary uninterrupted fluency, and thus imparts the motive to the feelings of the hearer with the most impressive distinctness. If we must regard that artistic form as the highest which can be comprehended entirely without reflection, and by which the conception of the artist is most clearly communicated to the emotions, then, if we desire to find this form in the musical drama (with the provisions already pointed out), *the orchestra* of the symphonist is the marvellous instrument that alone can make a presentation of this form possible. It is plain that the chorus, which has already mounted the stage in the opera, loses entirely, as opposed to the orchestra and its importance, the signification of the ancient Greek chorus; it can now be regarded only as one of the persons concerned in the action; and wherever it is not required as such, it must seem in future inappropriate and superfluous, inas-

much as its ideal participation in the action has altogether passed to the orchestra, and is shown by the
latter in a way that is always obvious, but never disturbing.

I again take to metaphor, in order to explain to
you, in conclusion, the characteristics of the great
melody that I have in mind—a melody that shall embrace the whole composition ; and here I confine myself to the impression that must be produced by it.
The endlessly varied detail in it must reveal itself not
only to the connoisseur, but to the simplest layman,
so soon as he has attained to the requisite mood.   It
should produce an effect upon his spirits like that
which a beautiful forest produces, in a summer evening, upon a lonely wanderer who has but just left the
town.   The peculiarity of this impression, which I
leave to the experienced reader to trace out in all its
effects upon the soul, is—the appreciation of a silence
that grows more and more eloquent with every moment.   It is enough for the objects of a work of art,
generally speaking, if it has produced this fundamental impression, and can by its means sway the listener
and bring him still further into a mood of higher purpose ; unconsciously he begins to share its elevating
tendency.   But the wanderer in the wood, when,
overcome by the general impression, he is fairly established in the lasting mood that follows it, develops
his mental powers into new capabilities of perception, listens ever more keenly as one who hears with
new senses, and becomes with every moment more
distinctly conscious of endlessly varied voices that are
abroad in the forest.   New and various ones constantly join,—such as he never remembers to have
heard before ; and as they multiply in numbers they
increase in mysterious power.   They grow louder and
louder, and so many are the voices, the separate tunes
he hears, that the whole strong, clear-swelling music
seems to him again only the great forest melody that

enchained him with awe in the beginning ; just as the deep blue heaven at night had riveted his gaze, which, the longer it remained absorbed in the spectacle, saw more distinctly, clearly, and brightly its countless hosts of stars. This melody will forever echo within him, —yet he cannot hum it over to himself; and to hear it again he must go again into the woods on a summer evening as before. How foolish would he be if he sought to catch one of these bright forest songsters, to carry it home with him that it might whistle for him some little part of that great forest melody! What else would he hear if he did so, but simply—a bit of melody, after all! You can easily see what an endless number of technical details I have left unnoticed in the presentation just given,—a hasty sketch, and yet perhaps a too minute one ; you will see this especially when you consider that the number of these details from their very nature is positively inexhaustible in any theoretic presentation of them. In order to make clear my views concerning all the details of melodic structure, to show how I wish them to be understood, their relations to the actual operatic air, and the possibilities of their development, as well for their periodic structure as in the matter of harmony,—in order to show all this, I should have to relapse at once into my former fruitless endeavor. I refrain therefore from laying before the willing reader anything more than the most general outlines, and indeed even in this paper we are drawing near to that point where nothing but the complete art product itself can give us a conclusive solution.

You would be mistaken if you should imagine that I intended in this last remark to refer to the approaching performance of my Tannhäuser. You know the score of my Tristan, and though it does not occur to me to desire that this shall be considered a model of my ideal, you will nevertheless grant me that I have made a far longer stride from the Tannhäuser to the

Tristan than I made from my first standpoint, that of the modern opera, to the Tannhäuser.   And whoever should consider this communication to you as nothing but a preparation for the performance of Tannhäuser, would therefore cherish expectations which would be in a great degree erroneous.

If I should have the pleasure of seeing my Tannhäuser favorably received by the Paris public, I am certain that I should have the easily recognizable connection of this opera with those of my predecessors (among whom I especially refer you to Weber) chiefly to thank for its success.   But you will permit me to briefly point out to you what it is that nevertheless distinguishes this work in some degree from the work of those who have preceded me.   It is evident that everything which I have here described to you as the logical consequence of an ideal process, must also have been always an intimate characteristic of our great masters.   These inferences as to the possibility of an ideal work of art by no means came to *me* from purely abstract reflection, but on the contrary, it was my observations on the works of our own masters that brought me to these conclusions.   Although there existed for the great Gluck only the narrowness and stiffness of the traditional operatic forms (which he did little to materially develop, and which still stand almost unimproved), yet his successors understood how to elaborate these forms step by step, in such a way that they already sufficed for their highest purpose, especially if a dramatic situation of real significance gave them proper opportunity.   No one is more willing than I to delightedly acknowledge the greatness, power, and beauty of dramatic-musical conception, which we find in many works of esteemed masters, and of which it seems to me unnecessary to cite numerous examples here ; for I do not disguise from myself that I have come upon particular effects in the feebler works of even insignificant composers, which

fairly astounded me, and which taught me still more
of that incomparable power of music of which I have
already spoken to you. It is a power which, by the
firm accuracy of its melodious expression, raises even
the least talented singer so high above the level of his
personal abilities, that he produces a dramatic effect
which must be impossible to even the most skilful artist in the merely *spoken* drama.

But what always discouraged me, especially in this
connection, was that I never found all these inimitable
advantages of dramatic music developed in the opera
into a style which should embrace all parts of the work
alike, and yet be pure. Even in the greatest works,
I found by the very side of the most perfect and noblest elements much that was inexplicably foolish,
expressionless, conventional, and even silly.

Though we have almost universally retained the
awkward alternation (so fatal to any attempt at a finished style) of the pure recitative with the simple air,
and thus find the flow of the music (which is itself
based upon an erroneously conceived poem) constantly
interrupted and checked,—yet we often find, in the
best scenes of our great masters, that this evil has
been, completely overcome. In these cases some
rhythmic and melodious significance is given to the
recitative, and it joins unnoticed with the greater
flexibility of the actual melody. And when we have
fully perceived the effectiveness of this method, how
disagreeably we must be affected when suddenly, and
entirely without preparation the chord comes in, giving us notice that now the dry recitative is to begin
again. And then again, just as suddenly, the full orchestra breaks in with the customary ritournelle that
announces the air,—the same ritournelle that has elsewhere been so appropriately and significantly employed by the same composer, in connecting passages
or in passing from one to another, that we found in
the ritournelle itself a significant beauty, which gave

us the most interesting explanation of the meaning of the situation. But what if a piece calculated only to flatter the lowest taste, follows immediately upon such a really artistic production ? Or if a strikingly beautiful and noble musical phrase suddenly terminates in the regulation cadence with the two customary runs and the forced final note, with which the singer unexpectedly abandons his position toward the person to whom that phrase was addressed, in order to turn directly to the *claque* and give it the signal for applause ?

It is true that these last-mentioned inconsistencies do not occur in the works of our *really* great masters, but among those composers with regard to whom we are only forced to wonder how they could possibly make themselves masters of such conspicuous beauties of style. But what seems so extraordinary in this phenomenon really consists in the fact, that after all the noble and perfect results which the great masters have succeeded in achieving, and by which they brought the opera so nearly to the perfection of a pure style,—these lapses could continue to occur, and their monstrosities appear more conspicuously than ever.

The humiliating regard paid to the character of the ordinary operatic audience (which is always the decisive element in weak artistic natures), is unquestionably the chief reason for this. I have heard from Weber, even,—from even this pure, noble, and thoughtful soul,—that sometimes when he was himself terrified at the results of his own nobly-conceived processes of composition, he would give his wife what he called the " right of the gallery " (*Recht der Gallerie*), and would let her make objections, just as the gallery would be likely to do, to certain of his conceptions ; objections which should determine him, now and then, not to be too severe in his style, but to make occasional prudent concessions.

I believe, however (I think I may take this much

credit to myself), that you will find none of these " concessions "—such as even my first beloved model, Weber, believed himself compelled to make to the operatic audience—in my " Tannhäuser ; " and, in so far as the structure of my work goes, this is perhaps the very point that distinguishes my opera from those of my predecessors. I needed no special courage to achieve this ; for from my own observations of what had been most successful in its effects upon the public in the opera of previous periods, I had derived an opinion of that public which had led me to take decid-. edly optimistic views. The artist who directs his work not toward the abstract but toward the intuitive perception, does not produce his work for the benefit of the art connoisseur, but purposely submits it to the public itself. The artist only has reason to fear, in so far as the public has absorbed the *critical* spirit, and has lost the purely *human* fashion of looking at things. I consider the kind of opera that has hitherto obtained as precisely calculated, by the very " concessions " which it contained, and which left the audience in un-certainty as to its purpose, to so mislead that audience as to force upon it the necessity of an unsuitable and false mental process, and to expose it to the danger of having its confusion heightened to the last degree by the chatter of those in its midst who affect to speak as connoisseurs.

If we observe, on the contrary, with how much greater decision the public expresses itself with regard to a merely spoken drama, and how nothing in the world can induce it, in this case, to consider a ridicu-lous plot sensible, an inappropriate speech appropriate, or incorrect accent correct,—we gain from this fact a decided ground for placing the opera also in a safe re-lation to *its* audience, and in one which cannot fail to be favorable to its comprehension.

As a second point in which my " Tannhäuser " may differ from the ordinary opera, I would suggest to you the *dramatic poem* that forms its basis. Without in the least desiring to ascribe any great value to this as a purely poetic product, I believe myself justified in affirming that, although based upon the legendary and marvellous, it contains a really logical dramatic devel‑ opment, in the conception and execution of which no sort of "concession" was made to the senseless de- mands of an opera-libretto. My object has been to first enchain the attention of the audience by the *dramatic* action, by the fact that it is never compelled for a moment to lose sight of this, but that on the con- trary the musical dress at first seems only a method used for the better display of it. And it was this do- ing away with all "concession" in the matter of the subject, which made it possible for me to also do away with it in the musical execution ; and in these things, taken together, you will perhaps find the best example of what my "innovation" really consists in ; you cer- tainly will *not* find it in a purely musical fancy which many have thought themselves justified in foisting upon me as a striving after a "music of the future."

Let me say to you in conclusion, that in spite of the great difficulties in the way of a perfectly just poetical translation of my "Tannhäuser," I lay my work before the Parisian public with confidence. And to that which a few years ago I should only have undertaken with the greatest hesitation, I now come with all the confidence of one who has in view not so much a spec- ulation as a matter in which his heart is interested. For this change in my feelings I have to thank, first of all, some acquaintances that it has been my privilege to form since my last visit to Paris. There was one among these that speedily filled me with glad surprise ; for you, my honored friend, permitted me to approach you as one to whom I was already known and with whom I already stood in confidential relations. Without hav- ing attended a performance of my operas in Germany, you had already, as you assured me, made yourself acquainted with my scores by careful reading. The knowledge thus gained of my works had aroused in you the desire to see them produced *here ;* and had even brought you to the opinion that by such production a favorable and not unimportant effect might be produced upon the susceptibilities of the Parisian public.

Since you, then, contributed especially to inspire me with confidence for my undertaking, may you not think ill of me for rewarding you by wearying you with this perhaps too detailed communication ! May you rather attribute my perhaps over-zealous desire to comply with your wish, to my earnest longing to simultaneously give the friends of my art here a somewhat clearer view of those ideas which I will not expect any one to search out for himself from among my earlier art-writings.

PARIS, *September,* 1860.

AN
ACCOUNT OF THE PRODUCTION
OF "TANNHÄUSER" IN PARIS.

PARIS, *March* 27, 1861.

I PROMISED you to give you a precise account of my whole experience in the Tannhäuser matter in Paris; and now that it has taken such a decided direction, and that I can look back over it all, it is a matter of justice to myself to come to some conclusion about it, by means of a quiet presentation of the whole affair—such a presentation as I should wish for my own benefit. You can only understand the subject in its true relations, if I refer at the very beginning to what really decided me to go to Paris at all. Let me begin, therefore, at that point.

After almost ten years' separation from every possibility of refreshing myself, if only at intervals, by taking part in really *good* performances of my dramatic compositions, I at last fairly felt myself compelled to take into consideration the project of emigrating to some place which could in time make it possible for me to have these necessary *living* relations with my art. I hoped that I might find such a place in some modest corner of Germany. I earnestly endeavored in the summer of 1859 to persuade the Grand Duke of Baden (who had already, with touching condescension, permitted me to produce my latest work at Carlsruhe under my personal superintendence) to manage for me, instead of the prospective temporary sojourn, a lasting residence in his country; for otherwise, I had no resource but to go to Paris; to make my permanent domicile there. But the fulfilment of my request was—impossible.

When, in the autumn of the same year, I finally did go to Paris, I still kept in view the production of my "Tristan," for which I hoped to be summoned to Carlsruhe on the third of December. I believed that when the work had once been produced under my direction, I could safely leave it to the other theatres of Germany ; and the prospect of being able to pursue the same course in future with my other works contented me. Paris retained, when I adopted this view, but one point of interest for me—the possibility of hearing there, from time to time, an excellent quartette, or a thoroughly good orchestra, and so of keeping myself in refreshing communication at least with the living organs of my art.

All this was suddenly changed, when I received news from Carlsruhe that the production of my Tristan there had proved impossible. But my difficult position at once suggested to me the idea of inviting some prominent German singers of my acquaintance to Paris for the following spring, in order by their aid to bring about the desired specimen performance of my new work in the salon of the Italian Opera. To this performance I also wished to invite the directors and managers of such German theatres as were friendly to me, in order to attain by it the same object which I had first had in view in the Carlsruhe performance. But, as the execution of my plan was impossible without a considerable participation on the part of the Parisian public, I had to endeavor first of all to induce them to take some interest in my music ; and for this object I undertook the well-known three concerts given at Les Italiens. The success of these concerts, though great, so far as applause and interest were concerned, could unfortunately have no effect on the chief undertaking I had in view, for the very difficulty of such an undertaking was revealed to me through them ; and on the other hand, the impossibility of bringing together at one and the same time in Paris, all the German singers whom I had selected, compelled me to abandon the design.

While, hemmed in on every side, I now turned my anxious glance again toward Germany, I learned, to my extreme surprise, that my situation had become the subject of zealous discussion and partisanship at the Tuilleries. The very friendly interest, till then unknown to me, which was felt in me by several members of the German embassy here, was the cause of this favorable movement. It extended so far that the Emperor, when a German Princess, whom he held in particular esteem, gave him a very favorable opinion of the best known of my works, Tannhäuser, at once gave orders for the production of that opera in the Grand Opera House.

I do not deny that, although at first much rejoiced by this entirely unexpected evidence of the success of my works in social circles from which I was so far removed, I nevertheless could only look forward with great anxiety to a performance of Tannhäuser at this particular theatre. For to whom could it be more evident than to me, that this great operatic theatre had long entirely alienated itself from every earnest artistic effort ; that far other demands obtained in it than those of true dramatic music ; and the opera itself had become in it only an excuse for the ballet ? Indeed, when I had received, during the last few years, repeated encouragement to look forward to the production of one of my works in Paris, I had never had the grand opera in view, but rather—as far as the experiment was concerned, at least—the modest *Théâtre Lyrique ;* and this for two special reasons,—first, because it takes its tone from no particular class of the public ; and secondly, because—thanks to the poverty of its resources—the ballet has not developed here into the central point of the whole performance. But the director of this theatre was compelled to give up a performance of the Tannhäuser, after having repeatedly entertained the idea, more especially for the reason that he could find no tenor capable of undertaking the difficult leading rôle.

Indeed, it became evident during my first interview with the director of the Grand Opera, that the introduction of a ballet (and this in the second act) was to be regarded as the most indispensable requisite for the success of a performance of Tannhäuser. I was only to discover the full meaning of this demand, however, when I declared that I could not possibly interrupt the progress of the *second* act by a ballet, which must appear senseless from every point of view if introduced in this place ; but that, on the other hand, I saw in the *first* act, at the luxurious court of Venus, a most perfect opportunity for a choregraphic scene of some real meaning—in a passage, indeed, where in my first conception of it I had myself thought I could not get on without the dance   I was even delighted with the task of thus remedying a weakness of my earlier score, and I drew up an elaborate scheme, according to which the scene on the hill of Venus should be raised to a position of great importance.

But the director refused this plan decidedly, and frankly informed me that it was not the mere *introduction* of a ballet that was important in the performance of an opera, but, more especially, that this ballet should be danced in the middle of the evening ; for it was only then that those subscribers to whom the ballet almost exclusively belonged entered their boxes, since they ordinarily dined very late. A ballet performed at the beginning, therefore, would not satisfy these people, because they never were present at the first act. These and similar explanations were afterward repeated to me by the Minister of State ; and every possibility of a favorable result was shown to be so entirely dependent upon the fulfilment of the conditions therein contained, that I began to believe I must give up the whole undertaking.

While I thought more earnestly than ever of return-
ing to Germany, and anxiously looked about for some
point which might be offered to me as a basis for the
production of my new works, I was suddenly to
appreciate the full meaning of the imperial decree, that
put the whole establishment of the Grand Opera, with
every engagement that I might find necessary, entirely
and unconditionally at my disposal.   Every requisition
I desired to make was at once carried out without the
least regard to cost ; and such care as I had never
before conceived of was exercised in regard to the
scenic setting of the work.

Under circumstances to which I was so entirely un-
accustomed, the idea that I saw before me, the possibility of a thoroughly complete and even ideal performance, soon increased its hold upon my mind.
The conception of such a performance, no matter of
which one of my works, had long seriously occupied my
thoughts,—ever since my retirement from our own
operatic stage.   What had never stood at my disposition before was now unexpectedly offered me in
Paris, and at a time when no endeavors would have
sufficed to procure for me on German soil a favor
· bearing any similiarity whatever to this.   I frankly
confess that this thought filled me with a warmth long
unknown to me—which was perhaps only increased
by a certain bitterness that mingled with it.   I soon
had nothing in mind but the possibility of a completely
beautiful performance ; and, in the lasting and earnest
anxiety to realize this possibility, I let every scruple
be powerless to affect me.   If I succeed—I said to
myself—in attaining that which I believe to be possible,
what does the Jockey Club and its ballet concern me ?

From this time forth I knew no feeling but anxiety
with regard to the performance.   The director informed me that there was no French tenor for the rôle
of Tannhäuser.   Being informed of the brilliant talent
of the young singer, Niemann, I designated him

(though I had never heard him myself), for the leading part; and especially as he had a good French accent, his engagement, for which there had been careful preparations, was decided upon at a great sacrifice. Several other artists, especially the baritone, Morelli, were indebted for their engagements to my desire to have them for my work. For the rest, I selected young people of talent, in preference to some of the singers already prominent here, because the too settled manner of the latter disturbed me, and I could more easily hope to form the former according to my own style. The care, quite unknown among us, with which vocal rehearsals with piano-forte accompaniment are conducted here, was surprising to me; and I soon saw our studies attaining a rare perfection under the intelligence and refined leadership of the *chef du chant*, Vauthrot. I was especially rejoiced when the young French singers gradually attained to a comprehension of the matter in hand, and acquired a pleasure in, and love for, their task.

I had myself gained renewed pleasure in this, my earlier work, and I went through the score again with the greatest care, wrote the Venus scene entirely new, as well as the ballet that preceded it, and especially endeavored to bring the music of the whole into the most exact accord with the translated text.

Though I had directed my whole attention to the performance, and in doing so had laid all other considerations aside, my troubles began at last, with the perception that after all, this performance could not maintain itself at the height which I had anticipated. It is difficult to accurately point out to you in what points I was finally compelled to see that I had been deceived. The worst of them was certainly this;— that the singer of the leading rôle, as a result of his necessary intercourse with the critics, who were constantly prophesying to him the failure of my opera, fell into an increasing mood of discouragement. The

favorable hopes that I had nourished during the pianoforte rehearsals, sank deeper and deeper the more we
came into relations with the stage and the orchestra.
I saw that we were again falling to the level of an ordinary operatic representation, and that all expectations that looked for anything much higher, must remain unfulfilled. In this view of the matter, which I
naturally did not at first permit myself to hold, the
very point was wanting which alone can serve such an
operatic performance as a special distinction ;—that is,
some really important singer of talent who is already
a favorite with the public ;—whereas I was to appear
almost entirely with novices. Finally, it especially
troubled me that I was not able to take out of the
hands of the regularly appointed conductor the leadership of the orchestra, with which I might still have
exercised great influence upon the spirit of the performance ;—and that I had to consent with saddened res-
ignation to a spiritless and forceless production of my
work (for my desired withdrawal of the score was not
permitted) is still a source of deep regret to me.

Under such circumstances, it was almost entirely a
matter of indifference to me what the reception of my
opera might be on the part of the public. The most
brilliant one could not have persuaded me to be present at an extended series of performances, for I should
have received from them far too little satisfaction. But
it seems to me that you have thus far been intention-
ally left in the dark with regard to the character of
this reception ; and you would be very wrong if you
should derive from it an opinion of the Parisian public, which, though it might be very flattering to the
German, would be in reality incorrect. I continue,
on the contrary, to attribute to the Parisian public very
agreeable characteristics, especially a very lively re-
ceptiveness, and a really magnanimous sense of justice.
I say *the public;* for to see a whole audience to whom
I am personally entirely a stranger, who have daily

heard the most ridiculous things about me through newspapers and idle chatterers, and who have been influenced against me with an almost unprecedented pains-taking care,—to see such an audience declare itself in my favor and against a clique, by repeated earnest demonstrations of applause, a whole quarter of an hour long—would of necessity, even though I were the most indifferent of men, have filled me with warmth. But on this evening there was assembled in the Grand Opera house, by the amazing efforts of those who had rendered it next to impossible for me even to give away the seats on the day of the first performance, and to have my few personal friends present,—there was assembled, I say, by their efforts, an audience which any cool observer would at once have seen to be intensely prejudiced against my work. Add to this, the representatives of the Paris press, who are officially invited on such occasions, and of whose hostile course regarding me you can judge from their reports,—and you can well believe that I believe myself justified in speaking of a great triumph, when I tell you truly, that the by no means enchanting performance of my opera was greeted with stronger and more unanimous applause than I had ever personally experienced in Germany. The real leaders of the opposition, and several—yes, all—of the musical critics here, who had up to this time done their best to distract the attention of the audience from the representation, evidently began, toward the conclusion of the second act, to fear that they would be forced to witness a complete and brilliant success for my "Tannhäuser," and began to break out with rude bursts of laughter at certain catchwords, which they had agreed upon at the rehearsals, by which means they brought about at the end of the act a sufficiently distracting disturbance to sensibly weaken the manifestation of applause at the falling of the curtain. These gentlemen had unquestionably observed, at the grand re-

hearsals, from which I had never succeeded in exclud-
ing them, that the real effect of the opera must be in
the performance of the third act.   A capitally painted
scene by M. Despléchin, representing the valley before the Wartburg in the gloaming of an Autumn evening, had, even during the rehearsal, produced an effect
upon the spectators, by which the frame of mind necessary for the proper comprehension of the succeeding scenes was brought about in spite of themselves ;
from the standpoint of the performers, these scenes
were the most brilliant point of the whole performance ;
the Pilgrim's Chorus was admirably sung and sceni-
cally presented ; Elizabeth's prayer, given entire and
with striking expression by Mlle. Sax ; the *phantasia*
to the evening star, produced with perfect and pathetic
delicacy by Morelli ;—these so successfully introduced
the best portion of Niemann's performance,—the account of the pilgrimage, which always secured the
heartiest recognition of that artist's powers—that a
very exceptional success seemed secured for this third
act at least, even with the most hostile opponent of
my work.

But precisely this act was now attacked by the leaders above referred to, and they sought to hinder the
production of the necessary absorbed spirit among the
audience by loud bursts of laughter, which must have
found their childish provocation in the most trifling
opportunities.   Undisturbed by these hostile demonstrations, my singers did not suffer themselves to be
in the least confused, nor did the audience permit itself
to be kept from giving its appreciative attention to
their brave endeavors, which were often rewarded by
hearty applause ; and at the end of the act the opposition was completely defeated, when the performers
were tumultuously called before the curtain.

The behavior of the audience on the evening of the
second performance, proved to me that I had not been
mistaken in considering the result of this first evening

to be a complete success; for by this it was decided with what opposition I was to have to deal in future, —namely, with that of the Paris Jockey Club, which I am certainly authorized to name thus plainly, since the audience itself openly pointed out my opponents by the cry "à la porte les jockeys." The members of this club, whose right to consider themselves lords of the Grand Opera, I need not now explain to you more fully, and who felt themselves deeply injured at the absence of the customary ballet at the time of their entrance to the theatre (about the middle of the performance), perceived with disgust that "Tannhäuser" had *not* failed at its first reception, after all, but had really won a triumph. From this time forth it became their business to prevent this balletless opera from being presented to them evening after evening; and for this purpose they had provided themselves, on the way from their dinner to the opera, with a quantity of hunting-whistles and similar instruments, with which they began, immediately upon their entrance, to operate against the "Tannhäuser" in the most shameless manner. Until that time (that is, during the first and up to nearly the middle of the second act) not a trace of opposition had made itself felt; and continued applause had accompanied unhindered those passages of my opera that had most quickly become favorites. But from this point no further demonstrations of applause assisted me; in vain did the Emperor and Empress themselves a second time demonstrate their appreciation of my work. The irrevocable condemnation of the "Tannhäuser" had been spoken by those who regarded themselves as masters of the theatre, and who all belonged to the highest aristocracy of France. Up to the very end of the piece, whistles and pipes accompanied every attempt at applause on the part of the audience.

Knowing the perfect powerlessness of the management against this club, and seeing the fear even of

the Minister of State himself of making the members of
it seriously hostile to him, I saw that I could not expect the stage-artists, who had stood by me so faithfully, to expose themselves long and repeatedly to the
shameful disturbances to which they were ruthlessly
subjected, naturally with the design of altogether
forcing them from the stage. I gave directions to the
management to withdraw my opera, and only consented to a third performance on the condition that it
should take place on a Sunday,—a day excluded from
the regular subscription,—and thus under circumstances which could not irritate subscribers, while they
would open the theatre freely to the real public. My
desire to designate this performance on the play-bill
as " the last " was not considered advisable, and there
remained no way for me to do but to privately announce to my own acquaintances that it was so. This
precaution, however, did not suffice to still the fears
of the Jockey Club ; on the other hand they imagined
they saw in a Sunday performance a bold and dangerous demonstration against their interest, after which,
the opera having once been brought forward with
undisturbed success, the hated work might easily be
forced upon them against their will. No one would
believe in the sincerity of my promise that in case it
really did attain such a success I would withdraw it
all the more quickly.

And so these gentlemen gave up their other amuse-
ments for this particular evening, and came back
again to the opera fully equipped, and renewed the
scenes of the second performance. This time the
wrath of the audience, which was entirely prevented
from hearing the performance, rose to an unprecedented pitch (so I was assured), and only the apparently
sacred social position of messieurs the disturbers of
the peace prevented them from being roughly han-
dled. Let me say briefly, that astounded as I was at
the unbridled conduct of these gentlemen, I was still

more impressed and touched by the heroic efforts of the true audience to secure justice to me, and that nothing can be further from my purpose than to lose confidence in the Paris public, whenever it is upon an impartial ground that truly belongs to it.

The withdrawal of my score, which I have now officially announced, has placed the management of the opera in a situation of really great perplexity. They declare loudly and openly that they consider the case of my ópera one of the greatest of successes, —for they cannot remember to have ever seen the audience so enthusiastically take the part of an assailed work. Large pecuniary gains appear secured to them by the "Tannhäuser," for the seats in the theatre have been taken over and over again, in advance, for its performances. They are informed of an increasing bitterness of feeling among the public, which sees itself deprived, by a comparatively small number of persons, of its right to hear quietly and without molestation, and to properly estimate, a new and much-talked-of work. I hear that the Emperor is still entirely in favor of the matter, and that the Empress will willingly become the guardian of my opera, and will insist upon guarantees against any further disturbances. At this moment a protest, to be sent to the Minister of State, is in circulation among the musicians, painters, artists, and authors of Paris,—a protest against the undignified proceedings at the opera-house ; and I am assured that it is receiving numerous signatures. Under such circumstances it might seem an easy matter for me to be encouraged to take up my opera again. But an important artistic consideration keeps me from doing so. Up to this time no quiet and collected presentation of my work had taken place ; the true characteristic of such a performance, which lies in a compulsion inherent in the work itself, and forcing the audience into a mood foreign to the ordinary audience at an opera, and capable of taking in the spirit of the whole, —such a mood has never yet been impressed upon my hearers. On the contrary, they seize upon only the brilliant and easily appreciated outward characteristics, that serve me only as a scaffolding,—they take note of these, and can appreciate them with true sympathy, as they have already done.

If a quiet and thoughtful hearing should now be secured for my opera, I fear, after all that I have told you of the character of the performance here, that the inner weakness and spiritlessness of that representation (which have been no secret to those who have become more closely acquainted with the work, and which it has been impossible for my personal interference to prevent), must be gradually revealed—so that I could not hope for a *true* and not merely outward success for my opera on this occasion.

May all the unsatisfactory portions of the present presentation, therefore, remain mercifully buried under those three evenings of defeat! And may many a one who bitterly disappointed the hopes I had founded upon him, content himself for this time with the belief that he fell in a good cause!

So, then, let the Paris "Tannhäuser" pass for this time. Should the wish of earnest friends of my art be fulfilled,—should a project be carried out which is just now pressed upon me from a very intelligent source, and which has for its object nothing less than the speedy founding of a new operatic theatre for the realization of those reforms which I have urged here, —then you may perhaps hear of "Tannhäuser" again —even from Paris.

As far as regards my work in Paris at this time, be assured that you have heard the full truth about it. This may be your security for the fact—that it is impossible for me to content myself with a mere *appearance*, if my inmost wishes remain unsatisfied by it; and these are only to be satisfied by the knowledge that I have produced a really intelligent impression.

THE
PURPOSE OF THE OPERA.

A WELL-INTENDED complaint on the part of some earnest friends of the theatre, attributes the decline of that institution to the opera. It is based upon the undeniable lessening of interest in the spoken drama, as well as on the injury to general theatrical performances which the influence of the opera has brought about.

The justice of this accusation must appear plain. It would only seem to be needful, to investigate how it came about, that ever since the first beginnings of the modern theatre, the development of the opera has constantly been undertaken ; and that the capabilities of that branch of dramatic art, through the one-sided development of which theatrical performance has assumed the guise of the present form of opera, have repeatedly received the serious consideration of the most brilliant thinkers.

Through such an investigation we might well be led to a point of view which would show us our greatest poets as in a certain sense the preparers of the opera. And if this view must be adopted with great caution, the result of the productions of our great German poets for the theatre, and their influence upon the spirit of our dramatic representations, must at least lead us to the earnest consideration of the question how precisely this influence—that is, the influence of those great poetical works upon the character of our dramatic performances, could be so powerfully assisted by the opera, with so overwhelming a shaping of popular theatrical taste. We may arrive at a distinct insight into this question, if we keep in mind, before all things in this investigation, the actual result which shows itself in the theatrical representation of the true drama, as it has been brought about by the influence of Goethe's and Schiller's plays upon the spirit of the performances of our actors.

We recognize the effect of this influence at once, as the product of a disproportion between the capabilities of the actors themselves, and the task that is set them. A full explanation of this disproportion belongs to the history of German dramatic art, and has already been undertaken in that branch of criticism, in several noteworthy essays. Inasmuch as we here consider this point as one part of our discussion, and reserve the deeper æsthetic problem, which lies at the basis of the whole evil, for the later progress of our investigation, it is only important, for the first matter, to
✓ point out that the ideal purpose of our poets is forced to choose a form for its dramatic representation, in which the nature and education of our actors cannot properly fit. It would need the rarest gifts of genius on their parts—such gifts as those of a Sophie Schröder —to completely fulfill a task which has been placed upon far too high a plane for our actors (accustomed as they have hitherto been only to the everyday, commonplace elements of German life),—too high for them not to fall into the direst confusion in the bold attempt to carry out their part. The much maligned "false pathos" owes its origin and development to the unfitness here pointed out. This was preceded, in the earlier days of German dramatic art, by that grotesque affectation peculiar to the so-called "English comedians," which was employed by them in the crude presentation of rudely prepared old English and even Shakespearean plays, and which we find, even now, upon the dying English stage. This tendency was opposed by the healthful reaction toward so-called "faithfulness to nature," which found its fitting ex-

pression in the presentation of the ordinary social
drama (*des "bürgerlichen" Dramas*). And it must
be remarked that even though Lessing, and even
Goethe (in his youth) contributed to this *bürgerliches
Drama*, it derived its chief support from pieces which
were written by the best *actors* of the period themselves. The narrow sphere and slight poetical value of
these products now challenged our great poets to the
broadening and elevation of their dramatic style ; and
if a desire for the continued preservation of the " faithfulness to nature " yet ruled, an ideal stamp was still
impressed upon them, which found its expression in
what could be called *poetic* pathos.

Whoever is at all acquainted with this branch of our
art-history, knows how our great poets were disturbed
in their endeavors to impress this new manner upon
the actors ; but whether they would have been finally
successful in their attempts even if there had been no
disturbing influences, is much to be doubted, inasmuch
as they had hitherto had to content themselves with
only the artificial appearance of this result—which was
nothing but a development of the old "*false* pathos."
And this remained (significant of the small degree of
talent possessed by Germans for the drama), as far as
the character of theatrical performances of dramas of
ideal tendency was concerned, the only gain that had
been derived—and a very doubtful one it was too—
from that influence of our poets which had in other
ways been so important.

What had found its expression in this " false pathos "
now became again the tendency of the dramatic conceptions emanating from our minor theatrical poets,
the whole contents of which was from beginning to end
as workless as that pathos itself ;—we need only recall
the productions of a Müllner, a Houwald, and the
whole series of similar pathetically-inclined writers
down to the present day. The only thing that could
be called a reaction against this tendency would seem

to be the constantly renewed and nourished domestic prose-drama or comedy of our own time,—if indeed the French sensational play had not gained such over-whelming influence among us in this direction, as to determine and rule everything else. By this, every recognizable purity of type in our theatre has been obscured, and what we have preserved in our modern play even from Goethe's and Schiller's dramas, is only the revealed secret of the application of " false pathos " —the " sensation."

If all that is written for and played upon the stage is inspired only by this tendency toward " sensation," so that all that does not possess this characteristic will go for naught, we need not be surprised if this is the only thing retained in the presentation of even Goethe's and Schiller's pieces ; for in a certain sense there lies concealed in these also an example in this direction, arising from precisely the disproportion we have pointed out. The necessity for poetic pathos inspired our poets with a poetical, rhetorical diction pur-posely designed to work upon the feelings, which, as its ideal object was neither understood nor carried out by our unpoetic actors, led to that in itself senseless, but nevertheless melodramatically powerful delivery, the practical result of which was precisely this same " sensational " effect—that is, the startling of the lis-tener's sensuous emotions,—as is practically proved by the " storm of applause."

This " applause," and the " exit-passage " which is designed to call it forth, have become the soul of all endeavors in our modern theatre. The " brilliant exits " in the rôles of our classic dramas are all counted over, and the worth of the piece estimated en-tirely by their number—like the worth of a part in Italian Opera ; and indeed one cannot take it ill in our priests of Thalia and Melpomene, thirsty for applause as they are, if they look with envy and covetousness upon the opera, in which these " exits " are by far more numerous, and the "storms of applause" conferred with far more certainty than in even the most effective dramas ; and again, as our dramatic poets get their living, in turn, from the effectiveness of the rôles of our actors, it is easily explicable that the operatic composer, who can produce all this so easily by the arrangement of an appropriate shriek at the end of any vocal phrase he chooses, should seem to them a rival to be greatly hated.

But seriously, the outward reason for the complaint with the consideration of which we began, as well as the characteristic most easily hit upon in our investigation of it, appears to be this and nothing else. I have already sufficiently pointed out that I am far from believing that I have in this touched the *deeper* reason for the complaint ; but if we desire to discover this more clearly, it seems to me advisable to get at the core of the matter by investigating the outward indications that lie open to universal experience.

Let us assume, then, that in the character of all theatrical representations there is a tendency which manifests itself in its worst shape as a striving after so-called *effect ;* and that this, however much it may belong to the spoken drama, can nevertheless satisfy itself most completely in the opera. The complaint made against the opera, on the part of the drama, is based upon the lowest motives,—upon annoyance at the latter's greater wealth of sensational methods. The serious annoyance of the actor, on the other hand, has a much greater appearance of justice, since it results from contrasting the visible lightness and frivolity of these effective methods with the always difficult endeavor which he has to make to attain any proper representation of the character *he* has to set forth. The drama, considered even in its outward effect upon the audience, can always claim the advantage that the action represented in it, as well as the plot that connects it and the motives that explain it, must be made intelligible in order to secure the sym-

pathy of the spectator ; and that a piece composed of
mere declamatory rhetorical effects, without a basis of
action which expresses itself intelligibly and thus fixes
the interest, could not be thought of for a moment. On
the contrary, the accusation may be brought against
the opera, that in it a mere succession of effects, designed to work upon purely sensuous emotions, suf-
fices, if there be only an agreeable variety of contrasts
presented, to successfully conceal the absence of any
intelligible or sensible action.

It is plain that this point of complaint is founded
upon a very serious consideration. And yet, with
closer investigation, doubts may arise concerning this
also. Composers have always, but especially in recent
years, felt so strongly that the so-called text of an
opera should be interesting, that it has been one of
their most earnest endeavors to procure a good libretto.
It has been necessary, especially in our own day, that
an opera, if it was to have much effect, should be
based upon a plot at least suitable to its character, or
even upon an interesting one ; so that it would be
difficult to entirely deny a dramatic character to the
loose arrangement of even an operatic text. We see,
in fact, that it was not possible to pursue a wholly
irresponsible course in this matter, from the circumstance that there is hardly any piece of Shakespeare,
and almost none of Schiller and Goethe, which has not
appeared to the opera just the thing to be adapted to
its purposes. But again, precisely this abuse in turn
might with considerable justice irritate our actors and
dramatic poets ; they might properly exclaim—" Why
should we trouble ourselves further to correctly render
our dramatic labors, if the public deserts us to flock to
where the same work is applied, with a frivolous abuse
of its nature, to the multiplication of mere vulgar
effects ?" It is true that they might be met by the
question, how it would· be possible to bring M.
Gounod's opera of " Faust " before the German pub-

lic, if our dramatic stage had succeeded in making
Goethe's Faust intelligible to them ? We can see
clearly that the public turned away from the singular
efforts of our actors to make something out of the
monologue of *our* Faust, and turned to M. Gounod's
air, with the joys of youth for its theme, and applauded it, while in the former case nothing resulted
from it.

No example could show more clearly than this, to
what point our stage has fallen. But even now it
does not seem entirely right to us, that this undeniable
decline should all be laid to the fault of the opera's increasing prosperity ; on the other hand, we should see
in this latter as well the weakness of our theatre, as
the impossibility of finding in its present limits and
the means now at its command, the ideal province of
the drama. Precisely here (in the opera), where the
highest ideal is associated with its own greatest abuse,
—as in the example cited,—the phenomenon must
seem most terrifying to us, and a deeper insight into
the nature of the problem we have to solve must force
itself upon us. We might still keep from us the necessity for seeing this, if we were only admitting a great
decline in the public taste in art, and were seeking
to find the causes of it in the broader field of our
social state. But since for us, coming upon the startling fact from this very standpoint, it is impossible to
proceed from the assumption of a regeneration of the
public taste to the indirect supposition of a favorable
influence from this quarter upon the preference of the
people in art matters, there ought rather to commend
itself to us the attempt to attain by direct investigation
of this at first sight purely æsthetic problem, to a solution which may lead us to believe in the possibility of
an influence from this *other* side, upon the whole spirit
of the public.

To definitely fix this object in view, let us lay down
a thesis, with the following out of which we may

chiefly concern ourselves.   It may be put in this way :
We grant that the opera has evidently shown the
decline of the drama ; if it appears doubtful that it has
actually *produced* this decline, it is nevertheless clearly
to be seen from the present superior influence of the
opera, that it alone can be looked to, to again *elevate* the
drama ; but that it can only truly succeed in this restoration, if it at the same time leads the drama to the
attainment of that for which its ideal scope is so peculiarly fitted ; that the German stage has suffered far
more from the hitherto unsuitable and insufficient development of these ideal functions, than the French
theatre, which did not possess such functions, and
which could therefore, in its narrower sphere, more
easily attain to real correctness.

A properly traced history of dramatic pathos would
make it clear to us, what has always been aimed at in
the ideal direction in the modern theatre.   And it
would be instructive to notice here, how the Italians,
who, as far as their artistic tendencies are concerned,
derived all their instruction from the antique, left the
recited drama almost entirely undeveloped, and constantly endeavored, on the other hand, to reconstruct
the antique drama on the basis of the musical lyric,
and thus, pursuing this course with constant digression more and more into a single path, produced the
opera.   In the meantime, while this was happening
in Italy, by means of the all-powerful influence there
of the finely-cultured artistic spirit in the higher social
circles of the nation, the modern *drama* was developed
among the Spanish and English, from the very spirit
of the people ; for here the tendency of the more
learned poets toward the antique had proved powerless as far as any living influence upon the country
was concerned.

Calderon was the first to lead the Spanish drama
from that realistic sphere in which Lope de Vega had
proved so presumptuously productive, to the idealistic

manner, in which he approached the Italians so closely that we may find in many of his pieces a decidedly operatic character. Perhaps the English drama would also have taken this direction, if the wonderful genius of a Shakespeare had not succeeded in presenting, in the field of realistic drama, the noblest figures of history and fable with such semblance of nature, that he was exempted from all comparison with a standard which had hitherto been erroneously derived from the antique. Amazement at the incomprehensible and inimitable power of Shakespeare contributed not less than the recognition of the true meaning of the antique and its forms, to determine our great poets in their creations for the drama. They took into account also the great capabilities of the opera ; but were necessarily met by the inexplicable nature of· the question, how the opera was to be approached from their point of view ? Schiller could not be directed to the discovery of a method of coöperation with the opera, even by the transporting influence which Gluck's " Iphigenia in Tauris " made upon him ; and Goethe seemed to clearly comprehend that this matter must be reserved for the musical genius alone, when he saw himself forced to regard those remarkable hopes for the musically-conceived drama which were raised in him by " Don Juan," as extinguished by the news of Mozart's death.

Through this attitude of Goethe and Schiller we gain a deep insight into the purely poetic nature. If on the one hand Shakespeare and his method must have been to them incomprehensible, while on the other hand they must leave to the musician, with an equal lack of understanding of his method, the task which he alone can carry out, of giving to the figures of the drama an ideal life, the question arises, in what relation they, as poets, really stood to the true drama, and whether, *as poets alone*, they could feel themselves capable of, and fitted for, dramatic composition. If we endeavor to

penetrate into the nature of this doubt, we might come
to acknowledge a certain insufficiency in the poetic
power,—which power, in its purity, is only to be comprehended as an abstraction, and only becomes a concrete fact through the material element of its creations.
If neither a sculptor nor a musician is supposable
without the poetic element, the question occurs to us
—how that power which, in these two, works as a lat-
ent force in the production of a work of art, might be
made in the case of the pure poet, and acting as a
conscious creative faculty, to lead to the same result ?
Without going deeper into the investigation of the
secret here touched upon, we must nevertheless bear
in mind that which distinguishes the poet of modern
culture from the natural poet of the ancient world.
The latter was, before all things, the inventor of
myths ; then the relator of them in the recited epic,
and finally their direct representer in the living
drama.   Plato was the first to gain a mastery of the
power of this threefold poet, in his so dramatically
vivid dialogue—scenes filled with mythic creation,
which may be looked upon first as the origin, and
then (especially in the splendid " Banquet " of the
poetic philosopher) as the unequalled model of real
literary poetry, approaching the didactic in form.
Here the forms of simple poetry are only used as yet
for the explanation of philosophic theses, in an ab-
stractly popular sense, and their consciously effective
design takes the place of the influence of a directly
presented living picture.   To apply this didactic design to the drama actually performed by living beings,
of necessity appeared to our great culture-poets (*Kul-
turdichtern*) to be the most valuable method for ennobling the popular drama as they found it ; and they
might well be led to this belief by the consideration of
certain special peculiarities of the ancient drama.
    As this latter had developed its tragic power from a
compromise between the Apollonian and the Diony-

sian elements, so, on the basis of a lyric that has become almost incomprehensible to us, the old Hellenic,
didactic hymn of the priests could unite with the later
Dionysian dithyrambus to produce that marvellous
effect so peculiar to the tragic works of art of the
Greeks. The fact that it was especially the Apollonian elements which entered into this combination,
which gave to Greek tragedy, as a literary monument,
a special importance for all time—and particularly to
that part appealing to philosophers and teachers—
could easily mislead our modern poets (who saw in
these tragedies only literary products) to the opinion
that the real dignity of the ancient drama lay in this
didactic tendency, and consequently that the popular
drama, as they themselves found it, was only to be
elevated to an ideal meaning by infusing into it the
same element.

The true art spirit inherent in them prevented their
sacrificing the living drama itself to this bare tendency;
but the only thing which ·could fill the drama with
spirit, and at the same time raise it to the elevation of
ideality, seemed to them to be this higher motive;
and this the more, since the only material at their disposal, the means by which they could make ideas intelligible—a language of *words*—made it only possible
or advisable for them to exercise an ennobling and elevating influence in this one direction.

The poetically expressed sentence could only convey the high *motive*, and the influence to be exercised
upon the purely sensuous receptive power, always
strongly affected by the drama, must be left to the
so-called poetic diction. But it is precisely this latter,
which, in the performance of their pieces, led to
just that false pathos the recognition of which must
have set our great poets to thinking gravely, when
they felt themselves, on the other hand, so moved by
the effect of Gluck's " Iphigenia " and Mozart's " Don
Juan."

What must have impressed them so strangely here, was that they saw the drama at once raised into the sphere of the ideal, by the influence of music ; and that from this the simplest feature of the action appeared to them in a clearer light ;—effect and motive, mingled in one direct expression, spoke to them with the noblest power.   Every desire to seize upon some *purpose* was stilled ; for the idea itself was realized before them, as an irresistible appeal to the highest sympathy.   " Man errs in all his striving," or, " Life is not the highest good," no longer needed to be *said*, for the inmost secret of the wise"t sentence presented itself to them without disguise, in distinct melodious form.   If the sentence said " It signifies "—the other said " *It* IS."   Here the highest pathos had become the soul of the drama ; and a picture of life appeared to us with appealing truthfulness, as though from some happy world of dreams.

But how enigmatical this work of art must have appeared to our poets ; for where in it could the *poet's* element be found ?   Certainly not in that very trait in which their own strength lay—in the thought and the poetic diction ; for in both of these the operatic texts were entirely deficient.   If it could not be the poet, then it must be the musician, to whom alone the art-product seemed to belong.   But, tried by their standard, as artists, it was hard for them to allow to the musician an importance proportionate to the immense influence which appeared to emanate from him.   Music appeared to them a senseless art—a half-wild, half-ridiculous element, not to be approached by any true art-culture.   Besides, the opera seemed such an insignificant, disconnected agglomeration of forms, without that intelligible, artistic unity whose arbitrarily combined parts might strive to attain to anything sooner than the consistency of a dramatic plan.   If it were truly a dramatic basis which had united, in Gluck's " Iphigenia," that scattered chaos of forms (*Formengewirr*) to so powerful a whole, the question arose, who could take the place of this operatic poet, and write the singularly thin text even for the arias of a Gluck, unless he were willing to give up at once his title of "poet"? The incomprehensible part of it lay in an effect of high ideality, whose artistic factors could not be discovered by the analogy of any other art. This incomprehensible element increased, when this particular piece of Gluck's (which, by its subject, taken entirely from the antique, and of the truest tragedy, was so elevated and full of thought) was left out of sight,—and even, then it must be admitted that the opera in general, no matter of how nonsensical or trivial plot it might be, had under certain circumstances an unequalled effect, even in the highest ideal sense of the word.

These circumstances were at once brought into play whenever a great dramatic genius mastered the rôles of such an opera. Think, for example, of that presentation of "Romeo" in Bellini's opera—a presentation never to be forgotten by many still living spectators —which was once given us by Schröder-Devrient. Every feeling of a musician must rebel against acknowledging that the utterly poor and insignificant music of the piece had any artistic value ; and besides, it was in this case fitted to an operatic poem of ridiculous poverty of thought. And yet, ask any one who saw it what impression Schröder-Devrient's Romeo made upon him, as compared with our best dramatic actor's Romeo, even in the great Englishman's own play?

In this case, however, it must be confessed that this effect did not lie in mere skill in singing, as it does in the similar successes of our ordinary *prime donne ;* but rather while this quality was here only slight and unsustained by any luxuriant vocal capacities, it lay solely in the *dramatic* performance. Yet this again could not possibly have secured the success of even one like Schröder-Devrient in the most perfect of

spoken dramas; and therefore it could only be successful through the one element of *music*,—lending an
ideal atmosphere, even when in this petty form.

Just such an experience as that just mentioned,
ought to put us upon the right path toward forming
an opinion, and discovering the real factor in the production of a dramatic work of art.

As the participation of the poet in this production
was so small, Goethe thought that the creation of the
opera was to be entirely attributed to the musician;
and in how far this has serious sense in it, should
be clear to us, if we investigate more closely the
second element in the drama that was incomprehensible
to our great poets—the peculiarities of Shakespeare
and his artistic method,—and seek for a correct conclusion in this matter also.

Even now Shakespeare seems to the French—representatives of modern civilization—to be a monstrosity.
Until a very recent period he has been for the Germans, too, a subject for continually renewed investigation, whose results have attained so little definiteness
that the most widely different views and opinions still
continue to strive for general adoption. Thus within
a short time the most consistent aims of the didactic
poet have been attributed to this enigmatical dramatist,
who but a short time before had come to be looked
upon as an entirely irresponsible, wild genius, without
any art-culture whatever. Goethe, who introduces
him in "Wilhelm Meister" as a "masterly writer,"
found in constantly repeated consideration of the problem a resting-place for his more and more cautious judg-
ments, in the fact that he discovered the higher tendency not in the poet, but embodied as character in
the persons represented by him in full action before
us. But the more he looked at these creations the
more enigmatically the process of the artist hid itself
from the eye of the investigator. If the main plan of
a piece were clearly perceivable, and a consistently-de-

veloped action not to be ignored (such an action, indeed, generally being contained in the material chosen for the play)—the extraordinary " incidental bits," in the carrying out of the plot as well as in the action of the characters, were ·nevertheless incomprehensible, according to the scheme of an artistic arrangement and a well-considered plan.   There was plainly obvious a sharpness of individuality which often seemed like inexplicable capriciousness, the true sense of which could only be discovered when the book was closed, and we saw the drama filled with life before us ; and then the true picture of existence, seen in a mirror with irresistible faithfulness, stood in our presence, and filled us with an awe like that inspired by an apparition of spirits. But how could this enchantment be measured by the characteristics of " a work of *art* " ?   Was the author of these things a *poet ?*

The little that we know of his life tells us with innocent naïveté—that he was an actor, who arranged and wrote these pieces for himself and his company ;—these pieces before which our greatest poets now stand amazed and in truly affecting confusion ; and which for the most part would not have descended to them, if the insignificant prompter's books of the Globe Theatre had not been saved from oblivion, just at the right moment, by being printed.   Lope de Vega, hardly less wonderful, wrote his pieces from day to day, in direct association with the theatre and its actors ; beside Corneille and Racine, the poets of a fashion, stands the actor Molière—the only one full of life and creative ; and Æschylus stood in the midst of his noble works, as leader of the tragic chorus.   •

It is not the nature of the *poet*, but that of the *dramatist*, that is to be investigated if the elements of the drama are to be clearly understood ; and the latter is no nearer to the ordinary poet than to the mere mummer, from whose nature he must fully emerge if he desires, as a poet, to hold the mirror up to life.

10

The very essence of the dramatic art, therefore, as opposed to the poetic method, appears to be at first sight entirely irrational ; it is only to be grasped by a complete change in the nature of the observer.   It should not be difficult for us to determine in what this change should consist, if we look at the *natural* method in the beginnings of *all* art—and this we find distinctly in *imprcvisation.*   The poet who should show to the improvising actor a plan of the action to be represented, would stand in much the same relation in which the author of an operatic text stands to the musician ; his work cannot yet have any artistic value whatever; but this will be most fully imparted to it, if the poet makes the actor's improvising spirit his own, and carries out his work completely in the character of an improvisation, so that now the actor can enter with all his own peculiarity into the higher thought of the poet.   Of course a complete change in the art-product itself must take place through this means ; and such a change could only be exactly described, if it were possible to have before us the ac- tually transcribed improvisation of a great musician.

We have the testimony of excellent witnesses to the incomparable impression which Beethoven left upon his friends by improvising at the piano ; and we can- not regard as exaggerated the regret expressed at the fact of not having been able to preserve these creations in writing ;—it cannot be called exaggerated even when we consider the master's greatest written works, if we remember the frequent occurrence, that even less gifted composers, whose compositions when written out·are characterized by stiffness and constraint, can, by free improvisation, throw us into genuine amaze- ment at a creative gift never before suspected and of- ten most productive.

In any case, we believe we shall greatly facilitate the solution of a very difficult problem, if we call the Shakespearean drama a *definitely-planned histrionic*

improvisation of the very highest artistic value. For
if we take this view we shall have an immediate explanation of the apparently remarkable inconsistencies
in the action and language of characters who are
created with the single purpose of *being*, now and at
the moment when they are before us, precisely those
characters they are *meant* to appear to us,—and to
whom no language could possibly occur which would
lie outside this *nature*, with which they are, as it were,
bewitched. And it would seem absurd enough, on
closer consideration, if one of these characters should
suddenly seek to appear to us in the character of a
poet. This element is silent, and remains a riddle to
us, as Shakespeare does. Yet its work is the only
true drama ; and we see what importance the drama
really has as a work of art, in the fact that its author
will always appear to us the deepest poetic nature of
all time.

To continue the considerations to which the drama
so strongly urges us, let us now look at those peculiarities of it which seem most serviceable for our purpose. Most prominent among these is the fact that,
apart from all its other value, it belongs to the class of
pieces which alone are effective in the *theatre*,—pieces
that have been arranged expressly for the theatre at
different periods, have proceeded *from* the theatre or
from authors standing in direct communication with it,
and have from year to year enriched the popular
French stage, for example. The difference between
them lies only in the *poetic* value of true dramatic products that have arisen from the same origin. This
difference seems, at first sight, to be determined by the
greatness and importance of the material selected for
their action. While not only the French have succeeded in most truthfully depicting upon the stage all
the events of modern life in general, but the Germans
(people of much less theatrical talent) have successfully
brought forward the occurrences of this life in its

smaller and more domestic circle, this truly reproduc-
tive force has failed just in proportion as the events of
a higher sphere of action, and the fate of historic heroes
and the myths concerning them (removed to a re-
spectful distance from matters of every-day life), were
sought to be produced. For this purpose the true poet
(that is, the inventor and former of myths) had to overcome the insufficient dramatic improvisation; and his
genius, especially fitted for such a task, must manifest
itself in raising the style of that improvisation to the
height of his own poetic purpose. How Shakespeare
succeeded in raising his players themselves to this
height, must remain a problem ; it is only certain that
the capacities of our modern players would at once fail
in the task thus set them. The assumption is possible,
that the grotesque affectation peculiar to the English
actors of the present day (to which we referred above)
is a remnant of an earlier power which, since it comes
from a trait lying undeniably in the nature of the nation, may have been able, in the most perfect period
of national life and through the noble example of the
poetic actor himself, to lead to so unprecedented a
point in theatrical art that Shakespeare's conceptions
could be for once fully carried out.

Or we may perhaps call to mind for the explanation
of this enigma, if we do not wish to accept so extraordinary a miracle as that just supposed, the fate of
the great Sebastian Bach, whose rich and difficult choral
compositions would appear to lead us to the theory
that the master must have had at command, for their
execution, the most incomparable vocal forces ; while
on the contrary we know from undoubted documen-
tary evidence his own complaints of the general
wretched composition of his choir of school-boys. It
is certain that Shakespeare retired very early from his
connection with the stage ; a fact which we can easily
explain by the very great fatigue the rehearsals of his
pieces cost him, as well as his despair at the flight of

his own genius beyond the possibilities that were open to him. The whole nature of this genius is, however, only clear to us through these very " possibilities," which certainly existed in the basis of the actor's nature, and were therefore very properly taken for granted by the author ; and, considering the efforts for culture (*Kulturbestrebungen*) made by the genius of humanity in one great connection, we can look upon it as the task which the great dramatist in a certain sense bequeathed to his successors, to really *reach* those highest possibilities in the development of the capabilities of histrionic art.

To labor at this task appears to have been the truest calling of our own great German poets. Proceeding from the necessary acknowledgment of Shakespeare's inimitability, this purpose determined a direction for every form of their poetic conception, which we can well understand if we keep this hypothesis in mind. The search for the ideal form of the highest work of art—the drama—led them of necessity away from Shakespeare to the renewed and always deeper consideration of the tragedy of the ancients ; we have seen in what way alone they thought to gain anything from this, and we observed that they were necessarily led from this more than doubtful path to that inexplicable new impression which the noblest creations of the opera (in other respects entirely enigmatical to them) produced upon them.

Two things were noteworthy in connection with this, namely : —that the noble music of a great master could give an ideal enchantment to the work of even little-gifted dramatic performers,—an enchantment which was denied to even the most admirable actors of the spoken drama ; while on the other hand a true dramatic talent could so ennoble utterly worthless music, that we could be struck by a performance which the same talent could not succeed in producing in a spoken play. That this phenomenon could only be explained by the power of *music*, was unavoidable. And this could be true only of music *in general;* while it remained incomprehensible how the peculiar flexibility of its forms could be attained without their subordination to the worst possible kind of dramatic poet.

We adduced the example of Shakespeare, to give us as much of a glimpse as possible into the nature, and especially the method, of the true dramatist. And mysterious as the greater part of this must be to us, we could nevertheless perceive that it was the actor's art with which the poet entirely united; and we recognized that this actor's art was the dew of life (*Lebensthau*), in which the poetic purpose must be bathed, in order that it might be able, as though by a magic transformation, to appear a true mirror of life.—Now if every action, even every ordinary event of life (such as not only Shakespeare but every true play-wright shows us), can reveal itself to us, when reproduced as a mimic drama, in the glorified light and with the objective effect of a mirrored picture, we must accept as proved as a result of our further considerations, that this reflection in turn shows itself in the pure light of the ideal so soon as it has been dipped in the magic fountain of music ; and at the same time is displayed to us as a pure form, freed from all realistic materialization.

It would no longer be needful, therefore, to take into consideration the *form of music*, but rather the forms of music *as historically developed*, if one desired to determine that highest possibility in the development of the actor's art, which seemed to the investigator and the worker a dark enigma, while on the other hand it pressed itself more and more upon him.

By " the form of music " we must undoubtedly understand *melody*. The development of this especially fills the history of our music ; as the need of it determined the development of the lyric drama attempted by the Italians, into the opera. The attempt being

first made to imitate in this respect the form of the
Greek tragedy, this seemed at the first glance to be
divided into two principal parts,—the choral song, and
the dramatic recitation which periodically rose into musical measure; and the actual " drama " was thus left to
the recitative, the oppressive monotony of which was
finally interrupted by the discovery of the " air " (an
invention approved by the academy). It was only
with this that music gained its independent form as
melody; and it thus (very rightly) won such an advantage over the remaining factors of the musical
drama, that this latter, no longer employed as anything but an excuse for the other, finally sank to the
place of a mere scaffolding for the exhibition of the
aria. It must be the history of melody, closely limited to this *aria* form, which must therefore engage
our attention, if we are not entirely content with the
consideration of those of its effects merely, which it
presented to our great poets when they felt themselves
so deeply impressed by its power, yet so much more
deeply at a loss in thinking of any poetic association
with it. It was indisputably only a special form of
genius that could so endue with life this narrow and
empty form of melodic expression, that it could be capable of a really powerful effect. Its extension and development was therefore only to be expected from the
musician; and the course of that development could
be distinctly seen by a comparison of Mozart's masterpiece with Gluck's. In this comparison a rich power
of purely musical invention is especially displayed as
the only thing which could make pure music powerful
in a dramatic sense; for in Mozart's " Don Juan "
there is an abundance of dramatic elements of which
the far less powerful composer Gluck had no conception. But it was reserved for German genius to elevate the musical form, by the highest inspiration of
even its least important parts, to the inexhaustible

variety and richness which the music of our great
Beethoven now offers to a wondering world.

The musical creations of Beethoven have traits
which render them as inexplicable from one point of
view as those of Shakespeare are from another. While
the powerful influence of both must be felt as different
in kind, though equal in effect, even this difference between them seems to disappear upon closer consideration, and in view of the incomprehensible peculiarities of their creations ; for the only way of explaining
the one appears to us in the explanation given for the
other. .

Let us instance in proof of this, and as the most
easily intelligible point, the peculiarity of the humor-
ous element in both ; and we shall see that what often
appears to us as an incomprehensible inconsistency in
the humor of Shakespeare's creations, appears in precisely similar features of Beethoven's work as a natural piece of high idealism—presented as a melody
which is inseparable from the mood of the listener.
We cannot escape here from the assumption of a primal
connection between the two, which we shall be able to
properly define if we do not look upon it as existing
between the musician and the poet,—but as between
one poetic actor or *mimic* (*Mime*),* and another.
The secret lies in the *directness* of the representation,
conveyed in the one case by expression and action,
and in the other by living music. That which both
create and form is the true work of art, for which the
poet only draws the plan—and even this unsuccess-
fully, unless he has taken it directly from nature.

We have seen that the Shakespearean drama is most
correctly comprehended under the name of a " definite
imitative improvisation ; " and we were obliged to as-

---

* In the sense in which Wagner uses it, this word is extremely difficult
of translation.   Our English "mime " does not express it.   He means,
of course, to indicate the actor in his character of pure imitator of nature.
—TRANSLATOR.

sume that the highest poetic value, though emanating at first from the dignity of the material selected, must be secured to such a work of art by the elevation of the *style* of that improvisation. We cannot be mistaken, therefore, in thinking that such an elevation, to the extent which is really needed, can only be found in that music which stands in just such a relation to it as does Beethoven's music to Shakespeare's dramas.

The very point in which the difficulty of applying music like Beethoven's to dramas like Shakespeare's is here most prominently to be seen, might, if properly adjusted, lead directly to the highest perfection of musical form, by freeing it from every fetter that may still hamper it. That which so perplexed our great poets in their consideration of the opera, and that feature in Beethoven's instrumental music which still distinctly shows the skeleton of a structure found rather in the same tendency that produced the opera *aria* and the ballet piece, than in the true nature of music, —these features of conventional composition, though endowed with such wonderfully vigorous life by Beethoven's use of melody, would thus most completely disappear before an ideal method full of the truest freedom. Thus music, in this respect at least, would adapt itself closely to the thoroughly life-filled form of a Shakespearean drama, which, when its noble irregularity is compared with the drama of the ancients, seems almost like a scene in nature beside an architectural work—while its thoroughly logical character nevertheless is revealed in the certainty of the effect the work of art produces. In this, too, would be shown the entire novelty of the form of such an art product which, only conceivable (as an idealized natural production) by employing in it the aid of the German language, the most cultured of modern tongues, could nevertheless deceive the judgment as long as a standard was applied to it which it had entirely outgrown; —whereas the fitting new standard would be derived

10*

from the impression which the unwritten improvisation of an incomparable composer would make upon one fortunate enough to hear it. The greatest of dramatists has taught us to give definite form to such an improvisation ; and in the highest conceivable work of art the noblest inspirations of both composer and dramatist should exist as the very essence of the world thus revealed to us in the mirror of the world itself.

If we adopt, for the work of art which we have in view, this designation :—" a dramatic-musical improvisation of perfected poetic value, embodied in a fixed form by the highest artistic thought," we shall find, if we follow the teachings of experience, a surprising light thrown upon the practical points connected with the actual execution of such a work.

In a very important sense, and interpreting the matter strictly, our great poets could only be chiefly concerned with the discovery of some method by which a heightened pathos could be added to the drama, and a technical means be found for embodying this. However certain it may be that Shakespeare derived his style from the instincts of the actor's art (*der mimischen Kunst*), he must nevertheless have been dependent for the presentation of his dramas on the accident of greater or less talent in his players, who must all have been to a certain extent Shakespeares, just as he himself was always to a certain extent the character presented ; and we have no reason for the assumption that his genius could have recognized in the performance of his pieces more than the mere shadow of himself cast upon the stage.

That which so strongly attracted our great poets towards music was the fact that it was at the same time the purest form and the most sensuous realization of that form. The abstract arithmetical number, the mathematical figure, meets us here as a creation having an irresistible influence upon the emotions—that is, it appears as *melody ;* and this can be as unerringly

established so as to produce sensuous effect, as the poetic diction of written language, on the contrary, is abandoned to every whim in the personal character of the
person reciting it. What was not practically possible
for Shakespeare—to be *himself* the actor of each one of
his rôles—is practicable for the musical composer, and
this with great definiteness,—since he speaks to us directly through each one of the musicians who execute his
works. In this case the transmigration of the poet's
soul into the body of the performer takes place according to the infallible laws of the most positive
technique; and the composer who gives the correct
measure for a technically right performance of his
work, becomes completely one with the musician who
performs it, to an extent that can at most only be
affirmed of the constructive artist in regard to a work
which he had himself produced in color or stone,—if,
indeed, a transmigration of his soul into lifeless matter
is a supposable case.

If we add to this wonderful power in the musician,
that capacity of his art which we deduced from the
facts we considered in the beginning—the facts that
even insignificant music (so long as it is not entirely
distorted into the vulgar grotesqueness of certain
kinds of opera now popular) makes otherwise unattainable performances possible to a great dramatic talent,
while noble music can almost *force* from insignificant
dramatic powers successes impossible in any other way
—when we add the results of these facts to the musician's power, we can scarcely feel a doubt as to the
reason of the complete failure which this view predicts
for the poet of to-day, if he attempts to succeed in
mastering the drama, in its noblest sense, by the only
means at his command—the capabilities of the same
language in which now even newspaper articles speak
to us !

In this respect, however, our assumption that the
highest perfection is reserved for the musically-ar-

ranged drama, should have a hopeful, rather than a
discouraging, influence upon us : for here we are pri-
marily concerned with the purification of a great and
many-sided department of art—that of the drama as a
whole,—the errors of which are to-day both increased
and concealed by the influence of the modern opera?
To gain a clear conception of this, and to accurately
measure the field of their future productiveness, our
dramatists might perhaps find it advisable to trace
back the descent of the modern theatre ; but not to
seek its origin in the ancient drama, which was in its
form a so completely original product of the Hellenic
mind, its religion, and even its form of government,
that the assumption that it had been imitated by later
forms would lead to the greatest errors.   The origin of
the modern theatre, on the contrary, shows us along
the path of its development such an abundance of noble productions, of the greatest value, that this path
may certainly be followed further without shame. The
genuine theatrical " play," in its most modern sense,
would have to be the only healthful basis of all further
dramatic efforts ; but in order to labor successfully in
this direction, it is necessary, first of all, to form a
right conception of the spirit of theatrical art, which
has its basis in the art of the *actor ;* and not to use it
for the formulating of tendencies, but as the reflection
of life-pictures such as are really seen.

The French, who have even recently contributed so
much that is excellent in this respect, did not, it is
true, look for the appearance of a new Molière among
them every year ; and for us too the birth of a Shakespeare is not to be read in every calendar.

As far as seeking to satisfy ideal demands is concerned, the limit to which such demands may properly
go seems to be set, for the influence of the all-powerful dramatic work of art which we have in view, with
greater certainty than has before been possible.   This
point may be distinctly recognized as existing where,

in that art product, song comes in contact with *spoken* words. Yet by no means an absolutely narrow sphere is indicated by this, but rather an entirely different and dissimilar one ; and we may at once gain an insight into this difference, if we call to mind a certain involuntary compulsion which forces even our best dramatic singers into excess ; and by which they feel themselves forced to *speak* an emphatic word in the very midst of their song. Schröder-Devrient, for example, saw herself compelled to this course by a fearfully highly wrought situation in the opera of " Fidelio," where, holding her pistol before the tyrant, she suddenly positively *spoke*—and with a terrible accent of despair— the last word of the phrase—" another step—and thou art—DEAD ! " The indescribable effect of this acted upon every one as a harsh break from one sphere into the other ; and the power of it consisted in this,—that as though by a flash of lightning we gained a sudden insight into the nature of both spheres,—one of them the ideal, and the other the real. It was evident that, for a moment, the ideal one was incapable of bearing a burden which it therefore cast upon the other ; and as especially passionate and excited music is so commonly credited with a purely morbid element inherent in it, it may easily surprise us to recognize from this example how delicate and purely ideal in form its sphere really is, so that the realistic terrors of actual life cannot be contained in it—though the soul of all reality finds pure expression in music alone.

Evidently, therefore, there is a side to the world which concerns us most seriously, and the terrible teachings of which are only intelligible to us in the field of observation, in which music must be silent. This field is perhaps best estimated, if we allow ourselves to be led into it by the great actor Shakespeare, as far as the point where we find him overcome by that despairing discouragement which we have thought it necessary to assume as the reason of his early retirement

from the stage. This field may be best called, if not
the basis, at least the manifestation of history ; and to
properly seize upon its real value for human knowledge, must always be left to the poet alone.

So important and distinct an influence as we could
only attempt to indicate here by the merest outline,—
an influence exercised not only upon that department
of the drama with which it is most closely connected,
but on all branches of art, deeply connected with the
drama in any way—such an influence could only be
possible for the musically-arranged and executed
dramatic work that we have referred to, if the latter,
in its production before the public, can render itself
outwardly intelligible in a consistent way, and thus enable an opinion of its characteristics to be formed with
the necessary freedom. It is so closely related to the
opera, that we feel we may rightly look upon it, as far
as our present consideration is concerned, as the province of that branch of art ; none of the possibilities suggested to us could have been clear to us, if they had
not been manifested for us in the opera in general, and
especially in the most admirable works of the great
operatic composers. And just as certainly, it was the
spirit of music which, in the constantly increasing
richness of its development, could have such an influence upon the opera that these possibilities could in any
way arise within it. And yet, if we desire to explain
the degradation which the opera has undergone, we
must seek its cause again in the peculiarities of music.
As in painting and even in architecture, the merely
" attractive " may displace the beautiful,—so it has
been not the less the fate of music to decline from a
noble to a merely pleasing art. If its sphere was that
of the purest idealism,—if it had so deep an influence on our emotions, and freed what was realistic
from everything disagreeable in its representation by
the very fact that it showed itself to us as pure form
alone, so that what threatened to disturb this fell or

was kept away from it—even if all this was true, yet this pure form, if not placed in an entirely appropriate relation to its environment, might easily seem only suitable for a pleasant plaything, and only be used for such a purpose. This would be the case as soon as it was used, in so unfitting a sphere as the basis of the opera could offer it, as a mere superficial method of giving pleasure to the sense of hearing or arousing the emotions.

But we are little concerned here with this view, for we began our essay with the complaint made against the effect and the influences of the opera, the unfortunate importance of which cannot be better shown than by pointing to the universal experience, that the stage of to-day has long been given up and viewed with complete indifference by the truly educated portion of the nation, who used once to look to it with every hope. If we wish, then, to secure for the work of art we have described, the only esteem which could be just and valuable for it—that of those who have turned with serious displeasure from the recent stage,—this can only be possible outside of all relation with that stage. The neutral ground, however, on which it can be done, though ever so completely separated *locally* from the field of influence of our theatres, could only bear proper fruit if nourished by the real elements of our histrionic and musical arts. In these alone lies the truly productive material for genuine dramatic achievement; every attempt of any other kind must lead not to art, but to an affected artificiality.

It is our actors, singers, and musicians upon whose own instincts all hope for the attainment of artistic objects must rest, even when these objects themselves may be incomprehensible to them. For they must be the ones to whom these objects will most speedily become clear, as soon as their own artistic instincts are put upon the right path toward their recognition. That these instincts of theirs have hitherto been only

guided, by the influences of our stage, toward the development of the very worst qualities of dramatic ambition,—this fact must inspire us with the wish to at
least occasionally free these otherwise invaluable dramatic forces from such tendencies, to permit their *good*
qualities to gain that practice which would quickly
and decidedly make them serviceable in the realization
of our proposed art-work.   For it is only the peculiar
will of this guild of actors, so singular in their erroneous course, from which the perfect drama we have indicated can come, just as indeed every excellent dramatic result that has ever appeared has emanated from
them.   The decline of theatrical art in our time has
been brought about less by them than by those who
have hitherto—though without any authority—been
their leaders.

If we desire to point out that thing which, of all on
German soil, is and continues to be least worthy of
the fame of our great modern triumphs, we must point
to *the stage*, the whole course of which has prominently and boldly shown it to be a very betrayer of
German honor.

Whoever makes any effort to sustain this course,
must submit to a judgment which will necessarily class
him with a part of our public life that is of a most
doubtful nature,—and from which it will be as difficult
to emerge into a sphere of pure art, as it will be to
rise from the opera to the ideal drama we have supposed.   It is certainly true that if, according to Schiller's remark (here apparently inexact), that " art has
only declined through the fault of the artists "—it can
only be *elevated again by the artists*, and not by those
by whose pleasure in art that art suffers injury.   To
help this elevation of the art-standard by artists—and
to help it from without as well—this effort should be
the national atonement for the national sin—the evil
influence of the modern German stage.

MUSICAL CRITICISM:

EXTRACTS ·FROM A LETTER ON THAT SUBJECT TO
THE EDITOR OF THE "NEUE ZEITSCHRIFT FÜR
MUSIK."

.

YOU desire me to express to you my opinion as to
what part a musical periodical should take with
respect to the trial which the music of our day must
necessarily undergo, and as to how, by taking part
in the trial, it might best subserve the common good.
At present it is impossible—and I heartily wish it
may evermore be unnecessary—for me to engage in
any further literary work ; still I will endeavor to explain to you my views as to the matter in hand in the
only way possible for me, viz., by giving you my opinion not as an absolute and binding one, but as one
that has proceeded from my peculiar theories, and has
had its origin in what must always remain my wish.
Hence I will tell you what I should myself do were I
from force of circumstances, or of my own choice, to
think of publishing a musical periodical ; it is only
by confining myself to this purely personal standpoint
that I can communicate my views to you impartially.

In the first place, I candidly confess to you that at
one period of my life I never looked at a musical periodical, and that afterwards, I had reason for regarding
that period as being, so far at least, one of the happiest of my existence. That was the time when, as
Kappelmeister in Dresden, I devoted all my energy to
the presentation of musical works of art, and when
accordingly I thought I must rest all my hopes for
the success of art upon the actual representation un-

der my management—on the practical realization of
my artistic conceptions.   During that period I was so
deeply averse to speaking or writing about art that I
could only very rarely bring myself to express myself at
all. This period I have called one of the happiest of my
life ; and it was so, because I could then suffer illusion.   What I wished to do I never could perform to
my full satisfaction ; of all the circumstances which
hindered me, I single out two as having a bearing on
the subject before us : the total perversion of the *public
taste*, and the brainlessness and the dishonesty of the
critics.   What the true artist most desires to find is
the ingenuousness of pure human sympathy ; he fails
to meet with this among our theatre-going public ;
then he is forced to seek for help from the side of the
cultured artistic intellect—he must engage the medi-
ation of criticism.   The disgust I soon conceived of
the public at length forced me into this needy attitude
towards criticism ; and it was precisely here, where
I even sought it, and therefore could not reject it,
that I came to fully understand the nature of our
modern criticism, and now was forced to engage almost
alone in opposition to it.

What I have since published concerning art does
not constitute, as many have supposed, an appeal to
popular opinion, but in these writings I turned from
the modern public, which I had to give up as a senseless, heartless mass, and set my face against criticism, *i. e.* against uncritical, false criticism, that criticism which is guided neither by sympathy nor by correct understanding ; which rests simply on the ignorance of the masses, which lives by this ignorance, and
even favors it from motives of self-interest.   I say I set
my face against this kind of criticism ; I did not appeal to it.   For the thought even of giving it a true
direction can never occur to any one who has already
been obliged to abandon his hopes of the public.   The
public is, at least, not wilful in its perverseness, whereas

criticism is of set purpose and radically perverse. Still I ever made my appeal, as was unavoidable in literary compositions, *only* to criticism, that is, to the new criticism of right reason ; in other words, the understanding, which never for a moment deserts its constant support, right feeling. Thus I did not appeal to the critical routine of the old method, which was quite divorced from feeling — a method based on the same perversion of feeling and the same stupidity which is seen in the public. My appeal was to the enlightened judgment of those cultured minds which, like my own, are as ill content with the modern public as with the criticism of the present day.

From that time forward, I again began to look into musical periodicals, and journals devoted to the interests of art in general, for I·felt that I must look elsewhere than to the public for men to whom I could turn for the gratification of my new desire for converse.

I had learned, that is, that any effort to appeal to the unrestrained emotions by means of a work of art itself, was entirely rash and fruitless, where such unrestrained and free emotions do not exist to receive the fresh creations of a living art ; I had seen, on the other hand, that it was necessary, above all things, to aim at the destruction of that constraint which we find among the public, hampering the feelings, and fatally destructive for the artist's purpose. Since I was compelled to see that the reason of this constraint was deeply-rooted in the elements of our political and social life ; and that only a complete change in that life could bring about the natural birth of that art which I had in mind ; since I had to make the demand for such a change, as the first thing to be striven for, and to lay special stress upon it, as I did in my earlier writings ("Art and Revolution" and "The Art-work of the Future *)—I must also, looking at the other

---

* Two of Wagner's earlier essays in support of his theories—*Kunst und Revolution* and *Das Kunstwerk der Zukunft.*—TR.

side of the matter, perceive that a *second* influence must be active in bringing about this new birth of art, viz., a *consciously existing desire* for such an art. And I must consider it the chief task toward which the endeavors of the artist should be directed, to awaken this conscious desire in all those who are dissatisfied with our present art and art-criticism. For he can derive the strength for his higher efforts, directed toward the production of the art-work itself, only from the desire of others—and at length of *many* others.

But this desire cannot be awakened until we come clearly to see that the present conditions of artist life are unsatisfactory, not because of any accidental circumstance (some direct result of artistic characteristics, for instance), but for reasons that are essential, and that depend on a long train of causes. And this clear view we now obtain by way of criticism that is analytical and synthetic, healthy, sympathetic and revolutionary, as distinguished from a criticism that knows neither analysis nor synthesis, and which is merely conservative, and desirous of restoring the past. Hence, the first thing we have to do, is to get clear ideas about the status of modern art and the causes why that status is so unsatisfactory. Until this is done, with perfect candor and honesty, we can only go further and further astray in our efforts to supersede our present art. On the contrary, so soon as we have given clear ideas on this point, we must also gain that strength of will that I have just spoken of, as necessary to *aid* in the birth of the art of the future, even though the latter may find the actual conditions that make its being possible, to exist only in actual life.

* * * * * * * * *

I am very decidedly of the opinion that the most decisive, because the most necessary, agency for bringing about the birth of the new art is to be found in a periodical devoted to this particular object, and the only question is, how far and within what limits, a simply *musical* periodical is fitted for a point of union for critical forces employed in this sense ?

Permit me to answer this question from my own point of view.

In the first place, I have to inform you that whenever, in recent years, I have now and then felt a desire to publish my views regarding one phase or another of our art life, I have sought in vain for a periodical in which such communications would be properly in place. I had either to take such as I found, or else suppress my communication altogether. Our æsthetic journals are devoted to the interests of literature—not to those of art ; and hence in their aim (if aim they have) they differ as much from *my* aim as literature differs from art. They never come in contact with art, properly speaking, but only with art criticism ; they are only kept alive by the possibility of this latter ; and as they heap criticism upon criticism, their office resembles that of the various grades of the police forces in Russia, which supervise each other, the presumption being that each grade needs watching. Now the relation between the people proper, or better, between art and these police forces, is the same as that between art and these artistic-literary journals. In the bureau of these various grades of police, a man would be esteemed a fool or a madman, if he were to give expression to his natural emotions ; and in like manner in these literary journals, the man who has to do only with art is set down for a crack-brained enthusiast. For even when those various grades of police take their broadest view of a subject, the dominant idea after all is *police ;* and our literary journals, when they do their best, cannot go beyond the idea of *littérateur.*

Our modern music has at least this advantage over literature proper, that it must absolutely be perceptible by the senses, must be heard in order to be an object of apprehension ; and hence a musical periodical would have one advantageous characteristic, in that at least it deals with the sensible phenomena of an art, which cannot be apprehended at all without such sensible impression; while on the contrary,.even poetic literature, for instance, only exists by being independent of this sensuous influence.

That music has had need of a literature to be devoted to its interests and to make men acquainted with it, and hence that there have been " Musical Periodicals," is a circumstance which exhibits its weak side; but the same is to be said of all our " fine " arts— architecture, sculpture and painting; for these arts also have had to call in the aid of periodical literature to diffuse a knowledge of their principles. But what we must aim at, while engaging literature in the service of music, is, so far as possible, to hide away this weak side, to recognize as a defect in our present musical art its dependence on literature, to investigate the nature and causes of this defect, and then resolutely to free music from her dependence upon literature, and place her in a position where she shall no longer need the aid of literature as an interpreter. A musical periodical which should accept this point of view, would possess a character such as must render it most welcome under the present circumstances, and is most necessary for the true interests of art.

You, my dear friend, have in your most recent utterances given us the assurance of your having come to such conclusions as are here indicated, and we have furthermore your promise that henceforth your literary labors will take the direction to which I have just referred. Down to the time of my receiving your announcement I must confess that I never could see the use of a musical periodical. Each new musical journal that made its appearance excited in me only feelings of disgust or of amusement. The opportunities they afforded for talking or scribbling about music, and talking and scribbling about this over again; then too the sordid business character of these publications—with no thought at all for music, but all for musical stock and musicians, not to speak of music-making machines; all this was evidence to me how low down into Byzantinism our music had fallen—a Byzantinism which in my opinion leaves it no more creative force than that of an emasculated creature.

But in your prospectus you disclosed your resolution to break utterly with this system; in other words to resist its influence, and so far as possible to break it down.

Inspired by this spirit, the journal will soon be forced to perceive how necessary it is to incorporate the *poet* with its work; for it is he who must unite with the real tone-artist, to bring forth the full concord from which the flower of true *Musical Art* shall spring. We must turn, therefore, to that poet who longs, for his own satisfaction, to free himself from the ruts of merely literary poetry, just as the musical artist, from his peculiar position, longs for the poet. We must open our arms to this poet; for we cannot feel ourselves justified in absolute hopefulness until we can receive him in the fullest spirit of love. We must see in his attentive approach to us, his gradual drawing near, only evidence of the fact that we, from our standpoint, are on the right and proper way toward the attainment of what we wish; and so long as we *cannot* perceive this approach on his part, we must be convinced that we are ourselves in just such an isolated and lonely position as that from which we seek to entice the purely literary poet. The poet cannot enter into association with us until we take away from him the same dislike toward the mere music-maker that we feel toward the mere *littérateur;* and he will nourish this dislike as long as he sees us lending our support to the modern trivial style of musical art. The first poet who gives us his hand and aid should prove to us that we have really and completely departed from the old ruts, and have freed ourselves from our unproductive egotism.

＊　＊　＊　＊　＊　＊　＊　＊　＊

The goal of the united efforts of three types of artist—the poet, the musical composer, and the actor, can only be a work of art made positively *real* to the senses by a life-like presentation ; in short, of a work of art that, as compared to the only one now known, shall be in truth " the Art-work of the Future " (*Kunstwerk der Zukunft*)—a work which only the *life of the future*, it is true, can enable us to produce. To prepare this art-work for the life of the future is the proper endeavor of the artist of the present ; and indeed, in this endeavor lies the security for the appearance of such a work in that life. Until it has become fully *living*, we have none of us reached our goal ; but when we have reached it in the production of this true art-work ; when what we have longed for stands completed, exercising its influence upon our emotions, our criticism, too, is at an end ; then we shall be released from the duties of critics to become artists and enjoyers of art ; and then, honored friend—then let your musical journal end—it dies, because the art-work lives !

Such an extraordinary, unprecedented, and yet (for our time) so *necessary* a task can, in my opinion, be performed by a musical periodical. It lies within its power to keep this task steadily in view ; within the power of its present and future editors to completely fulfil it. I am gladly prepared to place myself among these workers ; yet it is my strongest wish to learn that I shall be unnecessary to you. I can give assurance that I have done my best, in every way I had of proclaiming my sentiments, to build the way for the new school ; as well my purely artistic as my literary works will very possibly serve you and your collaborators for a while as material for the discussion and development of that school ; and thus I can claim to have done my part in advance for your periodical.

* * * * * * * * *

With the heartiest wish for the success of your undertaking in the new path, I commend myself to your always friendly consideration as, &c., &c.,

RICHARD WAGNER.

ZURICH, *January* 25, 1852.

11

THE
LEGEND OF THE NIBELUNGEN.

FROM the womb of night and of death there sprang a race, who dwelt in Nibelheim (Nebelheim, the place of mists), that is, in dim subterranean chasms and caves. They were called *Nibelungen;* like worms in a dead body, they swarmed in varying, restless activity, through the entrails of the earth; they wrought in metals—heated and purified them. Among them Alberich gained possession of the bright and beautiful gold of the Rhine—The Rheingold;—drew it up out of the depths of the waters, and made from it, with great and cunning art, a ring, which gave him power over all his race, the Nibelungen. Thus he became their master, and forced them thenceforth to labor for him alone; and so collected the inestimable treasure of the Nibelungen, the chief jewel of which was the Tarnhelm (helmet), by means of which one could assume any figure that he chose, and which Alberich had compelled his own brother, Reigin, to forge for him. Thus equipped, Alberich strove for the mastery of the world and all that was in it. The race of the giants—the insolent, the mighty, the primeval race, was disturbed in its savage ease; its enormous strength, its simple wit, were not enough to contend against Alberich's ambitious cunning. The giants saw with apprehension how the Nibelungen forged wondrous weapons, which, in the hands of human heroes, should bring about the ruin of the giant race. The race of the gods, rapidly rising to omnipotence, made use of this conflict. Wotan agreed with the giants that they should build for the gods a castle, from which they might order and rule the world in safety;

but after it was done the giants demanded the treasure of the Nibelungen as their reward. The great
cunning of the gods succeeded in the capture of Alberich, and he was compelled to give the treasure as
ransom for his life. The ring alone he sought to keep ;
but the gods knowing well that the secret of his
power lay in this, took the ring from him. Then he
laid a curse upon it, that it should prove the ruin of
all who should possess it. Wotan gave the treasure to
the giants ; but the ring he kept, to insure his own
omnipotence. The giants, however, forced it from
him by their threats, and Wotan yielded at the advice
of the three Fates (*Nornen*) who warned him of the
approaching downfall of the gods.

The giants left the treasure and the ring on the Gnita
plain (The plain of Discord) under the guardianship
of an enormous dragon. By means of the ring, however, the Nibelungen, with Alberich, were kept in slavery. But the giants did not understand how to make
use of their power. It was enough for their clumsy
ideas. to have once bound the Nibelungen. So the
dragon lay from time immemorial, watching with his
idle terrors over the treasure. The race of giants
faded and died away powerless before the new race of
gods ; the Nibelungen suffered on, wretched and ma-
licious in their fruitless activity. Alberich brooded
ceaselessly over the recovery of his ring. And now the
gods, in their high energy, regulated the world, controlled the elements by their wise laws, and devoted
themselves to the careful guardianship of the human
race. Their power ruled over all. Yet the peace
through which they held that power was not based
upon a reconciliation ; it was brought about by force
and deceit. The object of their high rule over the
world was a moral consciousness, but the wrong which
they had themselves wrought kept its hold upon them.

From the depths of Nibelheim the consciousness of
their wrong-doing rose up against them ; for the slav-

cry of the Nibelungen was not broken.   Alberich
had only been robbed of his mastery, and this not for
a high purpose ; and the soul and the freedom of the
Nibelungen lay buried uselessly beneath the body of
the idle dragon ; Alberich was right in his reproaches
against the gods.

But Wotan himself could not expiate the wrong
without committing a new injustice.   Only a free will
independent of the gods themselves, which could take
upon itself all the fault and do penance for it, had
it in its power to loose the enchantment ; and the gods
saw the capability of such a free will in man.   They
sought therefore to infuse their divinity into man,
that they might raise his strength so high that he, conscious of this power, might withdraw himself even
from the divine protection, in order to do, according to
his own will, what his mind suggested to him.   So
the gods educated men for this high purpose, to be
the expiators of their crime ; and their object was to be
attained when they had lost themselves in this human
creation—that is, when they must give up their direct
influence to the freedom of human consciousness.

And now mighty races of men, sprung from divine
seed, bloomed into being ; they steeled their strength
in strife and conflict ; Wotan's maidens watched over
them as guardian angels.   As Valkyres they led to
Walhalla those who had fallen in battle, there to continue in Wotan's companionship a glorious life of mar-
tial games.

But the right hero was still unborn, in whom independent strength should come to its full consciousness,
so that he should be able voluntarily, and with the
penance of death before his eyes, to call that boldest
deed his own.   At last this hero was to be born of
the race of the Volsungs.   Wotan blessed an unfruitful
marriage of this race by giving the wedded pair an
apple of Hulda to eat ; twins, Siegmund and Sieglinda, brother and sister, were the product of the mar-

riage. Siegmund took a wife, Sieglinda married a husband (Hunding); but both marriages remained unfruitful; and at length, to beget a true Volsung, the brother and sister themselves joined in wedlock. Hunding, Sieglinda's husband, discovered the crime, discarded his wife, and attacked Siegmund. Brunhilda the Valkyr aided Siegmund against the command of Wotan, who had decreed his destruction as a punishment for his sin. Siegmund had already, under Brunhilda's protection, drawn the sword which Wotan himself had given him, and was about to deal Hunding a deadly stroke, when the god. caught the blow upon his spear, against which the sword broke in two pieces. Siegmund fell. Brunhilda was punished by Wotan for her disobedience; he expelled her from the company of the Valkyres, and banished her to a barren rock where she, the divine virgin, should be given in marriage to the man who should find her there and wake her from the sleep into which Wotan had cast her. But she begged as a boon, that Wotan should surround the rock with the terrors of flame, that she might be certain that only the bravest of heroes could win her.

The banished Sieglinda, after a long pregnancy, brought forth in the wilderness Siegfried (him who through victory should bring peace). Reigin (Mime), Alberich's brother, hearing the cries of Sieglinda in her labor, went to her from his caves and helped her; after the birth she died, after having revealed to Reigin her fate, and confided to him the boy.

Reigin brought up Siegfried; he taught ‘him the arts of the smithy; told him of the death of his father; and procured for him the two pieces of the latter's broken sword, from which Siegfried, under Mime's direction, forged the sword Balmung. And now Mime urged the youth to the destruction of the dragon, telling him he would show his gratitude thereby. Siegfried, however, desired first to avenge the death of his father.   He sallied forth, attacked and killed Hunding, and not till then did he fulfil Mime's wish, and overcome and slay the giant dragon.

As he put his finger, heated with the dragon's blood, into his mouth to cool it, he involuntarily tasted of the blood, and by this means suddenly gained a knowledge of the language of the birds which were singing around him.   They praised Siegfried's wondrous deed,   pointed out to him the treasure of the Nibelungen in the dragon's cave, and warned him against Mime, who had only made use of him to gain the treasure, and who would now seek his life in order that he might possess that treasure alone.   Upon this Siegfried slew Mime and took from the treasure the ring and the helmet.   He then consulted the birds again, who counselled him to win for himself Brunhilda, the most beautiful of women.

Siegfried now again sallied forth and reached Brunhilda's rocky fortress, penetrated through the fire that raged around it, and awakened Brunhilda.   She joyfully recognized Siegfried, the noblest hero of the Volsung race, and yielded herself to him ; he wedded her with the ring of Alberich, which he placed upon her finger.   When the desire seized him of sallying forth to new feats, she communicated to him by her instructions her secret knowledge, and warned him of the dangers of treachery and faithlessness ; they swore truth to each other, and Siegfried left her.

A second race of heroes, also of divine origin, was that of the Gibichungen, on the Rhine.   Among them were Gunther, and Gudrun his sister.   Gunther's mother, Crimhilda, had once been ravished by Alberich, and she bore him a natural son, Hagen. As the desires and hopes of the *gods* rested upon Siegfried, Alberich based *his* hope of regaining the ring on Hagen, the hero whom he had begotten. Hagen was pale, serious, and gloomy ; his features hardened early ; he seemed older than he was.   Even

while he was a child, Alberich had secretly revealed to
him the knowledge of his father's fate and incited him
to strive after the ring. He was strong and powerful;
yet still he did not seem to Alberich mighty enough
to slay the dragon.

As Alberich was now powerless, he had not been
able to hinder his brother Mime, when the latter
sought to gain the treasure by means of Siegfried;
but now Hagen was to bring about Siegfried's ruin in
order to win from him at his death the ring. Hagen was
hostile to Gunther and Gudrun; they feared him, but
they esteemed his cunning and experience. The secret
of Hagen's wonderful birth, and the fact that he was
not his real brother, was known to Gunther; he had
once reproached Hagen with being a bastard. Gunther had been instructed by Hagen that Brunhilda
was of all women the most to be desired, and aroused
by him to a longing to possess her, when Siegfried
came among the Gibichungen on the Rhine. Gudrun,
inspired with love for Siegfried by the praise which
Hagen had lavished upon him, gave Siegfried, by
Hagen's advice, a goblet of welcome prepared through
Hagen's art in such a way that it caused Siegfried to
forget his life with Brunhilda, and his espousal with
her. Siegfried sought Gudrun for his wife, and Gunther
consented on condition that he should aid him to gain
Brunhilda. Siegfried agreed to this; they swore an
oath of brotherhood to one another, from which Hagen,
however, held himself aloof. Siegfried and Gunther
entered upon their journey, and arrived at Brunhilda's
rock-fortress; Gunther remained in their ship, and
Siegfried for the first and only time made use of his
power as ruler of the Nibelungen, by putting on the
helmet and assuming by its aid the figure and appearance of Gunther. So he penetrated through the
flames to Brunhilda. She, already robbed of her
maidenhood by Siegfried, had also given up her superhuman power; all her wisdom she had given over to

Siegfried, who made no use of it; now she was powerless as any ordinary woman, and could make only a
fruitless resistance to the new, bold suitor; he seized
from her the ring, with which she was now to be es-
poused to Gunther, and forced her into a room where
he slept by her side during the night, but, to her surprise, with his sword lying between them.   In the
morning he brought her to the ship, where he permitted the real Gunther to take his place unremarked
by her side ; and he transported himself by the
powers of the helmet at once to the Gibichenburg on
the Rhine.   Gunther reached his home upon the Rhine
with Brunhilda, who followed him in gloomy silence ;
Siegfried, at Gudrun's side, and Hagen, received them
when they arrived.

Brunhilda was filled with rage when she saw Siegfried as Gudrun's husband ; his cold, friendly indifference toward her filled her with amazement ; but she
guessed the treachery that had been wrought against
him, and demanded the ring which did not belong to
him, but which Gunther had received from her ; he
refused it.   She demanded of Gunther that he should
take the ring from Siegfried ; Gunther was perplexed
and hesitated.   Brunhilda asked—did Siegfried then
receive the ring from her ?   But Siegfried, who recognized the ring, said, " I received it from no
woman ; my own strength won it from the giant
dragon ; by it I am the ruler of the Nibelungen, and
I will give up its power to no man."   Hagan stepped
between them and asked Brunhilda whether she
certainly recognized the ring ?   If it was her ring,
then Siegfried might have become possessed of it by
treachery, and it could only belong to Gunther her
husband.   Brunhilda cried out with indignation at the
trick that had been played upon her, and a terrible
thirst for revenge against Siegfried filled her soul.
She cried out to Gunther that he had been betrayed
by Siegfried ;—" I am not married to thee, but to

this man; he received my favors." Siegfried reproached her with falsehood; declared that he had been
true to his oath of brotherhood—that he had laid his
sword between Brunhilda and himself; he demanded
of her that she should bear witness to this. Purposely,
and aiming solely at his ruin, she would not understand him; she declared that he lied, and falsely appealed to his sword Balmung, that she had seen hang-
ing quietly on the wall while he lay lovingly by her
side.

The men and Gudrun besought Siegfried to repel
the accusation if he could, and Siegfried swore a solemn oath in confirmation of what he had said. Brunhilda accused him of perjury; he had sworn so many
oaths to her and Gunther, she said, that he had
broken. Now he swore to a perjury to strengthen a
lie. All was in a furious excitement. Siegfried cried
out to Gunther to restrain his wife, who so shamelessly
maligned her own and her husband's honor; he himself departed with Gudrun into their chamber.

Gunther, in the deepest shame and wretchedness,
seated himself apart and covered his face; and Hagen
approached Brunhilda, who was consumed by the
most fearful rage. He offered himself as the avenger
of her honor; but she laughed at him, as powerless to
conquer Siegfried; a single glance from his glowing
eyes, such as had shone upon her even through his
deceitful disguise, would break Hagen's courage. Then
Hagen said he knew Siegfried's mighty strength full
well;—that she must tell him, therefore, how he was to
be overcome. She, who had hallowed Siegfried, and
had secured him, by secret charms, against wounds,
advised Hagen that he must strike him in the back; for
that as she knew the hero would never turn his back
to his foes, she had not made that also enchanted.

Gunther was informed of the plan of murder. They
called upon him to avenge his honor, and Brunhilda
covered him with accusations of cowardice and treach-

11*

cry, until at last he acknowledged his fault, and the
necessity of ending his shame by Siegfried's death.
Yet he was filled with horror at the thought of being
guilty of breach of his oath of brotherhood. Brunhilda scoffed at him bitterly; what breaches of faith
had not been committed against *her?* And Hagen
urged him on by the prospect of gaining the Nibelun-
gen-ring, which Siegfried would let go at his death.
At last Gunther consented; Hagen planned a hunt for
the next day, when Siegfried should be attacked; perhaps his murder could be concealed from even Gudrun. Gunther was anxious on her account, for Brunhilda's thirst for revenge was sharpened by jealousy of
her.—Thus Siegfried's death was decided on.

Siegfried now appeared with Gudrun in the hall,
brilliantly arrayed, and invited them to a sacrifice and
the marriage feast. The conspirators obeyed with
hypocritical readiness, and Siegfried and Gudrun rejoiced at the apparent restoration of peace.

On the following morning, Siegfried, following
the game, wandered into a lonely rocky defile on the
Rhine. Three water-sprites suddenly rose from the
flood before him; they were the wise daughters of those
depths from which Alberich had once taken the clear
Rhine-gold, to make from it his mighty mystic ring.
The curse and the power of this ring would be forever
at an end, if it should be given back to the waters, and
thus dissolved again in its original pure element. The
water-sprites longed for the ring, and besought Siegfried to give it to them; but he refused it. (He had
taken upon himself, while sinless, the sin of the gods,
and now he brought the penance of their wrong upon
himself by his pride and unyielding spirit.)

The sprites told him of the evil and the curse connected with the ring; he must cast it into the waters,
or he would not outlive the day. But Siegfried said
"you shall not cheat me of my power, ye cunning
women; I care not a hair for the curse or for your

threats. What my own courage suggests to me is my
first law ; and what I do according to my own beliefs,
that is decided for me. You may call this curse or
blessing, but I shall obey it, and shall not strive
against my own power." Then the women asked
him—"Willst thou surpass the gods ?"

And he said, "If you would show me the way to
overcome the gods, I would fight against them with
all my courage. I know three wiser women than you ;
and they know how the gods will some day be in bitter straits. It must be the care of those devoted to
the gods, to see that I then fight on their side.
Therefore I laugh at your threats ; the ring remains
mine,—and thus I cast life behind me," and he took
up a clod of earth and threw it backward over his
head.

Then the women made sport of Siegfried, who
thought himself as strong and wise as he was really
blind and dependent.

"He has broken his oath, though he knows it not ;
he has lost a thing of higher value than the ring,
though he knows it not ; runes and enchantments
have been taught him, and he has forgotten them.
Farewell, Siegfried ! We know a proud woman who
will have the ring to-day, when thou art slain. Let
us turn to her ! She will give us a better hearing !"

Siegfried looked laughing after them, as they floated
singing away, and cried, "If I were not true to Gudrun, I would have captured one of you !" Then he
heard his companions in the hunt approaching, and
wound his horn ; and the hunters, Gunther and Hagen
at their head, assembled about him. They took their
hunters' meal ; and Siegfried, in merry mood, made
sport of himself on account of his fruitless hunt ;—only
water-game had offered itself to him, for hunting which
he was unfortunately unprepared ;—otherwise, he
would have brought to his companions three wild
water-birds, who had prophesied to him that he would

die this very day.   Hagen, drinking, tc...
and asked him if he really understood ...
speech of the birds ?

Gunther was gloomy and silent, and 5 ...
to cheer him, relating in songs the sto ...
his adventure with Mime, his slaying ...
and how it came about that he unde...
of the birds.   In the remembrance wh...
to him he suddenly recollected the a...
had given him to seek out Brunhild...
gone to the flaming rock and awakene...
membrance grew clearer and clear...
Suddenly two ravens flew swiftly above his head.
Hagen interrupted him ;—" What do those ravens tell
thee ? "   Siegfried sprang quickly up; and Hagen
said, " I understood them that they hasten to announce thy coming to Wotan."   With that he thrust
his spear into Siegfried's back.

Gunther, guessing by Siegfried's story the truth of
his incomprehensible relations with Brunhilda, and suddenly recognizing from it Siegfried's innocence, had
seized Hagen's arm to save the hero, but without being
able to avert the stroke.   Siegfried raised his shield to
dash down Hagen with it, but his strength failed him,
and he sank groaning to the earth.   Hagen had
turned away ; Gunther and his men gathered sympa-
thizing and agitated about Siegfried, when he opened
λ his eyes once more and cried—" Brunhilda ! Brunhilda ! thou glorious child of Wotan ! How fair and
bright thou comest to me ! Thou saddlest thy steed,
smiling gravely and solemnly, thy steed that strides
dripping with dew through the heavens.   Thou guidest
his course toward me—for here there is a hero for thy
choosing !   O happy I, whom thou dost cherish as thy
husband !   Lead me now to Valhalla that I may drink
there, to the honor of all heroes, the mead thou offerest
me, thou glorious handmaid—the mead of the Great
Father !   Brunhilda ! Brunhilda ! I greet thee ! "

s   upon
w   olemn

ƒ   ibech-
r   on the
1   udrun
ɔ   d slain
u   v her-
h   ers of

pure and free ; for only he, the noble one, has had me to wife."

Then she had a funeral pyre built upon the bank to burn Siegfried's body; no horse, no slave was to be sacrificed with him ; she alone would offer her body to the gods in his honor.   But first she took possession of her inheritance ; the helmet should be burned with him, but the ring she herself put on.

And she said :—"Thou hero overbold, how didst thou hold me bound to thee ! I told thee all my knowledge ; thee, a mortal—and so I had to part with my own wisdom.   But thou madest no use of it—thou trustedst to thyself alone. And now that thou must needs give it up in death, my knowledge comes back to me, and I know again the runes of this ring.   I know too, the runes of the primal law, the old utterance of the Fates ! Hear then, ye glorious gods, your wrong is expiated ! Thank him, the hero, who took your fault upon himself!   He gave it into my hand to end the work ; the slavery of the Nibelungen is abolished—the ring shall bind them no more ! yet Alberich shall not receive it ; he shall enslave you no longer ; but he himself shall be as free as you.   For I give this ring to you, wise sisters of the watery depths ; the flame that burns me, shall purify the evil treasure. Dissolve it and keep it harmless—the Rhinegold that was stolen from you, that slavery and wrong might be forged from it !   Thou only, Father of all, shalt reign ! That thy power may be eternal, I lead him to thee ! Receive him nobly—he is worthy of it ! "

And amid solemn songs, Brunhilda mounted Siegfried's funeral pyre.   Gudrun bent in bitter grief over the murdered Gunther.   The flames rose above Siegfried and Brunhilda ; suddenly they streamed up in brightest lustre, and above a dark cloud of smoke arose a glory, in which Brunhilda, armed and mounted upon her steed as a Valkyr, led Siegfried by the hand.

At the same moment the waves of the Rhine rose to

the entrance of the hall ; the three water-spirits bore
away upon them the helmet and the ring. Hagen
rushed madly toward them to tear the treasure from
them ; but they seized him and bore him with them to
the depths below.

THE
OPERA HOUSE AT BAYREUTH.

— • • • —

I.

THE CIRCUMSTANCES LEADING TO ITS INCEPTION, AND TO THE FORMATION OF WAGNER-ASSOCIATIONS (WAGNER-VEREINE).*

THE kind reader has seen from the closing passages of the preface to my trilogy,† the hopeless mood which finally suggested to me the adoption of a course with regard to the completed parts of my musical composition, which was not much more consoling than that I had adopted when I sacrificed the poem itself as a purely literary product. If I extracted from my scores and carefully arranged a few fragments for a concert performance, I thought I might flatter myself, as in the case of my edition of the poem, with the idea that it was not altogether impossible to succeed by this method in attracting the necessary at-

---

* This account of the difficulties which he encountered in endeavoring to secure a production of the " Ring of the Nibelungen " (his great trilogy), is given by Wagner under the following title : " Bayreuth. I. Schlussbericht über die Umstände und Schicksale welche die Ausführung des Bühnenfestspieles ' der Ring des Nibelungen,' bis zur Gründung von Wagner-Vereinen begleiteten." It has been thought best to replace this long title by the briefer and equally intelligible one given above.— TRANSLATOR.

† Printed in the sixth volume of the German edition of Wagner's collected works, but not included in this translation.—TR.

tention to my work and the theories connected with
it. And indeed, it was surprising to see these fragments of a music which had come into being, unlike any
other in the world, solely with a view to a great dramatic whole, accepted by the public, even when they came
to them in this wretched way, with the most lively applause ; it was an experience that might have seemed,
looking at it fairly, to confirm with extraordinary
force the hitherto accepted view,—that in the plan of
my work I had completely fallen into the chaos of
obscurity and impossibility. But still the general
opinion prevailed that it was best to have nothing to
do with me.

Under such impressions my frame of mind at last
reached such a point that I felt compelled to undertake
something which should take me out of the atmosphere of all wishes, hopes, imaginings, and especially
efforts, in behalf of my great work. So I planned the
" Meistersinger von Nürnberg." But a small part of
the musical composition of this new work was finished,
however, when the prince whom I besought fate to
send to me,* really entered into my life's affairs.

No poetic diction, not even a whole poetic diction-
ary, could contain a phrase fit to describe the beauty
of the experience which suddenly, at the call of a
noble, thoughtful king, now began in my existence.
For it was truly a king who cried to me in my chaos :
—*" Come ! Finish thy work ! I wish it ! "*

The remote future, if my work should live till then,
cannot be prevented from learning the circumstances
which, from that decisive event until now, have hindered my work from becoming an accomplished
fact. It seemed as though, as soon as I was placed
with my artistic purpose in the full light of publicity, all the opposition to it that had hitherto

---

* In the passage of the preface to the " Nibelungen," referred to above.
—Tr.

nursed itself in secret, was to break forth with its full hostile power. It seemed as though there were no interest, among all those represented in our press and our society, which the carrying out of my work and the plan of its performance did not oppose in the most destructive manner. In order to evade the shameless direction which was taken by this hostility, proceeding from every sphere of society and directed against the patron as well as the protégé, I thought it incumbent upon me to tone down the conspicuous and vigorous character of the undertaking as it had at first been boldly conceived, and so to bring the matter into a state in which it would be able to conceal those of its characteristics which had drawn down the general rage upon it. I even sought to distract public attention from it altogether, by devoting some hardly gained leisure to finishing the score of my "Meistersinger," in order that I might show myself, by this work, to be apparently quite in accord with the ordinary course in theatrical matters.

But the lessons which I derived from the fate of this work (which was favorably received by the public), and my experience of the spirit of our German stage, decided me to entirely refrain from all further relations of any kind with the latter. The peculiar character of German art-ideas, so far as they express themselves in the public taste in theatrical matters, must make it manifest to any one of even the slightest critical ability, as soon as he came into any direct connection with the stage, that all his efforts for the improvement of that stage, in so far as he seeks the support of an energetic popular opinion to aid him, must be in vain, and can only excite indignation against him. And for this reason it remained impossible for me to persuade myself to take any further part in the efforts which I had myself begun (yielding to the storm), to have some detached parts of my great work performed. Even the result of these attempts has never been

stated to me in detail ; for my friends knew that I desired to be spared its recital.

But the very sacrifice that I have here described,
made it possible for me to obey the first words of my
noble benefactor—"complete your work." I had
gained anew that quiet shelter, far from every sound,
from which I had once looked out into the silent alpine
region,* as I formed my stupendous scheme, and began the execution of that which I was now permitted
to finish.

The strong and faithful protection which now watched
over the carrying out of my work, is the same which
made it possible for me to enter hopefully and trust-
fully upon the path which should bring my completed
composition to its originally-intended performance, in
the fullest sense. For if one class opposed the noble
decision of the single power that protected me, I
could now, with the work that had been completed
under the shelter of that power, turn to an entirely
different class, to which I could fully entrust it and the
possibility of its performance.

To this end I came forward with a "Communication
and Appeal to the Friends of my Art," † which I began with an explanation of my plan, such as was laid
down in the preface before referred to ; and I added
to it the following more accurate sketch of the character of my undertaking, and of the advantages which I
believed might be gained from it, for the German stage
in general.

" I have already sufficiently pointed out, in my explanation of my earlier plan, that under the peculiar
circumstances in which I found myself placed with my
principal work, I especially desired to secure an absolutely correct performance of it, inasmuch as it seemed

---

* See AUTOBIOGRAPHY, p. 23.—TRANSLATOR.
† *Mittheilung und Aufforderung an die Freunde meiner Kunst.*

to me the most lamentable feature of the modern stage, that all the performances that it brings before the public, with perhaps the exception of the lowest class, suffer under the cardinal sin of *incorrectness*. The reason for this has been several times pointed out by me in other places than this, and I will only speak of it here as lying in the lack of *originality* of our theatrical productions. That our theatrical perform- ances are only imperfect and often entirely distorted imitations of non-German dramatic art, can by no means be concealed by the fact that even our German authors are all imitators of foreign models in the con- ception as well as the style of their dramatic composi- tions. Whoever knows anything of our stage, must derive from this fact a false impression of theatric art in general,—an impression which leads, with really cul- tured people, to a contempt for it, and with the great and less critical theatrical public to a degradation of taste, the reaction of which upon the spirit of the stage forces this latter to a still greater lowness of tone.

" The only practicable way in which our stage can be even gradually improved, seems to me to be this :— that works which, on account of their very originality, require the greatest accuracy of detail in their produc- tion, in order to make the proper impression upon the public, shall not at present be committed to this stage, since it cannot assimilate to their tone without greatly lowering it, and making it practically unintelligible. But on the other hand such works *might* be made ex- ceedingly useful to our authors if performed outside of this stage and beyond its injurious influence, thus showing them, by perfect accuracy and unmixed purity, universally understood models of what was before unintelligible to them.

" The German stage cannot be helped by the mere laying down of artistic principles ; for the stage, in whatever condition it is, has become a *habit* with the people, and is therefore a power. Its errors are based upon its whole organization, which has established itself among us—a faulty imitation of foreign matter, like our French fashions in dress. If then we must confess ourselves too weak to contend against its existence, we must look to an entirely new institution, as far as possible withdrawn from the influence of the theatre, if we really have at heart the development of the true, essential German spirit in this branch of art—so incomparably powerful in its influence upon the public mind.

" My own difficulty suggested to me the conception of the leading features of such an institution. It would be in complete accord with the German nature, now developing itself politically in the newly-restored German Empire ; for the forces exerted in it would always belong to parts of a great whole. It should offer nothing more than a common place for the periodical meeting of the best theatrical strength of Germany, for the practice and performance of their art in a high and truly original German style, such as it cannot be made possible for them to attain in the ordinary round of their daily duties.

" In regard to the possibility of theatrical performances carried out in this sense, I relied especially upon the appreciation which my own dramatic works had met with among the German public ; for I assume that such appreciation would be extended in a still greater degree to my greatest work, if I declare that this is composed in a style the correctness of which I could only expect to prove by so correct a theatrical presentation as could only be secured by the carrying out of the plan I have proposed. I count with confidence upon a corresponding result, not of my work as such, but of the complete correctness of its performances, and I assume that this result would first show itself in a desire for the periodical repetition of similar performances, for which (and perhaps this might extend to all branches of dramatic art) only such works

should be selected as seem to be entitled by the originality of their conception and the true German nature
of their style, to a peculiarly accurate theatrical representation.

"As I have expressed myself more fully elsewhere
on the salutary and in every way beneficial results of
such an undertaking, if it should prove successful, I
will only indicate here the way in which it seems to
me that the project, destined to be gradually extended,
can be practically carried out.

"In the first place, I believe that I may appeal to
the energetic support of true friends of my art, by
asking them to give me the assurance of their aid in
the attainment of my object—a performance of my
great trilogy. I now formally request them to make
themselves known to me, by simply announcing to
me their favorable disposition toward my undertaking.
If I am so fortunate as to gain in this way a satisfactory hope of success, a simple plan will be suggested
to those who have announced themselves as friends of
my scheme, by which they will be enabled, as an or-
ganized society with a common aim, to make themselves patrons of and participants in the performances
I have in view. I should still venture to attribute to
this scheme, based upon a voluntary union of its supporters, the character of a truly national undertaking
in a high sense, even if friends of my art *outside* Germany should announce to me their support of the
plan ; for I may assume that, considering the great
attention now paid by cultured foreigners to the spirit
of German art in this branch, the purity and originality of its development are matters of great importance,
if the expectations of its beneficial influence formed
in other countries are to be fulfilled. At the same
time all this tends to benefit that which must be so important to us in the best *national* sense.

"If this first undertaking should be carried out, on
the basis of a voluntary union of its supporters, to the

immediate object indicated—that of a successful result, and one which I imagine would be very instructive as to the fate of my further schemes—then the plan would need to be considered of establishing, from this isolated project, a really national art-institution. As I have already given my views of the character and influence of such an institution, and especially of the differences between this and our existing stage, the only point now needing to be established is the belief that this in turn could be best accomplished by a union of all, or at least of the specially endowed, German theatres.

" If I entirely disregarded this point as far as the attainment of my *immediate* object was concerned, I did so from the well-founded knowledge that in the present state of the theatres and their directors, any appeal I might make to them would lead, at the best, only to the greatest misconceptions, and as a result of these, to a hopeless complication. Only the influence which I can look for from a successful result of my undertaking, could have a sufficiently enlightening effect here ; and of course a favorable influence could only be exerted upon the theatres by the permanent institution I have suggested, if that institution should be finally founded and supported by *the theatres themselves*.

" To lay down the right basis for such action, might then become the serious task of an imperial official, busied with the elevation of the national morality in its highest sense. For it is certain that the public morality can be easily judged by the character of the public art of a nation ; and no art has so powerful an effect upon the fancy and spirit of a people as the theatrical representations daily presented to it. Even if we have a doubt as to whether the very questionable influence of the German stage has been brought about through the condition of the nation's morality, and even if we desire to look upon the result of that influence hitherto as a mere misleading of the public taste, it may nevertheless be positively asserted that an ennobling of that taste, and of the morals necessarily influenced by it, can be most energetically directed and supported by the stage. And to have called the attention of the nation's leaders to these considerations, would not be the smallest part. of the satisfaction which I could receive from a successful result of the undertaking which I have herewith announced."

Although I consider that I expressed myself sufficiently clearly in the preceding notice, in regard to the importance I attributed to the undertaking in aid of which I appealed to the friends of my art, yet I desire now to more carefully point out the characteristics which I attributed to that " other class " to which I referred before.

Permit me first of all to repeat from my account of the fate of my " Nibelungen," a phrase in which I endeavored to explain my decision, in every subsequent art-undertaking, to turn for support from Paris to Germany. I said :—" It was my knowledge of the unexampled confusion and hopelessness of the Parisian art element, which sharpened my view of the secret that lay at the root of this." This " secret," in part existing clearly and truly in my own mind, has to be partly sought in that same demoralized public element, in order to make it as clear as that of which I was myself conscious. It was a great delight to me, after despairing endeavors which brought me into some singular relations, to recognize this secret as the true essence of the German spirit (*das wahre Wesen des deutschen Geistes*). Among perplexities of every kind I was forced to come to the decision that the repulsive shape in which this spirit exposed itself to popular criticism, was a complete distortion of it, and that it appeared so ill—in many respects so laughable—in its present guise, might be taken, on more careful examination, as an evidence of its original high character.

History teaches us for what a noble gain the German sacrificed his outward independence during more than two whole centuries. That for two whole centuries he was only known as " a German " among the nations of Europe, by the lack of independence shown in his outward bearing and by the awkwardness and even ludicrousness of his public behavior,—this fact is less ⬛⬛ considering the wretched circum⬛⬛ life, than if he had worn the garb ⬛⬛ with a grace and ease that would ⬛⬛ ecognizable in it,—as the Pole has ⬛⬛ f French culture. · It could be seen ⬛⬛ reeable characteristics of his social ⬛⬛ l character was not involved in ⬛⬛ as only manifested in what was ⬛⬛ as a distorted form. But not to ⬛⬛ nce of the pitiable distortion, re⬛⬛ ong a faith as the Christian has to ⬛⬛ o the illusions of the world. It ⬛⬛ at inspired a German statesman of ⬛⬛ rage to reveal to the world by his ⬛⬛ at he knew to be the secret of the ⬛⬛ ngth. The secret of the revelation ⬛⬛ contribute, consists in the fact that ⬛⬛ erman has a national type of *art*, ⬛⬛ f esteem.

⬛⬛ n the strength of this secret force ⬛⬛ ty of bringing it to light, required ⬛⬛ than that statesman needed, who ⬛⬛ te accurately the long-treasured art spirit embodied in an organization almost as strong as that in which the statesman found the military strength of the country.

What was most difficult and painful to overcome in the conflict in the case of the artist, was that in this very sphere (the nature of which I have sufficiently indicated) the corruption of the German art-spirit had extended not only to the æsthetic perception and judgment, and the disposition most receptive of such influences, but even to the *moral* sense of all those who shared in the gain received from this corruption. An art which no one of those practising it really understands and loves for itself, must diffuse, in all its contact with the public life, an atmosphere of frivolity which, the further the influence of such an art extends, poisons more and more widely all which it touches.

Where was I to look, then, among the deeply-seated forces of our elaborately and powerfully-organized social life, for the secret force which corresponded to that which I believed in? It would seem impossible to allow the statesman any influence here. We should soon see how frivolous and ludicrous everything in this matter appears, if we should imagine that one of our parliaments could discuss it. Those who, after their exertions in affairs of state,

"In Ruh' was gutes speisen wollen," *

can hardly be expected to see that everything in this department, too, is in as disgraceful a condition as were German politics before their great upheaval. We are only sorry that the gentlemen should find such bad and unnutritious dishes; but if we toil and make every sacrifice to furnish their table well for once, we cannot prevent their enjoying the bad to-morrow with as much zest as they show in the enjoyment of the

---

* " Want to enjoy a good meal in peace— " i. e., like to take their pleasure, (in the theatre, to which Wagner is referring,) without having that also a matter of work.—TRANSLATOR.

good to-day. It is this that disgusts us, and finally induces us to leave their dishes to the scullions.

Since I had to seek the German nature in its more
ideal side, the artist-world was more fitting for my
purpose than the great public. Here I could proceed
from the nature of the actual musician, and find encouragement and delight in the fact that he showed
such a capacity for grasping so quickly that which was
correct, as soon as it was intelligibly shown him.
Nearly in the same position, though involved in far
more destructive habits, I found the musical-actor
(*den musikalishen Mimen*), who, if really talented,
recognizes and readily enters the true sphere of his
art, as soon as the true examples it presents are properly set before him.

The view I had formed, then, that intelligent appreciation would not fail in the excellent performances of
the artists who must actually take part in my plan,
was based on these encouraging characteristics I found
in them. But a further necessary task which I must
undertake, consisted in awakening a similar hope of
such satisfactory attainment, among all those whose
assistance I needed in the accomplishment of my design. If, by all the exertions I have made in furnish-
ing examples of worthy artistic performances, and by
the explanation of problems which have become clear
to me, I have gained the active attention of a sufficient part of the German public to render my purpose
attainable—then I must recognize in this portion of
the public that new class which I needed to discover.
This class would then become the nucleus of that of
which I had conceived ; not confined to any special
order in society, but penetrating all ranks, it would
represent in my eyes the active, receptive element in
German feeling, appreciative of every manifestation of
the German nature in that branch of art which has
hitherto been abandoned to the most anti-German influences.

THE
OPERA HOUSE AT BAYREUTH.

II.

In the invitation I published some time ago, calling on the lovers of my art to join in my projected enterprise, I addressed to a general public, personally unknown to me, a question, the answer to which I awaited for my own instruction.

Only to a few of my more intimate friends did I make known, in any detail, my more definite views as to how the public interest in my enterprise was to take shape. The youngest of these friends, the unusually gifted and energetic Karl Tausig, seized the opportunity which here presented itself as setting before him a personally agreeable task. In co-operation with a lady of high rank, an earnest and thoughtful patron of my art, he drew up a plan for gaining the requisite number of parlors for my enterprise. He proposed to place at our disposal, by the sale of patronage shares of 300 thalers each, the sum of 300,000 thalers, which appeared necessary for the erection of a provisional theatre, an improved arrangement of the stage, and the procuring of perfect scenery, as also for the remuneration of the select artists who should be engaged in the performances. Hardly had he entered on the line of action marked out for himself, when premature death removed him from our midst in the thirtieth year of his age. My last word to him I had to inscribe upon his tomb : it will not be out of place to repeat it here.

EPITAPH ON KARL TAUSIG.

It was thy lot, thy daring choice, to gather
　Life's slow-grown fruit ere hasty spring was o'er ;
'Twas early ripe—but ripe for death ; so rather
　Must we thy lot, thy daring choice deplore.

Profoundly perplexed as I was now, my former question to a " General Public " became now a question
addressed to Fate.
The little circle of my friends, now so painfully nar-
rowed, toiled on unmoved in the path indicated by the
deceased. A personage of the highest rank was gained
as a patron, and unexpectedly there was manifested an
active interest on the part of those in less exalted station, and even of those of no official station, with a view
to materially assisting me by forming an association.
At Mannheim, a specially ardent lover of my art and of
my theories, who down to that time had been personally unknown to me, backed by his associates who
were equally well disposed, founded a society for the
promotion of the enterprise announced by me, and
this society, regardless of the derision this act called
forth, boldly assumed the name of " The Richard Wagner Society." Their example found imitators. In
Vienna a second society was formed, which assumed
the same name, and similar societies soon sprang up in
one German city after another. Nay, beyond the
German frontiers, in Pesth, Brussels, London, finally
in New York, societies with the same tendencies and
bearing the same name arose, and sent me greeting
and encouragement.
It now appeared to me that the time had come for
making the needful preparations for executing my
project. As early as the spring of 1871, I had quietly
and unnoticed had my eye upon Bayreuth, the place I
have chosen for my purpose. The idea of using the
Margravian Opera House was abandoned so soon as

I saw its interior construction. But yet the peculiar character of that kindly town and its site so answered my requirements that during the wintry latter part of the autumn of the same year I repeated my visit—this time however to treat directly with the city authorities. I need not here say how deeply indebted I am to the worthy, honored men, whose hospitable overtures secured to my enterprise a genial soil in which it will flourish as long as my own life endures. An unsurpassably beautiful and eligible plot of ground at no great distance from the town was given me, on which to erect the proposed theatre. Having come to an understanding as to its erection, with a man of approved inventive genius, and of rare experience in the interior arrangement of theatres, we could then entrust to an architect of equal acquaintance with theatrical building the further planning and the erection of the provisional structure. And despite the great difficulties which attended the arrangements for putting under way so unusual an undertaking, we made such progress that the laying of the corner-stone could be announced to our patrons and friends for May 22, 1872.

Then it occurred to me to present the assembled patrons, as an artist's return for the pains they were at in meeting at Bayreuth, as perfect an execution as was possible of the ninth symphony of Beethoven. My simple invitation to the most prominent orchestras and Sängerchors, as well as to the most celebrated artists, sufficed to bring together such a number of excellent performers as perhaps never before met on a similar occasion.

In this first success no one could fail to recognize a highly encouraging omen for the future prosperity of the grand theatrical performances themselves. Indeed so excellent was the effect produced upon the minds of those who had participated in the entertainment, that not even the unfavorable state of the weather, which interfered with the ceremony of laying the corner-stone, could check the flow of their spirits. In the box which was to be enclosed in the corner-stone, I placed besides a dedication to the exalted protector of my best efforts, and several appropriate documents, a few verses of my own composing :

> I bury here a secret deep,
> For centuries long to lie concealed ;
> Yet while this stone its trust shall keep,
> To all the secret stands revealed.

To the meeting I made the following address :
FRIENDS AND HONORED PATRONS :—By your favor I stand to-day where never artist stood before me. You believe in my vocation to found for Germans a theatre of their own, and you place in my hands the means of erecting this theatre in actual, material form before your eyes. The provisional building of which we lay the corner-stone to-day, is, for the beginning at least, to serve this purpose. When we come together here again, this structure shall greet your eyes, and in its characteristic peculiarities you will at once read the history of the thought which it embodies. You will find here an outer shell formed of the poorest material, which will best recall to your minds the hastily adorned halls, which from time to time used to be erected in German cities for the meetings of singing societies and other similar occasions, and which were taken down again after the festival was over. But the enduring element of this building will become clearer to you as soon as you enter its interior.

Here, too, you will first observe the extreme poorness of the material and the entire absence of ornamentation; you will perhaps even miss with surprise the simple decorations with which festival halls used to be beautified. But then, in the proportions and arrangements of the hall itself and the auditorium, you will find a thought expressed which will establish between yourselves and the play you came to sec, a new relation very different from that which previously existed. Should this effect be simply and completely produced, then the mysterious entrance of the music will prepare you for the unveiling and plain exposition of scenic paintings, which, appearing to come out of an ideal world of dreams, will acquaint you with the full reality of the ingenious deceptions whereof the art of painting is capable. Here nothing will even provisionally speak to you with mere hints ; so far as is permitted by the artistic possibilities of the times, the most perfect representation will be set before you in scenic as in mimic play.

This has been my plan ; and it puts all that portion of our building which I called the enduring element, into that part of it designed to produce the completest possible illusion. If I entertain any expectation of successfully executing this artistic design, my sole inspiration has been a hope which sprang from the midst of despair itself. My confidence is in the genius of the German people, and that genius I expect to see manifested even in those phases of our life wherein, as in our art, it has languished most pitiably. Above all I have faith in the genius of German music, knowing as I do how brilliantly it manifests itself in our musicians whenever it is aroused by the summons of the German Master. I have faith in our actors and singers, knowing as I do that they would, as it were, be animated with a new life when the German Master summoned them away from the vain trifling of an art whose only aim is amusement, and placed before their minds the true ideal of their high calling. I have faith in our artists—and this I may well say to-day when so many distinguished artists are assembled here from every quarter of the Fatherland, in compliance with my simple friendly invitation. While all these, oblivious of self in the delight inspired by a masterpiece of art, execute to-day as a festive greeting the wonderful symphony of our great Beethoven, we all may say that the structure whose foundations are this day to be laid, will be no delusive castle in the air, even if we artists can do no more than vouch for the truth of the idea to be embodied in it.

But to whom shall I now turn, in order to insure for this ideal work its permanence, and for the stage its monumental home ?

Of late our undertaking has been spoken of as the building of the "National Theatre at Bayreuth." I cannot accept this title as correct. Where is the "Nation" that builds this theatre ? When a little while ago the question of state support of the great Parisian theatres was debated in the French Assembly, the orators believed that it was their duty to advocate warmly the continuance and even increase of their subsidy, on the ground that the maintenance of these theatres was a duty they owed not only to France but to Europe, which received the laws of its mental culture from the French. Fancy the perplexity and confusion of a German parliament were a similar question to arise. The discussion would probably lead to the pleasant discovery that our theatres have no need of national support, the French National Assembly having already provided for all their wants. At best our theatre would be treated as but a few years ago the German Empire would have been treated in our various local parliaments—viz., as a chimera.

Even if I had in my mind the idea of the true German stage, I should have to confess that it were hopeless for me to go before the nation to advocate my idea. Perhaps some will say that while one man may fail to inspire confidence, an association may succeed, and that success would be insured if an immense joint-stock company were formed, which should commission an architect to build somewhere a splendid theatre, to which should be boldly given the title "German National Theatre," in the expectation that very

12*

soon a German national histrionic art would be spon-
taneously developed. The whole world nowadays
firmly believes in a continuous progress, so called,
which in our own times is supposed to be specially
active—but no one appears to have any clear idea as
to the direction in which we are progressing. On the
other hand, those who have really brought into the
world something new have never been asked as to
their relations to this progressive environment, which
set up hindrances and obstacles in their way. We will
not on this festive occasion recall the outspoken complaints, nay, the profound despondency of our greatest minds, whose work has pointed out the one path
of true progress; still you will permit me, to whom
to-day you pay such distinguished honor, to say how
grateful I am that my individual project has been appreciated and heartily adopted by a host of friends, as
your presence here to-day testifies.

To you alone, lovers of my special art and of my
most distinctive work, could I look for encouragement
in carrying out my project; only upon you could I call
for assistance in my work. To bring this work simply and fairly before the minds of those who have
been favorably disposed toward my art, though hitherto they could contemplate it only in a faulty and distorted representation — such was my desire, and I
thought I could make it known to you without presumption. And in this my almost personal relation
to you, my patrons and friends, do I even now recognize the groundwork upon which we are to lay the
foundation-stone which shall support the entire edifice
of our most exalted hopes for Germany. True, for the
present, this structure will be but provisional—but so
for centuries was the whole outer form of German life.
But it is a characteristic of German life that it builds
from within; the everlasting God lives within it long before He raises from it the temple of His glory. And
this temple will be in just so far a manifestation of the

spirit within, as it is consistent with it in its rich originality. Hence I will regard this stone as the magic
stone which has the power of revealing the hidden
mysteries of that spirit. Let it have for the present
no other accessories than those appropriate ones the
assistance of which is necessary to produce that illusion
through which you are to look into the true mirror of
life; yet even now it has the strength and the proper
adjustment which will enable it one day to support a
majestic edifice, so soon as the German people desires
to honor itself by entering with you into possession of
it. Be it therefore consecrated by your love, by your
blessing, by the profound gratitude I feel for you,
for all of you, who have aided me by your good
wishes, your countenance and your means. May it
be blessed by the genius who put it into your hearts
to comply with my invitation; who gave you courage
to repose full confidence in me despite all derision; who
could speak to you through me, for in your hearts he
might expect to recognize himself—by the genius of the
German Nation, who calls to you across the centuries
with that morning song of his that is ever young.

I need not here narrate the history of that happy
festival, the intent and significance of which is as I
believe sufficiently indicated in the foregoing address.
It inaugurated an undertaking which has been able to
endure the derision and obloquy of those who could
not understand the idea underlying it, as was to have
been expected of the majority of the people who nowadays busy themselves fatuously in earning a precari-
ous livelihood in art and letters. Whatever difficulties
may attend the progress of our enterprise herein, I
must recognize, and my friends no less than myself
must recognize, the self-same hardships which for a
long period, for centuries, have attended the healthy
development of a truly German culture. I need
not more fully describe these difficulties for whom-

ever has followed with interest the explanations I have made from my peculiar standpoint, and the discussion of the same. My view and hopes in this regard I will however set forth once more in one of the ideas which already seems to be currently implied by the name "Bayreuth"—which has come to indicate something partly unknown or misunderstood, partly waited for with expectation and confidence.

What our not always very ingenious witlings have hitherto dished up for their own amusement under the absurd name of " Music of the Future," has now quit the nebulous shape and has become a " Bayreuth" with actual walls, resting on firm foundations. Thus what was a cloud has acquired a local habitation, and has thus put on a very real form. The " Theatre of the Future" is no longer a " nonsensical idea" of mine, which I want to force upon the present stage, with myself as a sort of Musical Director General, or Intendant General; * but (probably just because I was bound never to succeed) it seems now that I want to plant this idea of mine in a certain locality; and let us see what this locality is. It is little, remote, unhonored Bayreuth. At any rate, then, I have not sought to have my theatre established in any populous city—though that would not have been so difficult as some people pretend to believe. Let the witlings deride the smallness of the place and the extravagance of our ideas; for all that, here is the object of their derision endowed with a local habitation. I accept now, with great pleasure, for my theatre, the name given to it by the witlings—"Bayreuth," just as I once accepted their very stupid phrase, " Music of the Future." If my friends could accept this latter phrase, as expressing their theories, in the same spirit with which the brave Netherlanders proudly ac-

* As was lately affirmed by the writer of the History of Music in Brockhaus's Konversations-Lexikon.

cepted the nickname " Gueux," then I may willingly
accept the name Bayreuth, as a word of good omen ;
it may serve to indicate the union of those elements
that have come together from the most widely separated quarters to aid in the realization of the work of
art I had planned.

The man who after long wandering has reached the
spot which he has chosen for his permanent resting-
place, closely observes every indication that presents itself to him, giving to each the most favorable
interpretation. If in the " Meistersinger " I made
my Hans Sachs eulogize Nuremberg as lying in the
centre of Germany, I thought that the same might be
said still more justly of Bayreuth. The immense
Hercynian Forest into which the Romans never penetrated, once extended hither. The name Franken-
wald still remains, showing that the whole region was
once a forest ; the gradual clearing away of which is
indicated in sundry local names, or made up in part
of the syllables " reuth " (*reuten*, to make a clearing). Of the name Bayreuth, two different interpre-
tations are given. According to one account, in early
times the land hereabout was given to the Bavarian
dukes and the Frankish king, and here the Bavarians
cleared away the forest and made a home for themselves. This interpretation of the word flatters a certain historic sense of justice, in that the land, after
frequent changes of owners, at last reverts to those to
whom it owes a portion of its culture. Another and
more sceptical explanation would have it that " Bayreuth " is simply the name of a hamlet built up ": beim
Reuth " (in the clearing). However this may be, the
" reuth " remains, indicating a place won from the forest, and made productive ; and here we are reminded
of the " Rütli " of old Switzerland, whence the word
derives a still more pleasing and more elevated significance. The land became the Frankish frontier of the
German empire against the fanatical Czechs, whose

more peaceable Slavic brethren had previously settled there, and had so far advanced in civilization, that to this day many of the names of places bear both the Slavic and the German stamp.   Here first did Slavs become Germans, without having to renounce their own peculiar characters ; and they peacefully share in the fortunes of the common population.   This speaks well for the peculiarities of the German mind.   After a long-continued rule over this frontier, the Burgraves of Nuremberg made their way into the marches of Brandenburg, where they were destined to found the kingdom of Prussia, and finally the Empire of Germany.   Though the Romans never penetrated hither, still Bayreuth was not uninfluenced by Roman civilization.   In ecclesiastical affairs, it broke boldly away from Rome.   The old city, often reduced to ashes, adopted the French taste, under princes with a liking for embellishment ; an Italian erected, in the shape of a grand opera-house, one of the most fanciful monuments of the rococco style.   Here flourished ballet, opera, comedy.   But the Burgomaster of Bayreuth "affected" (as her ladyship expressed it), "affected" to pronounce his speech of welcome to the sister of Frederick the Great, in pure German.

Who is there that does not recognize in these few outlines, a picture of German life and its history which might mirror for us, on a larger scale, the whole German-Empire ?   A rugged soil, enriched by the manifold populations which have settled thereon, with local names, that are often hardly intelligible, in short, hardly recognizable, save by the German tongue, which has been maintained with victorious constancy.   The Roman church obtruded her Latin, and an extraneous civilization its French.   The scholar and the noble used only the foreign speech, but the clown of a Burgomaster always " affected " his native German.   And the German gained the mastery at last.   Indeed, as we see from this story of the Burgomaster of Bayreuth and the Prussian princess, not only was German spoken here, but people even affected to speak " pure German "—a thing which must have deeply pained the illustrious lady, for when once she herself met the empress of Austria, the two could not understand one another's German, for each spoke the peculiar *dialect* of her own native place. The spirit of German culture, therefore, is expressed in the fact that the educated community of Bayreuth obviously took a strong interest in a revival of German literature, which could enable them so to follow the unprecedented development of the German mind, the influence of a Winckelmann, a Lessing, a Goethe, and finally a Schiller, that a widely esteemed contribution to the culture of that mind could rise up among themselves, in the productions of their own original Friedrich Richter, who calls himself " Jean Paul " as though in merry irony. And thus the ridiculous foreign element among the higher classes, who were continually exposed to French influences, became impotent and harmless.

Who is there that would not experience a thrill of pleasure, on listening to the grand strains of this wonderful ninth symphony, performed by German musicians, assembled at the festival from all parts of the Fatherland, as he remembered that the court of the Margrave, accompanied by his guests—the great Frederick at their head—had in the same place witnessed a ballet or a French comedy, or had listened to an Italian opera ? When from that gallery from which gallooned court trumpeters had blown their stated flourishes, enthusiastic German singers now proclaimed, " Seid umschlungen, Millionen ! " did there not arise before the mind a vocal, living tableau which distinctly announced the triumph of the German soul ?

It was permitted to me, without a dissenting voice, to give this meaning to our inaugural festival ; and to all who kept that festival with us, the name of

" Bayreuth," in this sense has become a precious
memory, a cheering thought, a frequent motto.

And such a motto we need in order to persist in the
daily struggle against the encroachments of a foreign
spirit.

The question, " What is a German ? " is one that has
long seriously occupied my mind. It has always come
up in new shape ; when I supposed I could answer it satisfactorily in one shape, the next minute there it was before me in a very different one, and oftentimes I was perplexed and could make no reply. A certain patriot, the
wonderful Arnold Ruge, when driven to desperation by
this query, at last thought the reply must be that the
German is " niederträchtig " (low). Whoever has once
heard this dismal expression, will find it recurring to
his mind in moments of such dejection, and it may perhaps then be compared to one of those potent arcana
with which the physician strives to overmaster a mortal distemper : it quickly shows us that we ourselves
are that " German" who retreats in fright from his own
degenerate nature. This indicates that he only can
recognize its distortion as such ; and what could make
this recognition possible for him, save his unshaken
consciousness of his *true* nature ? At all events he
can never again be deceived ; he can never again com-
placently practise self-deception or flatter himself with
false pretences which have no longer any weight. He
cannot find in any reality, in any actual form of existence, the elements of a *German* life, except in that
form in which it reveals itself as bad,—even as repulsive. Even his language—that one sacred heirloom of
his race, painfully acquired and handed down to him by
the greatest minds—he sees recklessly given over to
destruction. He sees how everybody conspires to
make good the arrogant prediction of the President of
the United States, that before long only one language
will be spoken throughout the world—which means,
when you look at the matter more closely, that there

will be a universal jargon, made up of all sorts of in-
gredients ; and the German of the period may be sure
that he has already made a handsome contribution to it.

One who might have been at the time deeply dis-
tressed by these lugubrious thoughts could not fail to
be encouraged on that day when, even in that wonderful rococco hall of the Bayreuth Opera House, he
was addressed with the "seid umschlungen, Million-
en !" and he probably felt that General Grant's saying
might be fulfilled in a way the illustrious American
had not thought of.

But it was plain to every one that the German *word*
that solves the problem in the sense of the great master of melody, must, in order to become an actual
deed, displaying itself in a definite form, have different
surroundings from those of the Franco-Italian operatic
theatre. And we have therefore laid to-day the corner-stone of a building, with the peculiarities of which
I will, in closing, endeavor to make my reader acquainted, in order to show him, in its peculiar construction, an example of what has suggested itself as a
result of my desire to prepare for the German mind
a theatre fitting and appropriate for it.

In explaining once again the plan of the Bayreuth
theatre, now in process of erection, it will be best for
me to repeat what I have elsewhere said of the necessity, first observed by myself, of concealing from view
the musicians : for from this one necessity has proceeded all the other alterations in the body of our New
European Theatre.

My views on the subject of concealing the orchestra
are already known to my readers from certain detailed
expositions of them in my previous essays ; and I
hope that their next visit to any Opera House of the
period, convinced them (if they were not convinced ·
before) of the correctness of my judgment as to the
unpleasant effect caused by the obtrusion of the technical apparatus of the music before the eye.

I have explained in my essay on Beethoven the reason why, through the power exerted over our emotions
by noble performances of ideally perfect musical works,
the evil I have denounced might be rendered unnotice-
able, as though the sight itself were neutralized. But
in a dramatic performance, on the contrary, the very
matter in point is to make the sight fully take in a
picture ; an effect which can only be brought about by
entirely freeing the vision from the observation of any
intervening sense of reality, such as is inevitable when
the technical apparatus for producing the picture is obtruded.

Hence, the floor of the orchestra had to be sunk to
such a depth that the spectators might have a full view
of the stage, without seeing the musicians. At the
same time it was determined that the places for the
spectators might consist of rows of seats rising gradually one above the other, the elevation of the hinder-
most tier being limited only by the possibility of having thence a fair view of the scenic representation.
Thus the whole system of private boxes was done away
with, because from their elevated position on the side-
walls near the stage, the orchestra would be in full view.
The arrangement of the sittings was therefore like that
seen in the ancient amphitheatre, excepting that
the form of the amphitheatre, extending far around
on both sides so as to form even more than a semi-
circle, could not be followed ; since it is not now
the chorus in the almost entirely enclosed orchestra
which forms the chief object of view, but the scenic
stage, only presented to the Greek audience as a pro-
jecting surface, but used by us in its full depth.

Hence, we had to follow strictly the laws of perspective, according to which the rows of sittings would
grow longer as they receded from the stage, while always directly facing it. For the rest, all further arrangements had to depend upon the proscenium ; the
frame of the drop-scene of necessity became the start-

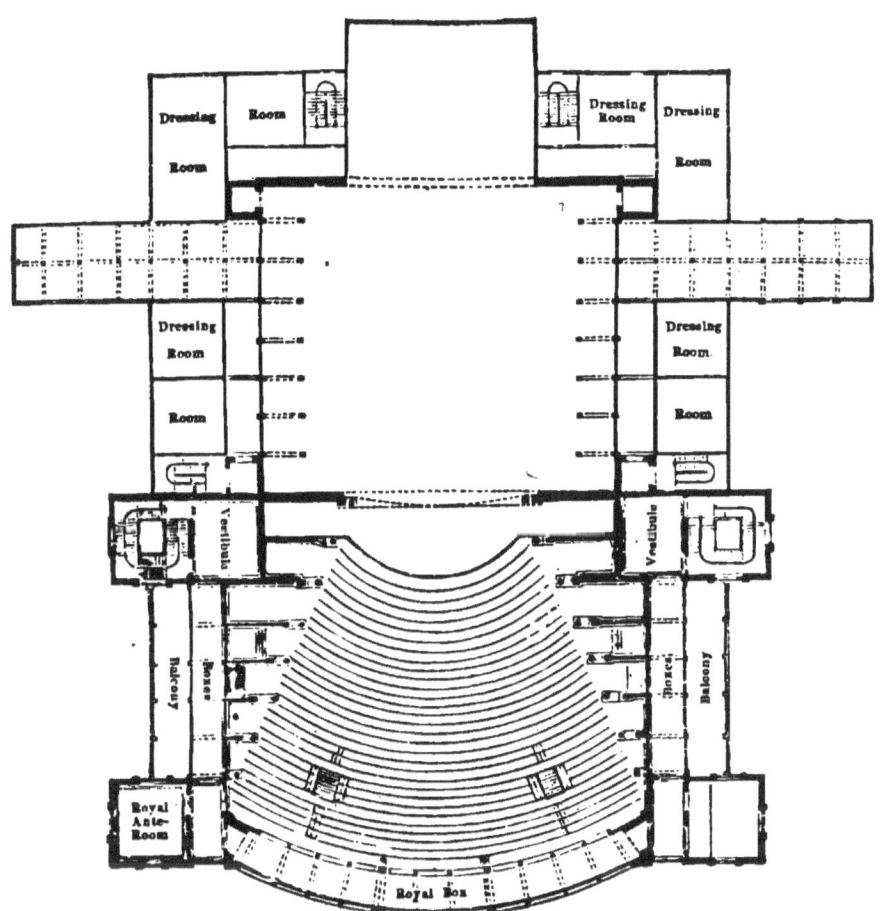

GROUND-PLAN OF THE BAYREUTH OPERA HOUSE.

ing-point for these arrangements. My requiring the concealment of the orchestra soon led the eminent and ingenious architect whom it was my privilege first to consult with upon the subject, to conceive the idea of a vacant space between the proscenium and the first row of seats. This we called the " mystic gulf," since it would seem to divide the real from the ideal; and the architect placed in front of it a second and wider proscenium, the effect of which was intended to be a wonderful illusion of the senses, the stage appearing to be more distant from the spectators than it really was, owing to the difference between its width and that of the second proscenium. Thus, though the spectator would see what took place on the stage, with all the distinctness of actual proximity, he would imagine that a considerable space intervened. From this would result another illusion, viz., that the dramatic personages would seem to be magnified into superhuman proportions.

The result of this contrivance might of itself suffice to show how admirably this new relation between the spectator and the scenic tableau works. On taking his seat, the spectator straightway finds that he is in a " Theatron " indeed; i.e. simply a place where one may witness a spectacle, and witness it straight before his eyes. Between himself and the spectacle there stands nothing that is clearly perceptible; only between the two prosceniums the skill of the architect has produced a certain indefinable effect of distance, which causes the tableau to retreat from the spectator, as in a dream; meanwhile, the music, as it comes forth like a spirit voice from the " mystic gulf," or like the vapor rising from the sacred bosom of Earth beneath the tripod of the Pythia, induces in him that spiritualized state of clairvoyance wherein the scenic representation becomes the perfect image of real life.

A difficulty arose as to what was to be done with the side-walls of the body of the theatre; being unbroken by rows of boxes, they presented a bare sur-

face which refused to harmonize with the ascending
tiers of sittings.   The eminent architect, to whom the
task was first assigned of planning the theatre, so
skilfully availed himself here of all the resources of
ornamentation to be found in the noblest Renaissance
style, that these surfaces disappeared and were trans-
formed into a real delight to the eyes.   But, inasmuch
as in the construction of this provisional theatre at
Bayreuth we had to renounce all thoughts of such
ornamentation as being adapted only to a building
constructed of costly materials, the question again
arose as to what was to be done with these side-walls.
The first of the plans given in the appendix exhibits to
us an oblong figure, narrowing as it approaches the
stage ; this is the space actually intended for the
spectators.   On each side are the walls, forming with
the proscenium an ugly angle, which could be used for
the purpose of giving to the spectators a convenient
passage to their seats.   To make as little obnoxious
as possible the troublesome, bare walls near the proscenium, and to reduce their disturbing influence to a
minimum, my present ingenious adviser hit on the
plan of interposing a third proscenium, placed still
further forward and extended still further out.   Struck
with the excellence of this idea, we soon went still
further, and found that we should only fully bring out
the idea of the width of the auditorium, gradually
narrowing, in accordance with perspective, toward the
stage,—if we should extend the gradually broadening
proscenium to the fullest extent, until its termination
at the gallery which crowned it; and thus open the
proscenic perspective to the audience from every
place that might be occupied.   For this purpose a
row of pillars was planned, corresponding to the first
proscenium, and gradually widening outward, forming
the end of the rows of seats.   These produced an
illusion with regard to the straight side-walls that lay
behind them; and the necessary steps and entrances

were usefully concealed by them. Thus we arrived at the decisive plan for the interior arrangement, as sketched in the adjoining drawings.

Our task being the planning of a *provisional* theatre, and our one óbject being to adapt the *interior* of the building to its intended uses, we were relieved from the necessity of conforming the exterior to any rules of architecture whatever.* Even if we had more costly materials than our means then afforded, for the erection of a florid monumental edifice, we should have shrunk from the task, and asked for assistance, though it is doubtful if we could have found it. For the work before us was the most novel, the most peculiar, and, inasmuch as it had never been attempted previously, the most difficult ever set before an architect of the present day (can it be harder even in the future ?). Our limited means restricted us to what was purely necessary for the attainment of the object in view, and that object consisted altogether in the relation of the interior of the auditorium to a stage which should be calculated according to the largest dimensions necessary for the erection of complete scenery. Such a stage must have three times the height it presents to the spectator in the body of the house, for the scenes have to be lowered as well as lifted. Hence the stage portion must stand twice as high as the body of the theatre, the latter being of the usual height. The result is a juxtaposition of two buildings differing very widely from one another both in form and size. To conceal as far as possible this incongruity, modern architects usually build up the body of the theatre to a consider- able height, and even on top of this build rooms to be used for painters' studios or for the officials, though they are seldom occupied owing to their great dis- comfort. In this design they were aided by the

---

* A slight condensation of the original text has been permitted here, to avoid repetition.—TRANS.

ranges of boxes rising often to a disproportionate height; the highest rising even above the height of the stage, since they could only be let to the poorer classes of the people, upon whom the difficulties of the dim bird's-eye view which they got of what was going on in the parquette, could easily be foisted. These boxes are wanting in our theatre, and no architectural inducement can induce us to direct the gaze upward over high walls—though this is, to be sure, done in Christian cathedrals. The earlier opera houses were built on the principle of presenting uniformity in the height of the building, and hence in the shape of a long box; of this we have a curious example in the Royal Opera House, Berlin. Here the architect had only to provide a façade for the front of the building, the sides being built into the two houses between which it stood. In our undertaking to erect an externally inartistic provisional theatre on an elevated, open site, I think that by steadily keeping our object in view, and providing only what was purely essential, we have succeeded in getting the problem clearly stated. This problem now stands before us clearly and definitely, exhibiting to us the conception of a theatre building which shall outwardly express the ideal object of its erection. In the main portion of this building we have the outward expression of the infinitely complex apparatus requisite for scenic representations of the highest attainable perfection; while the addition to this building constitutes merely a sort of roofed court, whence the spectators may conveniently witness the spectacle.

To us it seems as though in adhering of necessity to this simple plan, and in giving it artistic expression, without any reference to structures, such as palaces, museums, and churches, intended for very different purposes, we had set before the genius of German architecture a problem well worthy of study—nay, even perhaps the one problem which is peculiarly its own. But if for the sake of a grand façade, which by many is supposed to be indispensable, we are required to conceal the main purpose of the theatre by means of wings for ball-rooms, concert-halls, and the like, doubtless our plan will be condemned by all the canons of the unoriginal art of ornamentation now in vogue. Only the ideas of the Renaissance, with their unintelligent and unintelligible figures and ornaments, will occur to our sculptors and decorators, and finally —things will go on in such a theatre just as they do in the operatic theatre of to-day. It is for this very reason that I am very generally asked why I so absolutely need a *special* theatre for my purpose. Still, whoever has rightly understood me will readily perceive that architecture itself had to acquire a new significance under the inspiration of the Genius of Music, and thus that the myth of Amphion building the walls of Thebes by the notes of his lyre has yet a meaning.

Eventually, however, we had to go further, and to take into account what would be required by the German mind after it had been conducted into a path of original development, remote from all the disturbing influences of ill-understood and ill-applied foreign ideas.

It is the opinion of many intelligent men that the recent enormous successes of German statesmanship have done nothing whatever toward doing away with our stupid habit of imitating foreigners, or toward exciting a desire for conforming our existing institutions to the requirements of a peculiarly German culture. With the greatest difficulty-does our great German statesman withstand the pretensions of Rome in ecclesiastical affairs; but the pretensions of France remain unnoticed as regards the direction and forming of our tastes, and of our manners as influenced by our tastes. If a Parisian courtesan takes it into her head to give some strange shape to her bonnet, all the women in Germany must adopt the new fashion. Or some speculator on the Bourse suddenly makes a million, and at once he orders a villa to be built in the St. Germain style, for which the architect has a façade all ready designed. From all this it appears that the German has quite too easy a time of it, and that necessity alone can force him to return to a simple style peculiar to himself, and which ought to seem intelligible to him, if he should take into account his true and inner needs.

The characteristics of our plan for a theatre consisted in this : that in order to meet an altogether ideal need, we had to reject one scheme after another as unsuitable, and hence as not to be employed as in all previous arrangements of such buildings, and to devise a new arrangement, which again allowed of none of the usual ornament; and the result was that our building is now the perfection of simplicity. Trusting in the inventive power of necessity in general, and, in this case, of an ideal necessity for ornament, we are confident that, owing to the stimulus given by this problem, we shall yet find a German style of architecture which will not be unworthy of a structure sacred to German art—to art in its most popular manifestation, the drama—and which shall be distinctively and peculiarly German. We must wait until we have devised a style of monumental architectural ornament which shall to some extent compare in richness and diversity with the Renaissance or the Rococco ; there is no need of overhaste, for no doubt it will be long before the " Empire " makes up its mind to share in our work. Therefore, let our provisional structure, growing but slowly to its monumental proportions, stand for the present as a sign to the German people ; and let it set them to thinking of what has already been clearly grasped by those to whose sympathy, labor, and sacrifices it owes its erection.

There let it stand on that fair eminence at Bayreuth.

A LIST

OF THE PUBLISHED WORKS

OF

RICHARD WAGNER

WAGNER'S PUBLISHED WORKS.

By William F. Apthorp.

TO make a complete list of Wagner's works, from the material available in this country, is probably an impossible task. Such of his unpublished works as ever came to a performance have been virtually forgotten by the world for over thirty years, and the only imperfect trace of them that we can find is in scattered notices in contemporary newspapers, very few of which are now available outside of their own publishing offices. The earliest notice that we find of a work by Richard Wagner is the following paragraph in the *Allgemeine Musikalische Zeitung* for May 2d, 1832, criticising the " Subscription Concert " of April 18th :

" We were greatly pleased with a new overture by a still very young composer, Herr Richard Wagner. The piece received as full recognition as could be desired ; the young man really promises much. The work is not merely euphonious, it has sense and meaning, and is worked out with care and skill, evidently in successful striving after what is worthiest. We have seen the score."

In the *Allgemeine Musikalische Zeitung* for February 13th, 1833, we find the barest mention of a " Symphony (new), by Richard Wagner," at the Subscription Concert of January 10th.

In the *Allgemeine Musikalische Zeitung* for March 3d, 1841, we find the following : ".On February 4th, *M. Schlesinger* gave in Paris a superb concert to the subscribers to his *Revue et Gazette Musicale.* There appeared . . . . [here follow the names of several singers and instrumental performers, notably that of Charles Halle, the pianist] . . . and the composer, Richard Wagner, with an overture, having for its subject ' Columbus before and at the moment of discovering the New World.' It was well received."

The following list of the composer's published works, we have made out from Hofmeister's admirable catalogue of music published in Germany and the neighboring countries, the various numbers of which were put at our disposal by the courtesy of Mr. Carl Prüfer and Messrs. G. D. Russell & Co., of Boston.

The only works with opus number appear to be—

POLONAISE in D, for Pianoforte à 4m. op. 2. Leipzig : Breitkopf und Härtel.

OUVERTURE, *zur Jungfrau von Orleans* (to the Maid of Orleans), op. 31. Offenbach ^M : John André.

OUVERTURE, *zu Götz von Berlichingen*, op. 32. Offenbach ^M : John André.

This leaves a large hiatus which is probably to be filled out by unpublished works, or by works which originally had an opus number, but which were pub-

lished without one. The other published works are as
follows :

SYMPHONY, No. 2, in C. Leipzig : Breitkopf und
Härtel.
OVERTURE, No. 1, in C. Leipzig : Breitkopf und
Härtel.
OVERTURE, No. 2, in D. Leipzig : Breitkopf und
Härtel.
VARIATIONS, for Flute. Mainz : B. Schott's Söhnen.
SONATA in B♭ for Pianoforte. Leipzig : Breitkopf
und Härtel.
SONG from " *Das Liebesverbot* " (The Love-veto).
Hannover : Bachmann.
RIENZI, DER LETZTE DER TRIBUNEN. *Grosse tragische
Oper in 5 acten* (Rienzi, the Last of the Tribunes.
Grand Tragic Opera in five acts).
Pianoforte-score, 2 vols.
    "   à 4 m. arranged by C. G. Klück.
    ."   solo.
Overture in full score.
    "   for 2 pfts. à 8 m. arr. by K. Burchard.
Dresden : C. F. Meser.

(We can find no notice of the first performances in
the *Allgemeine Musikalische Zeitung.* We only find in
the number for November 16th, 1842, that *Rienzi* was
then in active rehearsal at the Royal Opera in Dresden.
Hector Berlioz, who was in Dresden during that winter, mentions in his letter [without date] to Ernst, the
violinist, having heard *Rienzi* and the *Flying Dutchman*, which latter opera was brought out January 11th,

1843, and *after Rienzi*. The principal features of the
cast were : *Rienzi*, Tichatscheck ; *Adriano*, Madame
Schröder-Devrient ; *Irène*, Mlle. Wiest. The opera was
brought out under Wagner's own direction, who had
just been appointed Royal Capellmeister, together
with Reissiger. Wagner received the Prussian order
of the Red Eagle for his *Rienzi* in 1847.)

DER FLIEGENDE HOLLAENDER, *Romantische Oper in* 3
Aufzügen. (The Flying Dutchman : Romantic Opera
in three acts.)
Pianoforte-score.
"   à 4 m. arranged by L. Röhr.
"   solo   "   "   C. Götze.
Overture in full score.
Dresden : C. F. Meser.

(The *Dutchman* was brought out at the Royal Opera
in Dresden, January 11th, 1843, under Wagner's personal direction. The principal features of the cast
were : *The Dutchman*, Wechter ; *Senta*, Madame
Schröder-Devrient.)

SONG, Les deux Grenadiers (*Die beiden Grenadiere*).
Mainz : B. Schott's Söhnen.

DAS LIEBESMAHL DER APOSTEL, *eine biblische Scene
für Männerstimmen und grosses Orchester*. (The
Love-feast of the Apostles : a Scriptural Scene for
male voices and grand orchestra.)
Full score.
Pianoforte-score.
Dresden : C. F. Meser.

(Brought out in the Frauen-Kirche in Dresden, at the great Men's Singing Festival, July 6th, 1843.)

TANNHÄUSER UND DER SÄNGERKRIEG AUF WART-
BURG, *romantische Oper in drei Acten.* (Tannhäuser
and the Singer's Contest at Wartburg : Romantic
Opera in three acts.)
Full score.
Pianoforte-score.
" à 4 m. arranged by Hans v. Bülow.
Overture for two pfts. à 8 m. arranged by K.
Burchard. Dresden : C. F. Meser.

(Brought out at the Royal Opera in Dresden, October 20th, 1845.)

Since the publication of the score Wagner has entirely remodelled the overture and first scene. This
later version alone is to be considered as authentic.
It is unfortunately not published.

GRUSS SEINER TREUEN AN FRIEDRICH AUGUST DEM
GERECHTEN BEI SEINER ZURÜCKKUNFT AUS ENG-
LAND AM 10. AUGUST, 1844, *für Männerstimmen.*
(Greeting from his faithful subjects to Frederick Au-
gustus the Just, on his return from England, the
tenth of August, 1844 : for male voices.)
Full score.
Arranged for a single voice, with pianoforte ac-
companiment.
Dresden : C. F. Meser.

WANN ? WO ? WIE ? *Duet aus Stadt und Land.*
(When ? Where ? How ? Duet from City and Coun-
try.)
Magdeburg : Heinrichshofen.

EINE FAUST-OUVERTURE (A Faust-overture).
Full score.
For 2 pfts. à 8 m. arranged by K. Klauser.
For pianoforte à 4 m.   "   " Hans v. Bülow.
For   "   solo   "   "   "   "
Leipzig : Breitkopf u. Härtel.

LOHENGRIN : *Romantische Oper in drei akten.*
(Lohengrin : Romantic Opera in three acts.)
Full score.
Pianoforte-score arranged by Theodor Uhlig.
"   à 4 m.
"   solo.
Leipzig : Breitkopf und Härtel.

(Brought out in Weimar, August 28th, 1850 [the an-
niversary of Goethe's birthday], under the direction of
Franz Liszt.   A fire broke out in the Opera House
during the last dress-rehearsal, but did not do enough
damage to prevent the performance.   The prominent
features of the cast were : *Lohengrin,* Beck; *Telra-
mund,* Milde ; *King,* Höfer ; *Elsa,* Fr. Agthe ;
Ortrud, Fr. Fastlinger.)

HULDIGUNG'S-MARSCH (March of Allegiance).
Full score.
2 pfts à 8 m.
Pianoforte à 4 m. arranged by Hans v. Bülow.
"   solo   "   "   "   "

(This march was originally written for wind instruments, for the coronation of Ludwig II. of Bavaria.)
Mainz : B. Schott's Söhnen.

TRAUERSINFONIE ZUR FEIERLICHEN BEISETZUNG DER ASCHE K. M. v. WEBERS, *nach Melodien der Euryanthe.* (Mourning symphony for the solemn burial of C. M. v. Weber, after themes from Euryanthe.)
Arranged for Pianoforte-solo by Ad. Blassmann.
Dresden : C. F. Meser.

GEDICHTE *für eine Frauenstimme mit Begleitung des Pianofortes.* (Poems for a female voice, with pianoforte . accompaniment.)
1. *Der Engel.* (The Angel.) ·
2. *Steh' still!* (Stand still !)
3. *Im Treibhaus.* (In the green-house.)
4. *Schmerzen.* (Sorrows.)
5. *Träume.* (Dreams.)
Mainz: B. Schott's Söhnen.

(Numbers three and five are sketches for *Tristan und Isolde;* the former for the introduction to the third act, and the latter for the love-duet in the second act at the words " *O sink' hernieder, Nacht der Liebe.*" A most sumptuous edition of these songs, with a lithograph portrait of the composer, has been published in Milan by F. Lucca, with the following title-page: " 5 *Canti di R. Wagner per voce di Soprano in chiave di Sol con accompto. di Pianoforte, Traduzione dal testo originale tedesco di Arrigo Boito.*" The separate

· **13***

songs have the following titles : i. *L'Angelo*, 2. *Fer-mati!* 3. *Nella serra*, 4. *Dolori*, 5. *Sogni*. The lithograph frontispiece is the only portrait of Wagner with which the composer himself is satisfied.)

TRISTAN UND ISOLDE : *Handlung in drei Aufzügen.*
(Tristram and Isoude : Action in three acts.)
Full score.
Pianoforte-score arranged by Hans v. Bülow.
"   à 4 m.
"   solo   "   " A. Horn.
Vorspiel for 2 pfts à 8 m. arranged by A. Heintz.
Leipzig : Breitkopf u. Härtel.

(After having gone through upwards of forty-seven rehearsals in Vienna in 1862, and having been given up as impracticable, this work was brought out in Munich under the direction of Hans v. Bülow on June 10th, 1865, with the following cast: *Tristan*, Ludwig Schnorr von Carolsfeld ; *Kurwenal*, Mitterwurzer ; *King Mark*, Zottmayer ; *Isolde*, Madame Schnorr von Carolsfeld ; *Brangäne*, Mlle. Deinet. Schnorr died before the year was out, of inflammatory rheumatism.   Many ascribed his death to the inordinate physical and mental exertions required by the rôle of Tristan.   But he himself says : " Oh, it is not the acting and singing in *Tristan* that are so exhausting, but the annoyances during the performance ; lying quietly on the ground in a profuse perspiration after the intense overheating and excitement of the great scene in the third act ; that is fatal to me ; for with all my pains I could not get them to shut the theatre against the frightful draught that blew over me like ice, as I lay motionless on the stage, catching my death of cold.")

DIE MEISTERSINGER VON NÜRNBERG. (The Master-
singers of Nuremberg.)
  Full score.
  Pianoforte-score arranged by C. Tausig. (The
    overture arranged by H. von Bülow.)
  Pianoforte à 4 m.
    "   solo.
  Vorspiel for 2 pfts. à 8 m. arranged by A. De-
    prosse.
  Vorspiel for piano à 4 m. arranged by Hans v.
    Bülow.
  Mainz: B. Schott's Söhnen.

(Brought out in Munich June 21st, 1868, under the direction of Hans v. Bülow. The principal features of the cast were as follows: *Hans Sachs*, Betz; *Walther*, Nachbauer; *Beckmesser*, Hölzel; *David*, Schlosser; *Eva*, Mlle. Mallinger; *Magdalena*, Mad. Dietz.)

DREI GESÄNGE *für eine Singstimme und Pianoforte.*
(Three songs for voice and pianoforte.)
  1. *Schlaf'ein, holdes Kind.* (Dors, mon enfant.)
  2. *Die Rose.* (Mignonne.)
  3. *Die Erwartung.* (Attente.)
    Berlin : Fürstner.

IN DAS ALBUM DER FÜRSTIN M. (1861), *Albumblatt
  für Pianoforte.* (In the Album of Princess M.
  [1861], album-leaf for Pianoforte.)
    Leipzig : E. W. Fritzsch.

KAISER-MARSCH *für grosses Fest-Orchester*. (The
.Emperor's march, for grand festival-orchestra.)
Full score.
2 pfts. à 8 m. arranged by August Horn.
Pianoforte à 4 m. "   " Hugo Ulrich.
    "   solo. "   " Carl Tausig.
Leipzig : C. F. Peters.

DAS RHEIN-GOLD (The Rhine-gold).
Full score.
Pianoforte-score arranged by C. Klindworth.
    "   solo.
Mainz : B. Schott's Söhnen.

(This work, the Introduction (*Vorabend*) to the trilogy, *Der Ring des Nibelungen* (The Ring of the Nibe-
lung), came to a public dress-rehearsal in Munich, August 25th, 1869, much against the composer's will.)

DIE WALKÜRE (The Valkyrie).
Full score.
Pianoforte-score arranged by C. Klindworth.
    "   solo.
Mainz : B. Schott's Söhnen.

(This, the first evening of the Nibelungen trilogy,
came to a public dress rehearsal in Munich, June 24th,
1870, with the following cast : *Wotan*, Kindermann ;
Siegmund, Vogl ; *Hunding*, Bauserwein ; *Brünnhilde*,
Frl. Stehle ; *Sieglinde*, Frau Vogl ; *Fricka*, Frl. Kauf-
mann.)

SIEGFRIED.
* Pianoforte score arranged by C. Klindworth.
" solo.
Mainz : B. Schott's Söhnen.

This completes the list of Wagner's published works up to October 1st, 1874. The third and last evening of the Nibelungen trilogy, *Die Götterdämmerung* (The Twilight of the Gods), is not yet published. The Pianoforte-scores of the earlier operas, from *Rienzi* to *Lohengrin*, are of about the same quality as ordinary pianoforte arrangements of modern operas, such as · Meyerbeer's *Robert* and *Les Huguenots*, and are of moderate difficulty. The pianoforte-scores of the later dramatic works from *Tristan* to the Nibelungen dramas, arranged by von Bülow, Tausig, and Klindworth, are to be ranked only with what is most perfect in pianoforte transcription, and are often extremely difficult. Among the hosts of pianoforte transcriptions, paraphrases, fantasias, and the like, that have been made of separate parts of Wagner's dramatic works, we would notice as peculiarly excellent—

A. By Franz Liszt :
Spinnerlied (Spinning-song), from the Flying Dutchman.
Leipzig : Breitkopf u. Härtel.
Ouverture zu Tannhäuser, Conzert paraphrase.
Dresden : C. F. Meser.
Einzug der Gäste auf Wartburg. (March and chorus from Tannhäuser.)
Leipzig : Breitkopf u. Härtel.

‹   *O, du mein holder Abendstern.* (Romanza from Tann-
häuser.)
Leipzig : Fŗ. Kistner.
Festspiel und Brautlied (Introduction to third act and
Epithalamium), and *Elsa's Traum und Lohengrin's
Verweis an Elsa* (Elsa's vision and Lohengrin's
rebuke to Elsa), from Lohengrin.
Leipzig: Breitkopf u. Härtel.
×   *Elsa's Brautzug zum Münster* (Elsa's Bridal Procession
to the Cathedral), from Lohengrin.
Leipzig : Breitkopf u. Härtel.
Isolden's Liebes-Tod. (Finale from Tristan.)
Leipzig : Breitkopf u. Härtel.
B. By Carl Tausig.
Drei Paraphrasen aus Tristan und Isolde. (Three Para-
phrases from Tristan u. Isolde.)
1. Love scene and Transfiguration.
2. Brangäne's song and Sailor's song.
3. Shepherd's Melody.
Berlin : Schlesinger.
Siegmund's Liebesgesang (Siegmund's Love-song) and
Der Ritt der Walküren (The Ride of the Valkyrior),
from Die Walküre.
Mainz : B. Schott's Söhnen.

*6 Scenes from Nibelungen In
Waldweben - Siegried Tod che
Wagner - Brassin.*

INDEX

OF NAMES, PLACES AND IMPORTANT WORKS MEN-
TIONED IN THIS VOLUME.

·

www.ingramcontent.com/pod-product-compliance
Lightning Source LLC
Chambersburg PA
CBHW060524030726
47498CB00004B/1069